Automotive
Cooling System Basics

Randy Rundle

Published by

krause publications

700 E. State Street • Iola, WI 54990-0001
Telephone: 715/445-2214

Please call or write for our free catalog of automotive publications.
Our toll-free number to place an order or obtain a free catalog is 800-258-0929 or please use our regular business telephone 715-445-2214 for editorial comment
and further information.

Library of Congress Catalog Number: 98-87287
ISBN: 0-87341-680-5
Printed in the United States of America

Contents

Introduction

This book is written to be both a reference guide and a how-to book. It explains in simple, common sense terms the basics of how an automotive cooling system works. Additionally, there are complete "how-to" instructions on troubleshooting all types of cooling system problems, including antique, classic, street rod, and performance/racing applications.

This book explains exactly what works, what doesn't, and why. By reading this book you will learn how to take advantage of modern technology to upgrade an older cooling system, as well as gain the knowledge and understanding necessary to design and build a complete automotive cooling system from scratch.

Also included are tech tips by the hundreds, and simple project ideas, to help you identify and solve your own cooling system problems. Most important of all is a special chapter dedicated to the Flathead Ford—whose reputation for overheating is well known. Upon your completion of reading this book, you should be well on your way to becoming a cooling system expert.

— **Randy Rundle**

Acknowledgments

I would like to thank the following companies and individuals for their efforts in helping to complete this book. Without their assistance there is little doubt that we would be forever lost.

Gates Rubber Co.	Paul Kosma
Prestone Products Corp.	Dave Lukkari
Texaco Coolant Products	Cornhusker Manufacturing
Evans Cooling Systems	Robertshaw Company
Michael Kirby Inc.	American Honeycomb Radiator Mfg. Co.
Rex Gardner	Robert Flake
Fluidyne Radiators	Steve Pressley
U.S. Radiator	Street and Performance Inc.
Total Performance	Brodix Manufacturing
Don "Packy" Rankin	Weiand Automotive
The BrassWorks	AE Clevite Engine Parts Co.
Brent Vandervort	Pro-Blend Motorsports Products
Red Line Synthetic Oil Corp.	Stant Cooling Products

Also a special thank you to anyone I may have missed. While you were not formally recognized, your help was greatly appreciated.

Foreword

Just as in the game of baseball where the batting coach decides who bats and in what order, I had to decide the order of the information contained in this book. So if things seem out of order to you, blame the batting coach. I also believe that to coach baseball you have to have a good knowledge of the game, know all of your players strengths and weaknesses, their assigned positions, and how they play together as a team. With that knowledge and understanding, you can then begin to make worthwhile improvements.

So it is with an automotive cooling system. You need to know the basic parts that make up a cooling system, what job each part does, and how those parts are designed to work together, before you can begin to make worthwhile improvements.

I also know many of you reading this book could care less about automotive cooling systems built before 1960. But in order to appreciate what we have now, you need to know a little bit about the past. By learning a little bit about where we came from, you can begin to appreciate what we have today and be less likely to make the same mistakes as others. Also, learning from someone else who has "been there and done that" will also save you lots of time and money—not to mention the mental aggravation involved. So unless you are into mental self-cruelty, you had better read the whole dang book! (By the way, now would be a good time to acquire the coolant beverage of your choice, to make the task of reading this book more enjoyable.)

Chapter 1: The Basics

In an ideal world, the laws of physics would not apply and automobile engines would be one hundred percent efficient. However, in the real world today, automobile engines are only about twenty-five percent efficient (up from fifteen percent prior to the mid-1950s). This means seventy-five percent of the potential energy you pour into your gas tank is wasted.

Most automotive engines since the 1920s (with a few exceptions) have all been four stroke engines. This means to get power from these engines there has to be an intake stroke (to draw the fuel in), a compression stroke (to squeeze the fuel mixture and compress it), a power stroke (in which the compressed fuel is ignited in the cylinder, creating the horsepower), and finally the exhaust stroke (in which all of the leftover fuel and heat is vented out into the atmosphere).

Officially, in the eyes of an engineer, an automobile engine is considered to be a "heat engine" which means that it burns fuel and air inside of a combustion chamber (located inside what we call the engine block), to produce horsepower. The working temperature inside of the combustion cylinder during combustion can reach as high as 5,000 degrees Fahrenheit. Part of that heat created as a result of the combustion process, is turned into horsepower (about 25 percent); part of it goes out the exhaust (about 35 percent); part of it is absorbed through the engine lubrication oil and friction loss (about 10 percent); and the rest (about 30 percent) is absorbed into the engine coolant and released into the cooling system.

As you might suspect, the only part of the "combustion heat" being produced that we really have much control over is the heat that is being released into the coolant. By controlling the makeup of the coolant, and the design (and arrangement) of the cooling system, we can attempt to control the temperature of the engine coolant, which can, in turn, affect the operating temperature of the engine and its overall efficiency.

> The working temperature inside of the combustion cylinder during combustion can reach as high as 5,000 degrees Fahrenheit. Part of that heat created as a result of the combustion process, is turned into horsepower (about 25 percent); part of it goes out the exhaust (about 35 percent); part of it is absorbed through the engine lubrication oil and friction loss (about 10 percent); and the rest (about 30 percent) is absorbed into the engine coolant and released into the cooling system.

Just Exactly How Much Heat Are We Talking About Here?

A modern automobile engine at operating temperature will generate about 150,000 BTUs of heat when traveling at sixty miles per hour. That is enough heat to warm and maintain a six room house at seventy degrees Fahrenheit, even when the outside temperature is a chilly zero degrees!

Regardless of how efficient an automobile engine is or is not, we still have to control the temperature by circulating coolant throughout the engine block. Without the coolant, the engine temperature would climb too high, causing the lubricating oil to boil and the engine to seize up and become a worthless boat anchor.

At the same time, we don't want the engine to run too cool. That would prevent the engine from developing full horsepower, and cause the engine to create an excessive amount of engine sludge (which is a nasty mixture of raw gas, exhaust blow-by, and crankcase moisture condensation). So the important job of regulating the operating temperature of the engine is done by way of the cooling system.

Ideally, we want to run the engine as warm as possible without overheating (causing the engine coolant to boil). This will make the engine as efficient as possible and, in turn, yield the most horsepower with the least amount of pollution. For example, in the Model T and Model A Ford days (cars of the 1920s and 1930s), 170 degrees Fahrenheit was considered the ideal engine operating temperature. Remember, plain water was the coolant of choice in those days, and in a non-pressurized cooling system water boils at or before 212 degrees Fahrenheit. It is because of these early engines that the established belief evolved that if your car engine is running hotter than 200 degrees Fahrenheit, it is overheating—regardless of coolant loss.

A Little Background On Gasoline

In the 1920s and 1930s, people often said that the gasoline available was of poor quality—which it often was. But if you didn't grow up in that era, you may not know exactly what they were talking about and why it affected car engines so much.

When petroleum (mineral oil) is heated, it gives off gases just as water does. During the refining process when petroleum is heated, these gases are separated from the mineral oil, then cooled to become liquid once again. These gases include gasoline, kerosene, benzine, naphtha and a few others. The main differ-

EFFECTS OF OVERHEATING ON ENGINE LUBRICATION

Among the various troubles that can result from an overheated engine, either in Summer or Winter, is damage to moving parts from failure of lubrication.

Excessively high temperatures cause rapid oxidation and breakdown of oil, and the formation of varnish on valves and pistons. Oil breakdown products can gum up moving parts of the engine.

There may be excessive wear and even seizure of moving parts, and serious damage may be done to bearings, wrist pins, pistons and piston rings, cylinder walls and other parts if lubrication is impaired. High piston temperatures accelerate oil breakdown and varnish formation.

Oil breakdown also causes the formation of acids which may corrode engine metals, especially bearings.

Water jacket passages, when clogged by rust scale, especially between cylinders, develop "hot spots" in the walls of the cylinders, and at the valve seats. These "hot spots" which create temperatures as high as 600°F., cause pre-ignition, detonation, burning of valves, localized lubrication failure, scoring of cylinders, pistons and valve stems and even engine seizure.

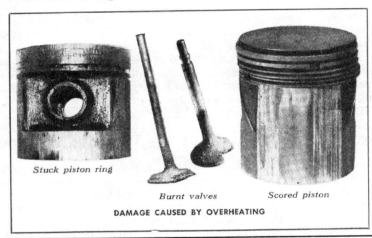

Stuck piston ring

Burnt valves   *Scored piston*

DAMAGE CAUSED BY OVERHEATING

ence between these gases is their volatility (ability to evaporate and burn rapidly). Gasoline is one of the more volatile gases, which is why it is used in automobile engines. (For you trivia buffs: Gasoline was once considered a waste by-product of refining kerosene. It wasn't until automobiles came along in the early 1900s that a use was found for gasoline.)

In the old days, it was difficult and expensive to refine gasoline into a pure form, therefore, the quality of the gasoline varied greatly. The test used in the old days to grade gasoline was done using a hydrometer. First a glass tube was filled with gasoline, then a hydrometer bulb was lowered into the gasoline. The gravity of the gasoline was determined by how far into the gasoline the hydrometer bulb sank. A scale on the upper portion of the hydrometer bulb indicated the specific gravity.

The scale had calibrations of between sixty and eighty. Gasoline in the old days typically had a rating of between sixty-four and sixty-eight, with the high quality gas being rated at seventy-two. Gasoline that was rated below 60 was considered a poor grade and caused hard starting, poor performance, a black smoky exhaust, and a stinky exhaust smell (kerosene).

Because poor gas was so common in the old days, many of the luxury cars had some form of preheater to help vaporize the poor gasoline. Poor gasoline also had a low octane rating, in part, because it was poorly separated from its petroleum base. This also explains why cars in the old days had such low compression ratios.

The hydrometer test is no longer used because modern gas is much better refined, and the additives used in today's gasoline would affect the outcome. (However a modern gravity test is still used to measure the volatility of the gasoline.) The cheaper gasoline sold today is often just that, plain gasoline with no detergent additives.

EFFECTS OF OVERCOOLING ON ENGINE LUBRICATION

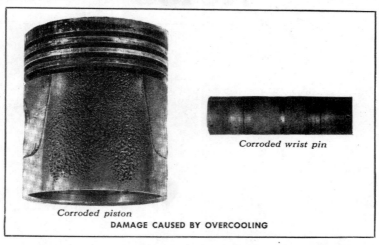

Corroded wrist pin

Corroded piston

DAMAGE CAUSED BY OVERCOOLING

Crankcase sludge is far more prevalent and serious in Winter than in Summer. In warm weather the steam in exhaust gas which blows by the pistons is generally removed by crankcase ventilation and heat.

In Winter, lower engine temperatures reduce the efficiency of crankcase ventilation, so that some steam condenses to form water.

This water mixes with the oil and partly burned fuel to form a thick sludge which clogs filters, screens and oil lines, stopping oil flow. It also hardens on pistons, valves and hydraulic valve lifters and causes them to stick. Lubrication failure and serious engine damage often follow oil sludging. Crankcase cleaning and regular oil changes are very important, especially in Winter.

In cold operating engines, exhaust gas blowing by the pistons into the crankcase dissolves in the water and forms very corrosive acids that may seriously damage engine parts. Corrosion of the working parts of the engine may be indicated by a rusty oil dip stick.

Crankcase water condensation and sludge in "cold" engines is increased by low speed driving, defective thermostats, or the removal of the thermostat. Proper engine temperatures, in Winter, can be best maintained by replacing low opening thermostats with the high temperature type which starts to open at 160°F. or higher.

And just so you know, the consistency of gasoline (even today) changes with the seasons. In the summer months a high gravity gasoline is produced, which vaporizes much easier—providing easier starting—in the hot summer months. In the winter months, a low gravity gasoline is produced, which is both a slower and longer burning gasoline.

For racing and high-speed engines, the high gravity gasoline is often used. High gravity has a high flame rate so the pressure in the cylinder rises rapidly and imparts a powerful push at the beginning of the power stroke. High gravity gasoline also has more heat units per gallon, but is more difficult to control, and more sensitive to carburetor adjustments.

In contrast, with low gravity gasoline, the explosion occurs more slowly and does not create the rapid shock common to high gravity fuels. The flame is more spread out and occurs during a longer portion of the power stroke. For medium operating speeds, where steam engine-like power is required along with good fuel economy, the low gravity fuel works best.

We have often heard the stories about how bad the gasoline was in those early days, but no one ever said what was bad about it. Now you know what they were talking about, and why compression ratios in engines were so low (6:1 being common). The key to finding the solution to a problem is understanding the entire problem.

OK, let's look at the parts that make up the cooling system....

Notes

Chapter 2: Parts Of A Cooling System

The **radiator** is the heart of the cooling system, transferring excess engine heat from the coolant to the atmosphere. Coolant enters the radiator through upper radiator hose and leaves through lower radiator hose. Warmed coolant enters the top of the radiator and travels through small tubes surrounded by thin metal fins. The moving car and the fan force air over these fins which dissipate excess heat into the atmosphere.

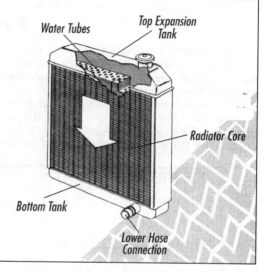

Water Tubes

Top Expansion Tank

Radiator Core

Bottom Tank

Lower Hose Connection

"PRESTONE" ANTI-FREEZE

The Prestone Co. was one of the first companies to offer ethylene glycol-based antifreeze/coolant.

Radiator

This part is the heart of the cooling system, and is designed to transfer the heat absorbed by the coolant into the atmosphere. The warm coolant enters the top of the radiator through the upper radiator hose assembly and travels down through the radiator, passing either "through the inside" or "around the outside" of metal "tubes" (depending on the type of radiator) that are surrounded by thin metal fins. The heat is then transferred from the coolant to the tubes, then from the tubes to the fins. While all of this is happening, air is being drawn through and past the radiator fins, often with the help of an engine driven fan. The air passing through the cooling fins draws off the heat from the fins and transfers it into the atmosphere.

The **radiator cap** serves two vital roles. First, it raises the coolant's boiling point by pressurizing the system. Every pound of pressure raises the boiling point 3 degrees. Most spring-loaded caps withstand about 15 psi, extending the coolant's operating temperature range by approximately 45 degrees. Secondly, by sealing the system, the cap prevents coolant loss due to evaporation.

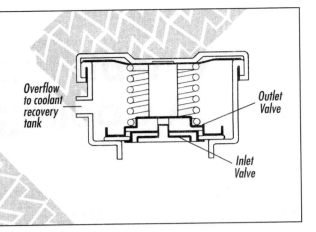

Radiator Cap

Located on the top side of the radiator, the radiator neck serves as the point where coolant is added. The early cooling systems of the 1920s through the early 1950s were non-pressurized systems (which means the system was not sealed to hold pressure). Beginning about the mid-1950s, sealed pressurized cooling systems became the norm. The radiator cap and filler neck were changed and used to seal the cooling system, causing pressure to build inside of the radiator. The pressure inside of the radiator helped to raise the boiling point of the coolant.

Since the 1940s, most engine coolant solutions have consisted of water and ethylene glycol, usually mixed in a 50:50 solution. Alcohol and various other solutions were once common to antifreeze mixtures prior to the 1940s, but the ethylene glycol antifreeze was proven to be superior over other solutions.

The **water pump** forces coolant through the system. Spinning blades draw coolant from the radiator, engine and heater, then pump it back to the cylinder block to absorb heat. From there, the warmed coolant circulates back to the heater and radiator where heat is dispersed.

Under normal operating temperatures and driving conditions, the water pump circulates up to 2,500 gallons of coolant per hour through the system. Typically, both the water pump and fan are powered by the same belt, unless the fan is electric. If the belt breaks or loses tension, the fan and/or water pump will stop operating, eventually causing the engine to overheat.

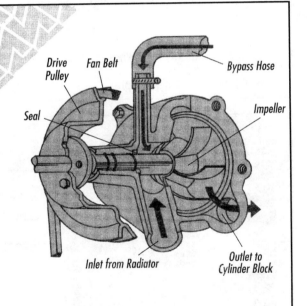

Water Pump

The water pump is an engine-driven mechanical pump that forces (pumps) coolant to circulate through the cooling system. (The early Thermo-Syphon cooling systems of the 1920s did not have a water pump, but instead relied on the heat expansion of the coolant.) Spinning blades or paddles located inside of the water pump housing are designed to force the circulation of coolant through the passages of the engine block and radiator.

It is common for an OEM (Original Equipment Manufacturer) designed cooling system to circulate up to 2,500 gallons of coolant per hour at highway speeds. In most cases, the water pump and the "engine-driven fan" are powered by the same belt, driven off the engine. As you might expect, a worn or loose fan belt is one of the number one causes of engine overheating.

Thermostat

The thermostat is designed to control the flow of coolant through the cooling system by using a type of valve called a "valve-plate" that opens and closes via a tiny internal piston. This tiny piston is raised and lowered by a sealed cup of wax-like material that is heat sensitive. This wax material expands when heated, and contracts when cooled.

When the engine is cool, the thermostat piston is in the closed position and coolant is allowed to circulate through the engine block only. As the engine warms, the thermostat begins to open allowing some of the warm coolant to circulate through the rest of the cooling system and on to the radiator. When the engine reaches full operating temperature, the thermostat opens completely and the coolant is circulated throughout the entire cooling system.

Coolant By-Pass Hose

The coolant by-pass hose is there so the water pump will always have a good supply of coolant to pump. When the thermostat is closed, the amount of available fresh coolant is limited and the pump could begin pumping air. To prevent this, a small amount of engine coolant is allowed to "bypass" the thermostat, and circulate through the system at all times.

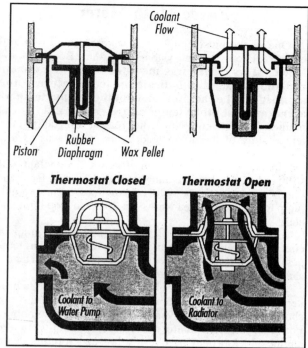

Coolant Flow

Piston — *Rubber Diaphragm* — *Wax Pellet*

Thermostat Closed — **Thermostat Open**

Coolant to Water Pump — *Coolant to Radiator*

Heater Core

The heater core works just like a small radiator, circulating warm coolant from the engine *after* the thermostat is open. (This is why you have to wait for the engine to warm before you can get any heat from your heater; you are waiting for the thermostat inside of the engine block to open.) After the thermostat opens, the warm coolant is circulated through the heater core. A fan or blower assembly blows air through the heater core, then on through the car's heating ducts, which warm your feet.

Heater Fan — *Heater Core* — *Windshield Defroster Duct*

Heater Supply Hose

Heater Return Hose — *Heater Floor Outlet*

Rubber Hoses

Rubber hoses are used to connect both the engine cooling system to the radiator and the heater system to the engine. Rubber coolant hoses have proven to be one of the most reliable ways to connect all of the parts of the cooling system together.

In most cooling systems, there is also what is called an expansion tank in both the upper and lower portions of the radiator. These tanks act as storage tanks (to store excess coolant) to help reduce the loss of coolant in the system. In addition, most pressurized cooling systems also have an additional remote expansion tank located on an inner fender area. This extra tank is used to catch the engine coolant as it expands during high engine operating temperatures. As the engine cools, the vacuum present draws the once-expanded coolant back into the cooling system.

Some sort of dash gauge or instrument is also used so the driver can monitor the temperature of the cooling system. Most early dash gauges were simply a mechanical thermometer with the bulb end mounted inside of the coolant passage of the engine block. Heat from the warm coolant caused the mercury to expand and rise, where it then registered inside a glass tube that was part of the dash gauge assembly.

Boyce Moto-Meter

One of the most unique devices associated with the early radiator cooling systems was the "Boyce Moto-Meter." **This device was mounted onto the radiator cap and was used to indicate the temperature of the air inside of the radiator, and not the coolant temperature, as most other temperature gauges did.** As explained by the company, the reason for taking the temperature of the air instead of the water was as follows:

1) Up to the actual creation of steam, the coolant will still read well below the danger (boiling) point. By reading the air temperature, when steam does occur, a quick jump to the danger area warns the driver to stop immediately.

2) On a thermo-syphon system, almost no jump in coolant temperature would occur since the coolant temperature hangs near 200 degrees anyway. It would take a sharp driver to notice the trouble ahead.

3) If measuring the coolant temperature alone, a broken water pump or stoppage of circulation would not show up in time to prevent damage to the automobile. For example, the radiator would remain cool while the engine block would be overheating and forcing steam out of the overflow tube.

Boyce brand Moto-Meters were once quite popular with automobile drivers and gained a well-deserved reputation for accuracy.

Examples of modern coolant hoses.

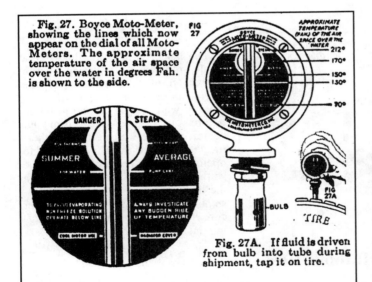

Fig. 27. Boyce Moto-Meter, showing the lines which now appear on the dial of all Moto-Meters. The approximate temperature of the air space over the water in degrees Fah. is shown to the side.

Fig. 27A. If fluid is driven from bulb into tube during shipment, tap it on tire.

The top line is danger; stop car and see if the overheating is due to lack of water, lubrication, too much gasoline being fed by carburetor, or loose fan belt.

The next lower line is an efficient temperature at which to operate an engine, especially of the thermo-syphon type during summer.

NOTE: "Summer average" represents a zone, not a line on the scale. It is quite impossible to give a definite line for all cars.

The next lower line for water-pump cars means the temperature at which most pump-equipped cars generally operate under summer conditions.

The next line is intended to show the bottom of the "summer average" zone, and a temperature above which alcohol non-freeze is likely to evaporate in winter.

Just as in shipment when they were new ... you will often times find Moto-Meters with the fluid from the bulb stuck up into the glass tube. To remedy this, simply tap the Moto-Meter on an inflated tire and the fluid will return to the bulb.

Notes

Chapter 3: Early Cooling System Designs— Thermo-Syphon Type

One of the earliest and simplest cooling system designs is called the "thermo-syphon" system. It works as the coolant is heated inside the engine to operating temperature. The heat causes the engine coolant to expand and fill the coolant passages inside of the engine. Once the coolant passages are filled, the heated coolant continues to expand until it begins to flow up into the top radiator pipe or hose. The coolant then continues to expand until it enters the top of the radiator.

When the warm coolant enters the top of the radiator, it begins to flow down through the inside of the radiator. The radiator, acting as a large cooling surface, begins to draw the heat from the coolant as it flows downward. As the heat is drawn from the coolant, it causes the coolant vapor to contract and return to a liquid. The coolant then becomes more dense (heavy), which causes it to fall to the bottom of the radiator. Once there, it enters the lower part of the engine block where it is then forced (pushed by the heated coolant behind it) back into the engine block and the process begins all over again.

Often times an engine-driven fan is used to help draw air through the radiator at idle and slow speeds; but the biggest difference between this type of cooling system and a more modern cooling system is that this system does not use a mechanical engine-driven water pump to help circulate the engine coolant. The coolant is moved through the system by the expansion of the coolant only.

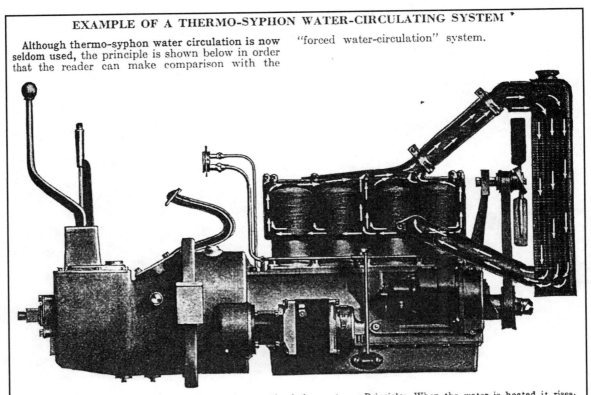

EXAMPLE OF A THERMO-SYPHON WATER-CIRCULATING SYSTEM

Although thermo-syphon water circulation is now seldom used, the principle is shown below in order that the reader can make comparison with the "forced water-circulation" system.

Internal view of a thermo-syphon principle of water circulation system. Principle: When the water is heated it rises and passes from the top of the water jacket at the top of cylinders, through the upper rubber hose connection, to upper tank of radiator, through radiator cores, whence it is cooled by air drawn through the radiator openings by the fan. The cooled water then passes to the lower radiator tank, up through lower hose connection, to lower part of cylinder water jackets.

The word "thermo" pertains to heat and the word "syphon" refers to drawing off a liquid from a higher to a lower level.

What Can Go Wrong With This Type of System?

Most important of all, the radiator itself must be mounted higher than the top of the engine, and at the same time also extend lower than the engine block itself, in order for this type of system to work. If the radiator is positioned either too high or too low, the coolant will not circulate and the engine will overheat.

The number one rule when working with a system of this kind is to keep the radiator full, so there is a slight resistance or back pressure to aid in forcing the water forward. It was considered good engine care at the time to check and add water frequently to the radiator instead of waiting until the level had dropped enough that circulation had slowed considerably or stopped.

Cavitation was one of the biggest problems with these systems. When cool water was added to the cooling system when the water level was low, a steam pocket was often created as a result of mixing the warm and cold water. This steam pocket would travel up inside of the engine block where it created a vapor barrier that blocked off the coolant flow. Because there was no water pump to force the circulation of coolant through the engine block, the steam pocket continued to grow in size. As the engine got hotter, more steam pockets formed, until the engine completely overheated from a lack of coolant circulation. When a thermo-syphon cooling system overheated you had no choice but to turn off the engine, let it cool down, and start over after everything had cooled. Ford, like many of the other manufacturers of the era, stated in its owner manuals that, "Slight boiling of the radiator is acceptable if the engine is under heavy load such as driving up steep grades, but the loss of coolant in normal driving is not acceptable, and the problem should be corrected immediately."

Considering the technology of the era and the low horsepower output of these engines, the thermo-syphon cooling systems worked okay, but didn't have much of a margin for error. Keeping the system full of water was a must and could be quite difficult, especially when these engines were under heavy load on a hot summer day.

> The number one rule when working with an early "thermo-syphon" system is to keep the radiator full, so there is a slight resistance or back pressure to aid in forcing the water forward. It was considered good engine care at the time to check and add water frequently to the radiator instead of waiting until the level had dropped enough that circulation had slowed considerably or stopped.

Chapter 4: Forced Water Circulation System Design

Following the "thermo-syphon" cooling system came the forced circulation type of cooling system. This system was different from the thermo-syphon system because it used a mechanically driven water pump, usually powered by the engine, to force the circulation of coolant through the engine block and radiator. The mechanical water pump provided more reliable coolant circulation, and would continue to circulate coolant even if the coolant level dropped below the acceptable level of a thermo-syphon system. The mechanical water pump was a step in the right direction.

Different Radiator Types and Designs

Unlike today, in the beginning there were many different radiator designs. Automobile manufacturers wanted not only the most efficient radiator design, but also the most cost effective to manufacture. Here are some of the more common types used in the early days:

Tube-Type Radiators

Tube-type radiators are constructed using vertical tubes placed between an upper and lower radiator tank. The coolant is designed to pass down through the inside of the tubes. If one of the tubes becomes clogged (due in part to hard water deposits and lime buildup), the coolant then must pass through the remaining tubes. This can slow circulation and be a cause of overheating. **The important thing to remember about this type of radiator is the design, since the coolant passes through the inside of the tubes.**

Cellular-Type Radiators

Cellular-type radiators are designed so that the air passes through the horizontal tubes and the coolant flows down and around, on the outside of the tubes. This is in contrast to the tube-type radiators in which the coolant flows on the inside of the tubes.

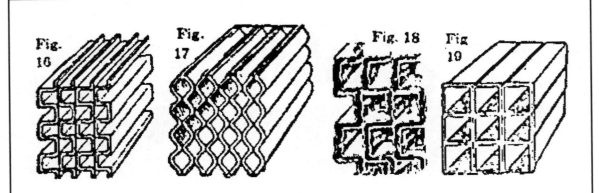

Variations of construction of the tubular type radiator are shown in Figs. 16, 17, and 18. Note that the appearance is similar to the cellular type, but the water flows through the tubes, whereas, with a cellular radiator, the water flows around the tubes.

Honeycomb Radiator

The **honeycomb** radiator design we commonly refer to, is actually a generic name for a group of different radiator designs that may, at first glance, look to be of the same design. Below are the different radiator designs and their official names. Our thanks to Neil Thomas of American Honeycomb Radiator Mfg. Co. for sharing his knowledge with us.

Because honeycomb radiators are such a mystery to so many people (including me), I thought it would be good to explain the different types of radiators and also what is involved in the restoration process of one of these vintage radiators. So again, with the help of Neil Thomas, here is the step-by-step process, along with a few before and after pictures.

Neil is able to completely duplicate a vintage radiator from scratch, as well as repair and restore an original radiator. Unique to his business is the number of vintage aircraft radiators he has done. In addition to the vintage aircraft radiators, Neil has completed a number of projects for vintage car collectors and museums. If you are in need of honeycomb radiator repair, it looks like American Honeycomb Radiator Mfg. Co. would be the place to call.

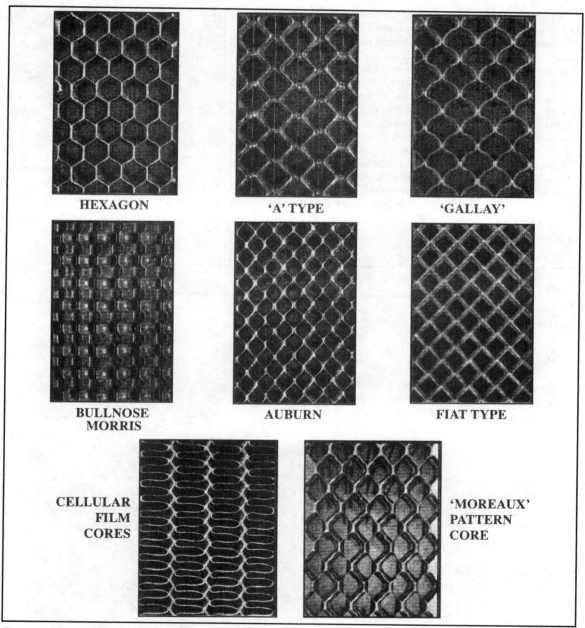

Examples of honeycomb radiator designs.

The American Honeycomb Radiator Mfg. Co. is able to manufacture Round, Honeycomb, or Square Tube Cartridge-type radiator cores. Cellular cores can be made into a honeycomb style radiator, which is much cheaper to manufacture. As an example, Rolls-Royce started using (V) cells in the mid-1950s, because they were cheaper to build than the honeycomb design used in the earlier years.

The major problem with a cellular core is that it is difficult, if not impossible to repair if seriously damaged. A cellular-designed radiator has vertical passages only and no cross-flow. Therefore, the cooling capacity can be seriously reduced in the event major damage occurs to the radiator.

So, given all that, the forced circulation cooling system design proved to be the most reliable. Typically, in general service, engineers of the day reported that the forced circulation cooling systems carried a coolant temperature of 170 degrees Fahrenheit.

In contrast, the engine coolant temperature of the thermo-syphon cars ran about 200 degrees Fahrenheit. In a non-pressurized system, as these cooling systems all were, water boiled at or before 212 degrees, which resulted in a loss of water in the radiator as the water turned to steam and escaped out the overflow or radiator cap. Once the boiling got started it was difficult to stop, especially with less coolant left in the system.

It is easy to see that as close to the boiling point as thermosyphon cars typically ran, boil-overs and loss of coolant was a common problem. It also becomes quite clear why the alcohol-based antifreeze had to be removed for summer driving—if you didn't, it would just simply evaporate.

Which brings us to antifreeze solutions. Like everything else in the old days there were no standard ingredients for engine coolant. And because of the Depression in the 1930s, there wasn't always money to buy commercial antifreeze anyway. As a result, car owners used whatever was handy.

Berg DI Aviatik 1916

The following pages contain product information and examples of the work of the American Honeycomb Radiator Mfg. Co.

Square Tubing

We can supply square tubing for Mercedes-Benz, Alfa Romeo and other early cars. Available in 1/4" and 5/16" o.d. Other sizes on special request.

Almost all "square tube" radiators are cellular in construction and contain no "tubes" at all! Additionally, many "square tube" radiators have only vertical spacers for water passage. Cross flow occurs only where segmented sections are joined.

We can duplicate this cellular construction with actual square brass tubing.

American with 5/16 square tubing

20

Dimensional Information

We require accurate dimensions of height, width, depth and contour. You may, if you wish, ship to us prepaid, the whole core you want duplicated. Our cartridge-type handcrafted cores are made of individual tubes, expanded at each end to hex, square or round shapes. These are assembled into a core shape the exact size you require. Conventional depths vary between 3" and 6", however depths as large as 12" present no problems. If you are not sure of the exact dimensions, give us the maximum measurements. We will manufacture a large square which you can then have reduced to the required size and shape locally.

Photographs are always helpful and are required when the core is complex in any dimension or contour, or where shipment to us of the old core is impractical. Clear, glossy, photographs of right and left, top and bottom, and, of course, front and rear views are usually sufficient. Polaroids well made are sometimes adequate.

An early World War I trainer can take to the air again.

An SE5a of the Royal Flying Corps.

Workmanship and Materials

All cores are made of brass. Tubes are 1/4", 9/32", 5/16", or 3/8" o.d. as required to duplicate the original. These are expanded on the ends to hex, square or round shapes. The resulting inside diameter of the hex, as measured across the flats, is slightly larger than the original outside diameter of the tubing used. Tube thicknesses are often greater than the original because:

1. Thicker walls guarantee longer life to the core.

2. Thicker walls are more resistant to road and/or runway damage.

Heat transfer is not greatly affected. We feel the extra long life more than offsets any minimal heat transfer loss.

Cores are face dipped with a solder alloy that combines good flow for clean frontal appearance and high yield strength. Because the quantities of brass tubing involved are so large, we use only those suppliers who can guarantee constancy in quality control.

Recoring

This is, of course, the main focus of our business. In some cases, as with this Bugatti, the radiators that come to us are so devastated that it is tantamount to a complete manufacture.

The more usual request for a new core is shown on the opposite page. Often, as with the Mercer, a "cellular" core of honeycomb configuration needs replacement. Our cartridge type hexagonal swedged tubes produce a near duplicate when asembled.

These pictures tell quite clearly how far we can go.

1925 Bugatti

1921 Mercer cellular care as received.

Recored with hexagonal tubes.

1916 Pierce Arrow shows its age and multiple leaks!

1916 Pierce Arrow recored, ready for years of service.

Aeroplanes

Here we have a special affinity because building the replica World War I SE5a fighter started us in the cartridge type "honeycomb" radiator core business.

We are especially pleased that the Smithsonian Institution asked us to build a complete radiator, shown right and below, for their 1912 Benoist aircraft. Both this and the SE5a radiator were built from sketchy old drawings and photographs of the originals.

The Curtiss Robin radiator was a complete manufacture duplicated from one lent to us by an old time pilot and restoration enthusiast.

1912 Benoist at Smithsonian

Curtiss Robin

1912 Benoist top tank.

More About Complete Radiators

We are primarily manufacturers of hand-crafted cartridge-type cores. We will on request make complete radiators. Shown here and elsewhere in this brochure are some of the many radiators we were asked to manufacture where no parts or remains were available.

Still, considerable saving can be effected if you use nearby craftsmen to complete your radiator. Local tinsmiths can easily make up simple tanks and coppersmith hobbyists can make compound curved external tanks quite readily. By restricting our services to an area of singular expertise we can give you real cartridge-type honeycomb radiator cores at the lowest possible price.

An early bird Curtiss A-11.

Left, this Fokker D-VII may oppose the SE5a.

Restorations/Repairs

We are often asked to polish up and repair radiators that are believed by the owners to be in serviceable condition.

What we find, more often than not, is a need for extensive refurbishing and repair of multiple leaks. Still, the core was not replaced and the radiator remains at least 50% original. A risky business at best but repairs can sometimes be effected.

1903 Meiselbach with oxidized imcomplete shell.

1903 Meiselbach refurbished with new tubes and shell.

BEFORE

1909 Maxwell

AFTER

1909 Maxwell

Shipping Information

Your new core, hand crafted especially for you, will be shipped by United Parcel Service prepaid and fully insured against loss. We will return your new radiator by air, if you wish, for an additional fee. Your old core shipped prepaid to us for examination and/or duplication will be returned to you, **collect**, if you wish to have it back. Lead time for completion of your core is 1 to 4 months depending on market conditions.

You will always be notified by telephone of any delays beyond the promised date should delays occur.

Upon receipt of your payment and written authorization to begin, we will start the manufacture of your handcrafted cartridge-type core.

Empty shells of P-40 radiators.

Price and Cost Reduction

The price of metals varies almost from week to week. Because of this unstable condition a price quoted to you will be good for 30 days only.

Price increases beyong 30 days are never excessive but do run from slight to moderate. We are sorry that economic conditions do not permit a more lenient quotation position.

To help you reduce costs to a minimum you may, if you wish, order cut and formed tubes to assemble into a cartridge-type core yourself. You should be a skilled and patient mechanic for this operation.

Recored, ready for shipment.

Aeroplane radiators we have manufactured for various museums and private collectors:

- 1912 Benoist — National Air & Space Museum
- 1916 Berg Aviatik D-1 — Champlin Fighter Museum
- 1911 Curtiss A-1 — Private Collector
- 1911 Curtiss Model D — United States Air Force Museum
- Curtiss Robin — Private Collector
- Curtiss P-1 — United States Naval Museum
  (from Private Collector)
- Curtiss P-40 — Champlin Fighter Museum
  2 for Private Collectors
- 1916 Caproni Bomber — United States Air Force Museum
- 1924 DH-4 — United States Air Force Museum
- 1917 Fokker DVII — Fokker Aircraft Company Museum
  Champlin Fighter Museum
  4 for Private Collectors
- 1912 Fowler-Gage — National Air & Space Museum
- 1917 JN-4 — Owl's Head Museum
  5 for Private Collectors
- 1917 S.P.A.D. XIII — Champlin Fighter Museum
- 1917 S.E. 5a — Private Collector

Automobile radiators we have manufactured or re-cored for private collectors:

American	Gardner 1925	Packard 1916
Alfa Romeo		Packard 1926
Arrow 1916	Hudson 1929	Pierce 1912
		Pierce Arrow 1916
Babcock 1910	Invicta	Plymouth 1928
Bentley 1959	Isotta-Fraschini	Pontiac 1927
Brush 1908		Premier 1922
Bugatti 1925	Marion 1910	
Bugatti 1933	Marmon 1928	Republic 1926
Buick 1912	Maserati 1937	Rolls Royce (17 assorted)
	Maserati 1957	
Cadillac 1906	Maxwell 1909	Seagraves 1918
Cadillac 1931	Meiselbach 1903	Simplex 1913
Chrysler 1928	Mercedes 1903	Standard 1917
Chrysler 1942	Mercedes 1913	Stevens Duryea 1910
Cleveland 1920	Mercedes Benz 540K	Stutz 1922
Crane 1912	Mercer 1921	Sunbeam 1919
Cunningham 1925	Morgan	
	MG 1935	Walker 1930
DeSoto 1929		Winton 1917
Dusenberg 1931	Oldsmobile 1917	White 1915
	Oldsmobile 1920	
Fiat 1913	Overland 1909	
Fiat 1914		

For more information about American Honeycomb Radiator Mfg. Co., see Appendix B in the back of this book.

Chapter 5:
What About Antifreeze?

Back in the thermo-syphon days, many motorists elected to drain the water out of their cars and put them in storage during the winter months. Considering the roads of the day and the weather in some parts of the country, that was a pretty good idea.

In contrast, some motorists elected to add a solution called "antifreeze" to their cooling systems, and kept on driving. This antifreeze solution was designed to prevent winter freeze-ups, which allowed the car owner to keep on driving through the cold winter months with no damage to his car's engine block or cooling system. The more successful antifreeze solutions of the day consisted of denatured alcohol (188-200 proof), methanol (synthetic wood or methyl alcohol), glycerin, or combinations thereof.

Some of the more creative antifreeze solutions in the early days included calcium, magnesium, chloride, sodium silicate, and substances such as honey, glucose, moonshine (white lightning to some of you, which also replaced gasoline in some parts of the country during hard times), cooking oil and kerosene, none of which worked very well and some of which were dangerous.

The bad side of using an alcohol-based antifreeze solution is that you had to remove it in the spring, or it would quickly evaporate when the weather got warm. Often times during the summer, when the coolant temperature got up near the boiling point, the alcohol would suddenly evaporate, causing the engine to overheat rapidly from a sudden loss of coolant. Alcohol also has a lower boiling point, 180 degrees Fahrenheit, than that of water (212 degrees Fahrenheit, as mentioned previously). Glycerin was another solution used as antifreeze, although it had a tendency to shrink the rubber coolant hoses causing leaks. Tightening the hose clamps was a regular duty if you decided to use a glycerin-based antifreeze.

> The more successful early day antifreeze solutions consisted of denatured alcohol (188-200 proof), methanol (synthetic wood or methyl alcohol), glycerin, or combinations thereof. Some of the more creative antifreeze solutions in the early days included calcium, magnesium, chloride, sodium silicate, and substances such as honey, glucose, moonshine (white lightning to some of you, which also replaced gasoline in some parts of the country during hard times), cooking oil and kerosene, none of which worked very well and some of which were dangerous.

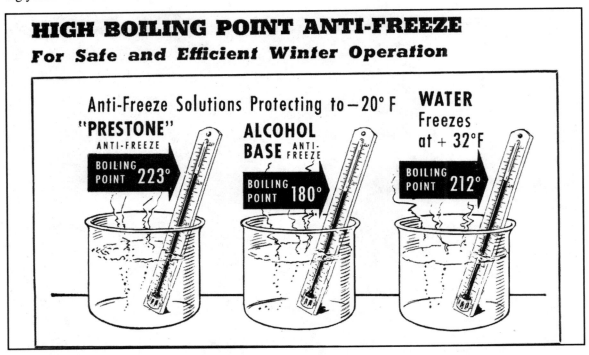

HIGH BOILING POINT ANTI-FREEZE
For Safe and Efficient Winter Operation

Anti-Freeze Solutions Protecting to −20° F

"PRESTONE" ANTI-FREEZE — BOILING POINT 223°

ALCOHOL BASE ANTI-FREEZE — BOILING POINT 180°

WATER Freezes at + 32°F — BOILING POINT 212°

Another problem with glycerin was that it tended to thicken in cold weather. The solution had to be re-mixed often in the winter months, to prevent the solution from getting thick and falling to the bottom of the radiator. If the solution was allowed to thicken it slowed down or sometimes stopped the circulation of

CAPACITIES OF COOLING SYSTEMS...Passenger Cars
The Capacities given are approximate. Newer models may change and older models vary.

MAKE and YEAR	MODEL	Capacity of Cooling System in Quarts
BUICK		
1953	40 (Synchro)	12
	40 (Dyna)	14
	50 (Synchro)	17
	50 (Dyna), 70	18
1951-52	40,50 (Synchro)	14
	40,50 (Dyna)	18
	70	18
1950	50 (Synchro)	12
	40 (Synchro)	13
	40,50 (Dyna)	14
	70	18
1949	40,50 (Synchro)	13
	40,50 (Dyna)	14
	70	17
1946-48	40, 50	13
	70	17
CADILLAC		
1949-53	All Models	20
1946-48	All Models	25
CHEVROLET		
1946-53	All Models	15
CHRYSLER		
1951-53	6	15
	8, V8	25
1949-50	6	17
	8	21
1946-48	6	17
	8	26
CROSLEY		
1949-52	All Models	4
1946-48	All Models	5
DE SOTO		
1952-53	6	15
	V8	22
1951	All Models	15
1946-50	All Models	17

MAKE and YEAR	MODEL	Capacity of Cooling System in Quarts
DODGE		
1953	6	14
	V8	19
1951-52	All Models	14
1946-50	All Models	15
FORD		
1952-53	6 (OHV)	15
	8	22
1949-51	6	16
	V-8	21
1946-48	6	15
	V-8	22
FRAZER		
1948-51	All Models	14
1947	All Models	15
HENRY J		
1951-53	6	10
	4	11
HUDSON		
1953	Jet	15
	Wasp and Hornet	19
1951-52	All Models	19
1950	6	15
	8	17
1948-49	6	17
	8	18
1946-47	6	13
	8	18
KAISER		
1951-53	All Models	13
1948-50	All Models	14
1947	All Models	15
LINCOLN		
1952-53	All Models	23
1949-51	All Models	35
1947-48	All Models	25
1946	All Models	27

MAKE and YEAR	MODEL	Capacity of Cooling System in Quarts
MERCURY		
1946-53	All Models	22
NASH		
1950-53	Rambler	12
	Statesman	15
	Ambassador	18
1949	"600"	15
	Ambassador	18
1946-48	"600"	14
	Ambassador	17
OLDSMOBILE		
1951-53	All Models	22
1949-50	6	19
	8	22
1946-48	6	19
	8	21
PACKARD		
1951-53	All Models	20
1949-50 (23rd Series)	"8"	18
	Super, Custom "8"	19
1948-49 (22nd Series)	Taxi "6"	14
	"8"	18
	Super, Custom "8"	20
1946-47	Taxi, Clipper "6"	14
	Clipper and Deluxe Clipper "8"	17
	Super Clipper, Custom Super Clipper	20
PLYMOUTH		
1951-53	All Models	13
1949-50	All Models	15
1946-48	All Models	14

MAKE and YEAR	MODEL	Capacity of Cooling System in Quarts
PONTIAC		
1953	6	18
	8	19
1950-52	6	18
	8	20
1949	6	18
	8	21
1946-48	6	18
	8	20
ROLLS ROYCE		
1950-53	Silver Wraith, Silver Dawn,	19
	Bentley (Mark 6)	18
1947-49	Silver Wraith	19
	Bentley (Mark 6)	18
STUDEBAKER		
1951-53	Champion	10
	Comm., Cruiser	17
1950	Champion	10
	Comm.	14
1949	Champion	11
	Comm., Cruiser	13
1946-48	Champion	10
	Comm., Cruiser	13
WILLYS		
1953	All Models	11
1952	4, 6 Model 685, 675	11
	6 Model 673 S.W.	9
1950-51	4	11
	6	9
1949	4	11
	6	10
1948	4	11
	6	9
1946-47	4	11

INSTALLING "PRESTONE" ANTI-FREEZE

First, be sure the cooling system is clean, leak-tight and in proper working order. Completely drain system by opening all drain cocks on engine and radiator. These vary in number from one to four. Be sure to locate all of them. Make sure underseat heater and other cooling system accessories are drained. Then flush with water.

Close all drain cocks and drain openings. Pour about ¾ gallon of water into radiator and then add "Prestone" anti-freeze. Finish filling with water to proper level. If concentrated "Prestone" anti-freeze is found difficult to pour from can at 10°F. or below, warm the can slightly or place it in a heated room for a while. *Shake can before pouring.*

Use only water in preparing solution. Avoid water containing large amounts of minerals and impurities. Soft or rain water is ideal.

Never fill radiator to the top—allow sufficient room for the solution to expand when it warms up.

Run engine to release trapped air and to mix solution thoroughly before driving car or exposing it to freezing temperatures then, if necessary, add more water to fill to the proper coolant level. Mixing of solution takes more time in systems without water pumps.

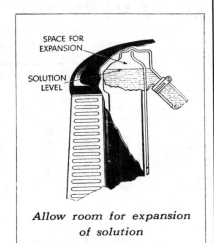

SPACE FOR EXPANSION

SOLUTION LEVEL

Allow room for expansion of solution

the coolant. That left the top part of the radiator filled with water ready to freeze.

There were, of course, two types of glycerin available in those days: the drugstore glycerin that was 95 percent chemically pure, and the automotive glycerin that also had a rust inhibitor added. People used both kinds with limited success.

And then there was kerosene. If you really wanted to stink up the neighborhood, you put kerosene in your radiator. While it worked well in really cold climates (it was often recommended for use in the radiators of farm tractors), it smelled terrible when it got warm, and the vapors it gave off when heated were flammable and could easily cause a flash fire!

Other bad points of kerosene are that it rots radiator tubing and deposits a dirty gray mist over the car and the driver. Its worst aspect, though—it forms gas pockets that build up and explode causing a bulge in the radiator.

Also, beginning in the 1920s, a solution called ethylene glycol was being offered by the Prestone Co. It was advertised as having a higher boiling point (223 degrees Fahrenheit) as compared to alcohol-based antifreeze, which had a boiling point of 180 degrees Fahrenheit. Also, the Prestone solution would not evaporate. Both solutions claimed freeze protection to minus twenty degrees Fahrenheit. The Prestone solution eventually became the basis for the "permanent antifreeze solutions" we use in automobiles today.

Now that you have the basics of antifreeze, let's move on to more "heady" subjects.

MIXING ANTI-FREEZE SOLUTION AND REMOVING TRAPPED AIR

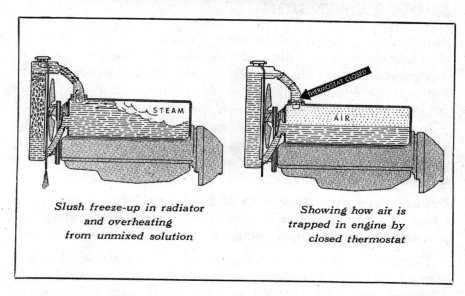

Slush freeze-up in radiator
and overheating
from unmixed solution

Showing how air is
trapped in engine by
closed thermostat

After installing, and before driving the car, always run the engine until the solution warms up, opens the thermostat, and starts circulation between the engine and the radiator.

This is necessary to thoroughly mix the anti-freeze with the water before exposing the car to freezing temperatures, otherwise the unmixed liquid in the radiator may form a slush which stops circulation and causes overheating and loss of solution. (This is similar to the slush freeze-up which occurs when the cooling system is under-protected.)

Another important reason for warming up the engine before driving the car is to release any air trapped in the engine water jacket by the closed thermostat. Though the radiator may appear to be full, the engine may be short as much as a gallon of liquid, and if the car is driven in this condition serious overheating may result.

When the thermostat opens, the trapped air is released and the water jacket fills. This lowers the solution in the radiator and more water may be added to fill to the proper level.

Be sure hot water heater control valves are open, to permit flow of coolant liquid through the heater.

These precautions should also be observed when making additions to a very low solution, and whenever the cooling system is drained, and flushed.

OVERFILLING THE RADIATOR AND LOSS OF SOLUTION FROM EXPANSION

Anti-freeze solution as well as water takes up more room when hot than when cold. If the radiator is filled too full when cold (Fig. 7), expansion when hot may overfill the radiator, and solution will be lost out the overflow pipe (Fig. 8). Adding unnecessary water weakens the solution and may lead to a freeze-up.

In many cars you cannot see deeply into the radiator, due to high baffle plates or "elbow" filler necks. If you check the solution level when it is cold you may not be able to see it, and may think it is low when it really is not.

Preventing overflow loss of solution from expansion
—First be sure that engine is warmed up to normal operating temperature, then with engine stopped, check solution level.

Never add any water as long as the hot solution level is well above the top of the radiator water tubes, or in the case of elbow fillers, as long as the hot solution level is in sight in the elbow. Follow car factory directions for inspecting coolant level in cars with radiator pressure caps.

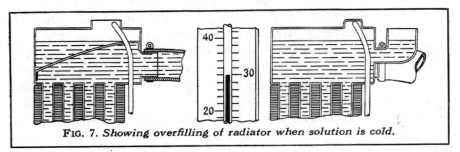

FIG. 7. *Showing overfilling of radiator when solution is cold.*

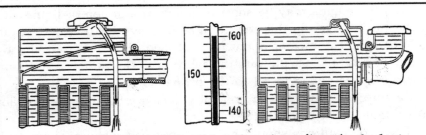

FIG. 8. *Showing how solution is lost through overflow pipe by heat expansion when too much water is added with solution cold.*

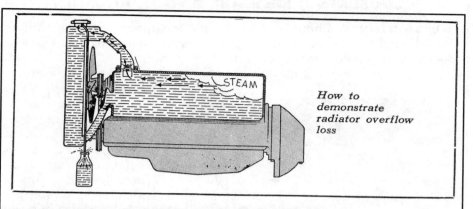

How to demonstrate radiator overflow loss

LOSS OF SOLUTION THROUGH RADIATOR OVERFLOW PIPE

Car owners often blame unobserved overflow losses on leakage.

Hidden Causes of Cooling System Overflow Loss

1. "Hot Spots" in rust and lime clogged engine water jackets, causing steam which forces solution out radiator overflow.
2. Corrosion damage to water distribution tube in engine block, or tube out of position, which causes overheating and boiling from improper circulation of solution at exhaust valves.
3. Rust clogged radiators causing engine overheating.
4. Air in solution, as from leaky water pump suction
5. Exhaust gas leakage into system at loose cylinder head
6. "Pumping over" from defective radiator baffle plate.
7. Overheating from clogged bug screens and damaged air baffles.
8. Thermostat stuck in closed position.
9. Water pump impeller corroded or loose on shaft.
10. Collapse of radiator hose or rotting of rubber lining.
11. Defective radiator pressure cap.

Radiator Overflow Tanks, designed to prevent "after boil" losses of alcohol, are undependable if system is not leak-tight. Sudden development of steam pressure may overfill tank and cause overflow of solution onto hot engine.

Radiator Pressure Caps — Most of the newer cars have a normally closed valve in the radiator cap which permits 4 to 13 pounds steam pressure in the system. This pressure increases the leakage tendency at hose connections and water joints. When the valve opens and the pressure drops, sudden boiling and large overflow losses may occur. *If the engine is hot, remove pressure cap slowly to avoid possible flash of steam and hot cooling liquid that would scald face and hands as well as spot car finish.* To avoid possible damage to system from excessive pressure, these valves should be regularly inspected for proper operation.

PREVENTION OF FOAMING, RUST LOOSENING, SEEPAGE, AND CORROSION

Defoaming — There is always some air mixed with the cooling liquid particularly during high speed driving, *and this causes serious foaming in glycol anti-freezes that trap and hold air*, as shown in FIG. 1 where the radiator hose is replaced with a glass tube.

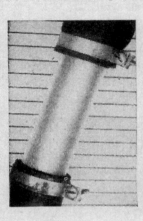 

FIG. 1
Foaming in glycol anti-freeze

FIG. 2
No foaming in "Prestone" anti-freeze

The solution is so full of fine air bubbles that it looks milky, and the lines on the background cannot be seen through the glass. This foaming can cause overflow loss of solution, as much as ½ gallon per 1,000 miles of driving, and the foaming may get worse with continued use. Foaming losses in high boiling point anti-freeze can be as serious as "after boil" losses in low boiling point alcohol, and replacements are more expensive.

Prevention of Rust-Loosening—A rusty solution is an indication of rust "on the move" from the engine water jacket where it forms, to the radiator where it settles out and clogs the small tubes

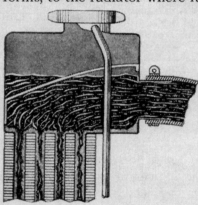

FIG. 3. *Loosened rust depositing in radiator tubes*

(Fig. 3). It is therefore important that anti-freeze should have no more rust loosening action than water. The physical film inhibitor in "Prestone" anti-freeze completely eliminates this *natural nuisance property of glycols*—in fact reduces rust-loosening to *less* than that of water. "Prestone" anti-freeze solutions stay clearer and more rust-free than anti-freezes lacking this film inhibitor, thus avoiding rust clogging and loss of heat transfer. Years of usage in cooling systems have proved this. Demonstrations in bottles prove nothing, and may be misleading.

Correction of Seepage — Anti-freezes which loosen rust will open up small leaks previously rust-plugged when using water, resulting in seepage loss of solution. Seepage is another reason for avoiding anti-freezes that make solutions rusty. The physical film inhibitor in "Prestone" anti-freeze stops rust loosening, and the leakage rate by actual test is 50% less than that of water.

Notes

39

Chapter 6: Stuff To Make Your Head Hurt

There is something else that can effect the boiling point of the coolant in your engine. It is called atmospheric pressure. It is a pressure found naturally in the atmosphere that is created as a result of gravity holding down the gasses such as nitrogen and oxygen to the earth.

What all that means to us, is that there is a natural pressure in the air around us. To establish a standard unit of measurement for this pressure, most "atmospheric pressure readings" are based off of the pressure at sea level. As an example, the pressure at sea level is about fifteen pounds per square inch. This fifteen pounds of pressure at sea level is known as one atmosphere of pressure. Often times, mercury (because it is the heaviest and densest liquid) is used to measure atmospheric pressure.

The official measurement of atmospheric pressure is done using an instrument called a barometer that contains a tube full of mercury, and is calibrated in "inches of mercury" using sea level as a reference point. And in case you were wondering, the normal or average atmospheric pressure at sea level is thirty inches of mercury.

There are also **three basic things** that can affect atmospheric pressure: temperature, humidity, and altitude. Let's look at each one separately.

Temperature

Warmer air lowers the atmospheric pressure because the molecules in the air move about faster and separate farther from each other. This decreases the density of the air, which lowers the air pressure. In contrast, colder air moves the molecules closer to each other, increasing the density of the air, which raises the air pressure.

Humidity

Humidity is the amount of molecules found in a given space of air. As water molecules come into the air they push away the heavier molecules of gases, creating a less dense air. This lowers the atmospheric pressure. So the key thing to remember is **the higher the humidity the lower the atmospheric pressure will be**. And in contrast, **the lower the humidity, the higher the atmospheric pressure will be**.

Location

The final thing we need to worry about is our location above sea level. Since we now know that sea level is the basis for measurement of the atmospheric pressure and the boiling point of water, we need to know what happens to the boiling point of our coolant as the atmospheric pressure changes.

The atmospheric pressure will become greater as altitude decreases, so the greatest air pressure can be found at sea level, which is why sea level is used as a reference point. Think back to when you were riding in a car through the mountains on vacation with your parents. Remember how your ears popped, and your mom gave you gum? The same thing also happens today when you fly on a commercial jet. What is causing your ears to pop is the change in atmospheric pressure.

Okay, based on what we just learned, we know that water boils at 212 degrees Fahrenheit at sea level (considered an official standard). Suppose we live in a city 2,000 feet above sea level; will we have a lower or higher boiling point? If you said lower because the atmospheric pressure is lower, you are correct!

Another key factor to remember is that **the boiling point of water is the temperature at which the vapor pressure is equal to the atmospheric pressure**. The following are some common examples of boiling points at different altitudes. Remember also the temperature and humidity factors. As you look at some of these boiling points, imagine a Model T Ford truck from the 1920s loaded with supplies (with a thermo-syphon cooling system of course) trying to climb a steep mountain grade to reach a work camp, located at 7,000 feet above sea level. If the truck's driver is making this trip in July or August, what are the odds he will make it without a boil over?

All of this information and technical stuff about atmospheric pressure is important and effects most everything we try and do to a cooling system. The important thing to remember for now is, how it works and why. We will learn how to figure out the rest of it later on. Another benefit to learning all of this: The weather report on television will make more sense, especially when the meteorologist talks about the barometric pressure readings.

Sea Level	212.0 degrees Fahrenheit
1000ft+	210.2 degrees Fahrenheit
2000ft+	208.4 degrees Fahrenheit
3000ft+	206.5 degrees Fahrenheit
4000ft+	203.8 degrees Fahrenheit
5000ft+	201.9 degrees Fahrenheit
7000ft+	198.2 degrees Fahrenheit
10,000ft+	193.7 degrees Fahrenheit

Chapter 7: Cooling System Hoses

At first glance you may think about skipping over this section; after all, what is there to learn about hoses? But don't do it! You will learn something, I promise.

While it is true that the basic design of cooling system hoses hasn't changed much over the years, the materials that make up the hoses have changed greatly. For you engineer types, a coolant hose is made up of three parts: the tube, the reinforcement, and the cover. The tube conveys the coolant, the reinforcement prevents the tube from rupturing under pressure, and the cover protects the entire hose assembly from harsh elements such as heat, oil, grease, abrasion, ozone, and ECD.

Hey, What's ECD?

ECD, or **electrochemical degradation**, takes places whenever a conductive fluid (water in this case) comes in contact with the different types of metals that make up the cooling system. This chemical reaction is caused by the pH balance of the coolant having a higher than normal acid balance. When the pH balance of the cooling system goes to the acidic side, the acids begin to attack and destroy the parts of the cooling system, including the radiator, heater core, water pump, head gaskets, freeze plugs, and the coolant hoses.

As an example, over the road diesel truck engines are prone to ECD problems. If the coolant in these engines is allowed to turn acidic, the ECD can "eat through" a cylinder liner .005 thick in just 30,000 miles. That is not many miles for an over the road truck. And time wise, it can happen in less than a month.

To prevent the pH of the coolant from turning acid, most antifreeze solutions contain a base stock that neutralizes the harsh acids of the water and the ethylene glycol (which is also an acid solution in its original form) so the cooling solution will be a neutral or a base solution. But as time goes on, the base stock of the antifreeze wears out (just like motor oil does), allowing the antifreeze to return back to its original acidic form.

Over the road trucks use a coolant filter along with a recharging element to protect the cooling system. These filters must be changed on a regular basis in order to protect the cooling system from damage.

Mixing Antifreeze Solutions

Normally, if you read the directions on a jug of antifreeze it says use a 50:50 mixture of antifreeze and water (which is freezing protection to minus thirty-five degrees). You might ask, "Do I still have to do that even if it never gets below thirty-two degrees where I live?" Yes, you should. The reason is that **if you have protection to minus thirty-five degrees you also have a correct mixture of 50:50 antifreeze and water**. That 50:50 mixture also means the pH of the cooling system is now above 7.0. Water by itself has a pH of about 7.0, while new antifreeze out of the jug has a pH above 12.0.

Anything above 8.0 is acceptable in most systems. But a higher number is always better. Oftentimes, the water mixed with the antifreeze will have an acid pH number. If that is the case, it may be necessary to add a pH concentrate (available at any full line auto parts store) to correct the acid condition. It is still a good idea to check the pH of a cooling system at least every two years or 30,000 miles.

So Why Not Just Add More Antifreeze to Correct the pH Factor?

Water is the best disperser of heat there is, because the molecules in water are spaced far apart, which makes it easy for the heat to be absorbed into the water. The problem with water by itself is that it is corrosive to the metal parts of the cooling system, and it freezes in the winter months.

So antifreeze solution is added to prevent freezing, protect the metals and coolant hoses from ECD, and lubricate the moving parts in the cooling system such as the water pump and thermostat. If you were to use more antifreeze to correct the pH factor, the engine would likely overheat. This is because the molecules in antifreeze are packed tightly together and do not absorb or transfer heat well.

In effect, the molecules in antifreeze are exactly the opposite of water. But keep in mind that originally, the engineers were more concerned with the freezing of water in the radiator than boil-over protection, so that is the property they looked for. Antifreeze up until the 1960s was used for just that to keep the engine coolant from freezing in the winter, and was usually removed in the summer months.

If you think back prior to the 1950s, antifreeze was never advertised or intended to be a permanent year-round additive. Water was the primary engine coolant, with antifreeze just being used as protection against winter freeze-up. It wasn't until the 1960s that antifreeze became a year-round additive.

Cooling Hose Enemies

As we mentioned before, there are five basic enemies of coolant hoses: ECD, heat, oil, abrasion, and ozone. Let's look at each of these separately.

ECD: As we explained earlier, ECD is the damage caused by the electrical charge created by the engine block and related components, and transferred by the coolant throughout the system. ECD-resistant coolant hoses are available, check the product label.

Heat Damage: Coolant temperatures normally do not exceed 260 degrees Fahrenheit, however the under hood temperatures of many vehicles may be close to twice that. Heat damaged coolant hoses will typically have a hardened glossy cover with surface cracks showing on the outside. On the inside, the interior yarn fiber may be damaged, causing the coolant hose to feel soft in places, or it may bulge and burst. Defective radiator caps can also cause excessive pressure buildup that may damage the coolant hoses.

Oil Damaged Hoses: Damaged hoses are often caused by a nearby accessory leaking, such as a power steering unit that drips power steering fluid onto the coolant hose. Also, many years ago, coolants contained a soluble oil that served as a rust inhibitor and water pump lubricant. This oil additive readily destroyed coolant hoses, and therefore, is no longer used in name brand antifreeze. However, it is still buyer beware, as it was and still is a cheap additive.

Abrasion Damage: This type of damage is most often a result of a cut or puncture from road debris, or by coming in contact with a part of the engine, such as a fan blade or spinning pulley. This is a common occur-

ECD Damaged Hose

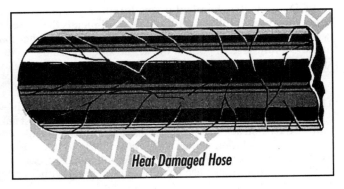

Heat Damaged Hose

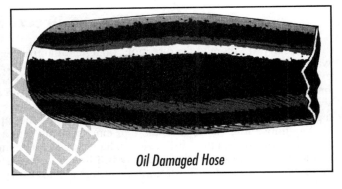

Oil Damaged Hose

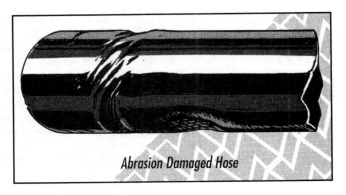

Abrasion Damaged Hose

rence when a "universal" hose is used to replace the correct molded hose.

Ozone Damage: Ozone is an oxygen compound found in small quantities in the atmosphere. Increased concentrations of ozone are found in polluted air, such as under the hood in the engine compartment. Ozone attacks the bonds in certain rubber compounds, which can damage coolant hoses, especially at stress points. It is also partly why your coolant hoses deteriorate when your car is just sitting unused in storage.

Ozone Damaged Hose

Now for the Tricky Stuff— Specialty Hose

Most of us know what a heater hose and a radiator coolant hose look like, and we all have seen flex hoses. But check out this hose from the Gates Rubber Co.; it would be perfect for a street rod or custom car application where the engine compartment is tight already. It is called a "branched hose" and is available in many different configurations.

A Trivia Lesson: The Green Stripe Story

The Gates Rubber Co. is one of the best known belt and hose companies throughout the world. Most of us have seen the "Green Stripe" found on the Gates brand of heavy-duty belts and hoses. Did you ever wonder how it came to be?

It was early in World War II that Gates

Example of branched coolant hose.

began supplying rubber products to the military, primarily for combat vehicles. After the war, these battle-field-tested belts and hoses became popular with commercial truckers. These belts and hoses were so tough they often outlasted the engines they were installed on. The commercial truckers were reported to have said that these military grade belts and hoses had "definitely earned their stripes" and the name stuck.

From then on, the military grade belts and hoses became known as the Gates "Green Stripe" Heavy-Duty Belts and Hoses. That tradition continues today, as the Gates brand of heavy-duty belts and hoses are still known by their Green Stripe markings.

Coolant Hose Installation Tips

You might think that you know all there is to know about coolant hose installation, but follow along anyway and you'll save yourself time and frustration:

1) The old radiator hose should be removed using a firm hand grip and a twisting action (after you have loosened the clamp). If the hose clamp itself is stuck, use a pair of tin snips to carefully cut the band of the clamp to release it. If the hose is stuck, do not force it or try to pry it off using a prying-type tool (screwdriver). Instead, carefully cut the hose lengthwise and then peel off the hose from the fitting.

2) After the old hose is removed, check the radiator's outlets or "nipples" as they are officially called, for any sharp edges or burrs. Next, clean the "nipples" with a wire brush to make sure all of the old hose residue and rust is gone.

3) Lubricating the "nipple" with coolant will make the hose installation go much easier. Clamp the hose into position between the outlet bead and the hose end. **CAUTION:** Do not tighten the hose clamp over the spline wire or outlet bead. Damage to the coolant hose could be the result. In other words, pay attention to what you are doing!

Now that you know all of the official rules concerning coolant hoses and their installation, it's time to learn a little about the hose clamps themselves.

All cooling system hoses are basically installed the same way. The hose is clamped on to inlet-outlet nipples on the radiator, water pump or heater.

The most common clamp is the worm-drive type which uses a simple screwdriver for tightening and loosening. The notched band won't cut the cover as a wire can. A worm-drive clamp also won't distort the pressure applied to the hose end when tightened.

When replacing a coolant hose, drain the cooling system below the level you are working. Loosen or cut the old clamp and slide the old hose off the fitting. If the hose is stuck, don't pry it off. You might damage the inlet/outlet nipple or the attached component. Use a knife to carefully cut off any pieces of the hose, then clean the remaining particles with a wire brush.

The fitting should be clean and smooth when you install a new hose. Burrs or sharp edges could cut into the hose tube and lead to premature failure.

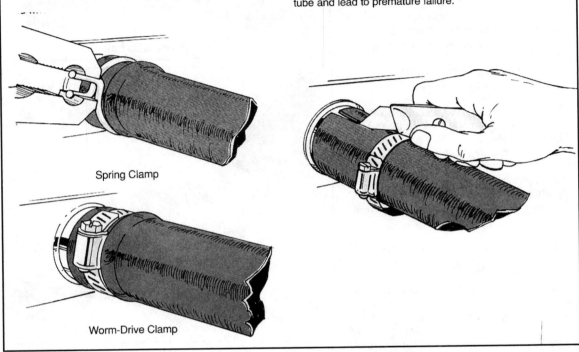

Spring Clamp

Worm-Drive Clamp

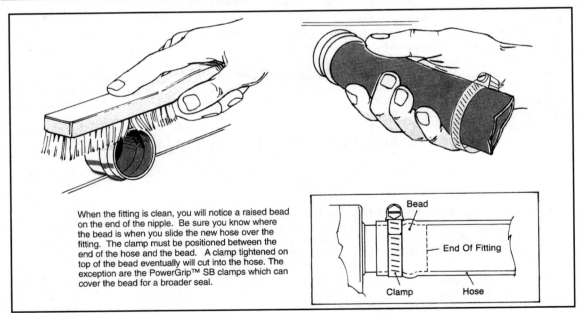

When the fitting is clean, you will notice a raised bead on the end of the nipple. Be sure you know where the bead is when you slide the new hose over the fitting. The clamp must be positioned between the end of the hose and the bead. A clamp tightened on top of the bead eventually will cut into the hose. The exception are the PowerGrip™ SB clamps which can cover the bead for a broader seal.

Bead

End Of Fitting

Clamp   Hose

Hose Clamps 101

Quick, name the five common types of coolant hose clamps. Gotcha! I know you have seen most of these types of clamps in service, but do you really know their strengths and why there are so many different clamps in the first place?

Clamp the hose into position between the bead and the hose end.

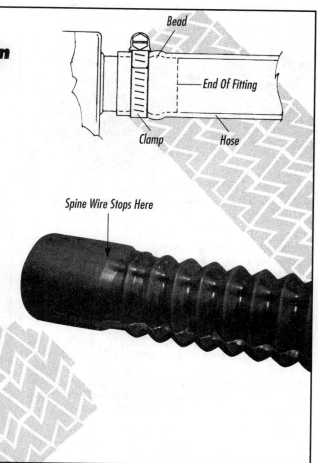

Bead

End Of Fitting

Clamp

Hose

Spine Wire Stops Here

Caution: A clamp tightened over the bead will eventually cut the hose tube. Extra care should be given when positioning a clamp on a Flex-N-Fit® hose. **The clamp's tightening device should not be positioned over the spine wire.**

In some cases, if the replacement hose is not an exact original-equipment duplicate, slight twisting or bending of the hose may be required for proper installation. This will not damage the hose as long as it does not kink or collapse. Also, avoid routing hoses into abrasive or high-temperature environments without protective sleeving.

Some automobile manufacturers use a **_spring clamp_** which can be carefully loosened or tightened with ordinary pliers. Spring clamps, although easy to adjust, tend to be weak and are rarely used in many applications.

Spring Clamp

Spring Clamp: This type can be loosened or tightened with ordinary pliers. While they are easy to adjust, they tend to be weak and are better suited for use on your washing machine.

Screw Tower and Twin Wire Clamps: These clamps are much stronger than spring clamps; you can, in fact (if you're not careful) easily over-tighten these clamps, causing the wire band to cut into the coolant hose. This style of coolant hose clamp is by far the toughest clamp, so don't get carried away when you tighten it.

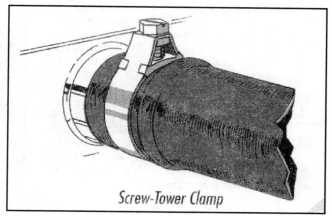

Screw-Tower Clamp

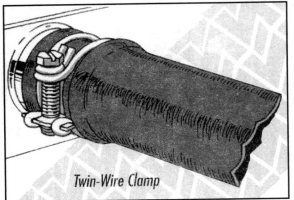

Twin-Wire Clamp

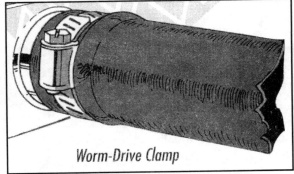

Worm-Drive Clamp

Worm Drive Clamps: Being the most common and fool-proof type of hose clamps, they can be easily adjusted with a screwdriver or nutdriver, and will easily hold the coolant hose in place. The band will not cut the hose the way a wire clamp can.

Constant Tension Clamps: Simply put, these are the most reliable tension clamps. By design, they are self-adjusting and maintenance free. They eliminate leaks by providing a constant clamping pressure. Often considered the best choice for coolant hose applications.

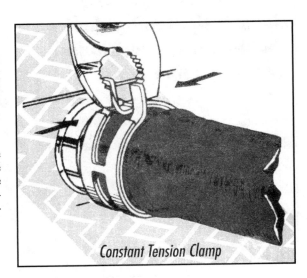

Constant Tension Clamp

Cooling System Service

The following are some of the official rules for cooling system service, established during the 1930s, and most are still true today:

1) When adding water to the cooling system, the water should be as near neutral in pH as possible (distilled water works well). Soft water is better than hard. Rain water, if clean, is usually soft, etc.
2) Avoid water containing lime, alkali, or impurities. If you must add water that is alkaline or hard, adding a pint of rust inhibitor (available at the local auto parts store) will go a long way towards keeping your system clean. Then be sure and check the pH level when you are through. What's that? You say you don't know how to do that? Keep reading and you will.
3) It was once considered good practice to flush out the cooling system twice a year: in the spring, and in the fall. This helped clean out the loose scale and rust particles that had accumulated over the seasons. Nowadays, with better additives, at least every couple of years is still required.

Inspect cooling systems regularly

46

Cooling System Tune-up

Each spring and fall it was also recommended that the following locations be checked for leaks: drain cocks, cylinder head bolts and nuts, hose clamps, water pump packing (lubricating the pump with waterproof grease if necessary), water pump mounting bolts, and, finally, radiator hold-down brackets and hardware.

It was also suggested that one should look for leaks in the radiator itself, and around all connecting hoses, core plugs, gaskets, and tin cover plates, replacing as necessary. A cooling system tune-up should be performed at least twice a year and before venturing out on any long trips.

Keep in mind that if you own and drive a collector car built before the 1950s, this information still applies to you. You may want to check your owner's manual or shop manual for more specific details.

HERE ARE THE THREE NEW "PRESTONE" BRAND COOLING SYSTEM PRODUCTS

DEVELOPED IN THE SAME LABORATORIES THAT PRODUCED "PRESTONE" ANTI-FREEZE!

Early cooling system products.

COOLING SYSTEM CLEANERS

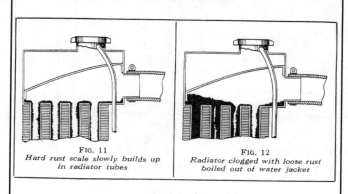

FIG. 11
Hard rust scale slowly builds up in radiator tubes

FIG. 12
Radiator clogged with loose rust boiled out of water jacket

Formerly, nearly all radiator cleaners were of the alkaline type, such as washing soda, or were the solvent type, such as kerosene. These materials may cut grease and remove loose rust but they have no solvent action on the rust itself, and therefore do not remove hard rust-scale in the radiator core or in the engine water jacket.

An effective cooling system cleaner such as "Prestone" brand cooling system cleaner is capable of removing both hard rust-scale and grease by dissolving action. This cleaner attacks rust deposits and grease but is harmless to cooling system metals and hose connections.

Iron rust and water scale usually build up together in the cooling system. Laboratory study of deposits from clogged radiators has shown that the clogging material is usually more than 90% iron rust with some grease and small amounts of water scale. No cleaner has rapid action on hard water scale, but "Prestone" brand cooling system cleaner dissolves the rust and breaks up the water scale so that it can be flushed out.

Periodic flushing with water may remove loose rust but flushing alone is not effective for removal of hard, adherent rust scale or grease. The use of a cleaner, to loosen and dissolve the scale, is necessary before flushing can be effective.

Overheating Problems

Aside from the usual leaking radiator and hoses, sometimes overheating is caused by a more serious problem. A leak in a cylinder can be caused by a faulty or damaged gasket or maybe a crack in the cylinder itself, either on the inside or the outside of the cylinder. Oftentimes, by warming the engine and *carefully* removing the radiator cap you can watch for bubbles at the cap hole. Bubbles are caused by the compression leaking out of the cylinder and into the coolant passages. Taking a compression test of each of the cylinders will usually find the bad cylinder. **CAUTION:** Be careful to never try and remove a warm cylinder head from the engine; there is a strong chance you will warp the head. Instead drain the cooling system and let the engine block cool naturally. Also, do not pry on the gasket surface area with a large screwdriver or chisel, as you will damage the smooth gasket surface area, causing the new cylinder head gasket to leak.

 Back off the cylinder head bolts or nuts and crank the engine over a few times. The compression will usually pop the cylinder head loose. Then use a block of wood or similar soft object to pry the cylinder head loose from the engine.

TO THE COOLING SYSTEM

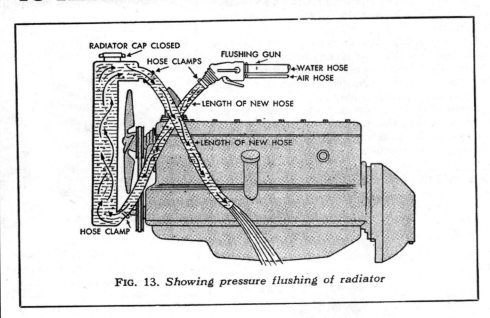

FIG. 13. *Showing pressure flushing of radiator*

To pressure flush cooling system, open the upper and lower hose connections, remove thermostat, and screw radiator cap on tight.

For applying the flushing gun to the radiator see Fig. 13. The hoses from the car may be used for attaching the gun, but a length of new hose may be more convenient. Use curved hose in tight places. Flush the radiator separately from the block whenever possible, and work on the radiator first to give the engine time to cool off.

A hose clamp is recommended to avoid leakage and to prevent the gun from being blown out of the hose when the air pressure is applied.

To carry the flushing stream away from the engine, a length of new hose may be attached to the upper radiator opening.

NOTE—In a few car models the water pump thrust seal seats against the impeller instead of against the pump housing. According to the makers of these cars this seal may be unseated by pressure. Although we have never encountered this condition, if there is any question, remove the water pump before pressure flushing the water jacket.

PRESSURE FLUSHING the COOLING SYSTEM

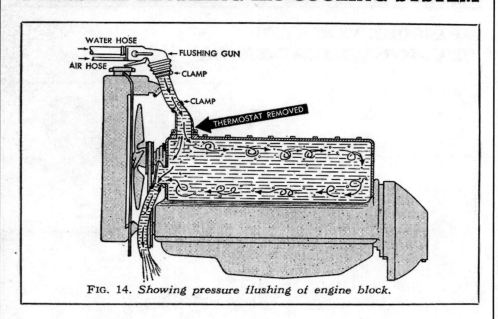

FIG. 14. *Showing pressure flushing of engine block.*

First flush in the opposite direction to normal flow as shown in Figs. 13, 14 and 15. Then flush in the other direction also. In systems containing very large quantities of rust, pressure flushing may be beneficial *before* cleaning as well as after.

Flushing Radiator — With the radiator cap on tight, and the gun clamped in the lower radiator hose, turn on the water and let it run till radiator is full. (Fig. 13.) Then apply air pressure gradually to avoid possible damage, especially when the radiator is clogged. Shut off air, again fill radiator with water and again apply air pressure. Repeat operation until water comes out clear.

Flushing Engine Block — The engine block requires flushing just as much as the radiator. Follow the procedure shown in Fig. 14. Partly close the opening at the water pump to fill engine with water before air pressure is applied. For cleaning out badly clogged engine water jackets remove core-hole plugs or cylinder head studs and flush through holes with small flexible tube attached to gun nozzle.

Service After Flushing — After flushing cars with sealed cooling, be sure that the valves in the radiator cap are free from sediment and properly seated.

Following the cleaning operation be sure to check thermostat, lubricate water pump, clean out overflow pipe, and blow insects and dirt from radiator air passages, radiator grille and bug screen.

PRESSURE FLUSHING THE HOT WATER HEATER

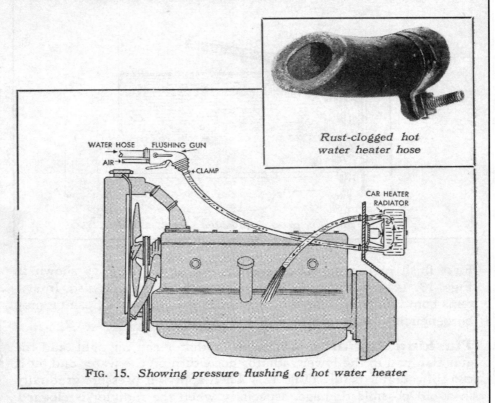

Rust-clogged hot water heater hose

FIG. 15. *Showing pressure flushing of hot water heater*

Hot water heaters and connections also collect rust, sediment and grease, and should be cleaned and pressure flushed whenever the cooling system is given this service.

Disconnect both heater hoses at the engine, and apply gun as shown in Fig. 15. If coolant flow through this heater is manually or thermostatically controlled by a valve, make sure the valve is wide open before flushing heater cores.

First flush the hot water heater in the direction opposite the normal flow through it, and then flush in the other direction. Follow the same special procedure as for the car radiator, applying air pressure gradually to avoid damaging the heater radiator.

CAUSES OF RADIATOR LEAKAGE

Seam leakage of radiator core

About 14% of all cooling system complaints are due to radiator leakage. Most of the leakage is in the soldered seams of the core and between the core and tank, and is caused by breakage from strains and shocks resulting from front end and engine vibration, rough road driving and pressure in closed systems. These same conditions sometimes are severe enough to fracture the joint where the radiator inlet and outlet pipes are attached to the tank.

Extreme changes of temperature in Winter driving also cause strains which open up leaks.

When the seams break, the solder corrodes out, but breakage rather than corrosion is the primary cause of seam leakage. Another cause of radiator leakage is perforation of the thin water-tube metal by electrolytic corrosion. Salt anti-freezes, some types of stop-leaks, mineral impurities in water, and cleaning solutions left in indefinitely, all increase electrolytic corrosion.

A common problem encountered in heavy-duty cooling systems is the occurrence of cold water leaks. This leak usually happens shortly after a new clamp or hose has been installed. Here is what causes the problem:

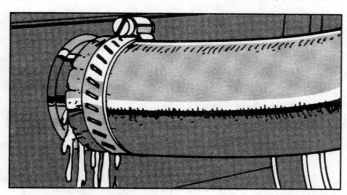

1. Both the radiator and engine block inlet and outlet tubes (metal) are susceptible to heat expansion and contraction. As the coolant and under-hood heat rises, these tubes begin to expand.

2. If a common band clamp is installed when the engines cool and it is tightened to the normal torque value, leaks probably will not occur when the engine is brought up to operating temperature. Then, because the inlet and outlet tubes have expanded, the hose will be squeezed between the clamp and the tube **in excess** of the normal compression.

3. This squeezing of the hose causes what is known as "compression set"; that is, the hose will "set" in the compressed position caused by the extra pressure of the expanding metal tube.

DAMAGE FROM OVERHEATING

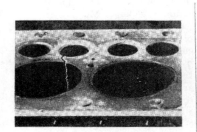
Cracked engine block
Courtesy of "Commercial Car Journal"

Damaged thermostat

Engines cannot be operated at excessive temperatures without injury. Cracked cylinder heads and engine blocks often result from operating an overheated engine or from adding cold water to a hot engine. Warn your customers to keep an eye on the temperature indicator, and to stop driving at the first sign of overheating.

Cylinder heads and engine blocks are often warped and cracked by terrific strains set up in the metal by overheating, especially when followed by rapid cooling. This applies to both iron and aluminum cylinder heads. Damaged thermostats, burnt valves, scored pistons, cylinders and bearings, are other overheating penalties.

WATER PUMP TROUBLES

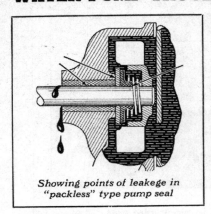
Showing points of leakege in "packless" type pump seal

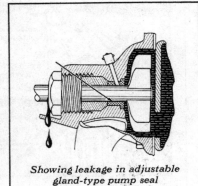
Showing leakage in adjustable gland-type pump seal

Water pump leakage is a very common cause of rust formation, antifreeze loss and overheating damage. In the adjustable packing-gland pump and also in the "packless" or automatic seal type, leakage is usually due to neglect of necessary repairs.

Tightening the packing nut or replacing the packing does not always stop leakage of adjustable gland-type pumps. Often a worn shaft or bearing is the real cause of leakage and must be replaced.

Leakage in the "packless" pumps occurs at the thrust washer seal and also at the shaft seal. This type of pump seal is self-adjusting. The seal, including the rubber part, has a limited life requiring renewal, and it may also be necessary to replace the pump bearing and shaft or even the complete pump assembly.

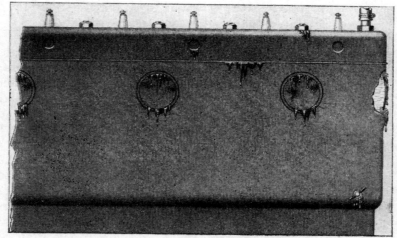

OUTSIDE LEAKAGE OF ENGINE WATER JACKET

Engine block leakage can be avoided by regular servicing

Core-hole plugs, engine drain cocks, water jacket cover plates, studs and capscrews, cylinder head and other water joints in the engine are often sources of very troublesome leakage, even in comparatively new cars.

Any leakage in the engine-block water joints is aggravated by pressure in sealed cooling systems, or by pump pressure in the water jacket which may run as high as 35 pounds per square inch.

Leaky core-hole plugs should always be replaced as soon as the leakage is noticed. Clean the core-hole plug seat and coat it with a suitable sealing compound. Use recommended tool for driving new plug in place.

Water jacket cover plates, where used, are generally made of light gauge steel. Merely tightening the bolts may start leakage, if it does not already exist, due to the thin plate bending under the bolts and breaking the old gasket.

It is better to replace old leaking gaskets, and to use the best quality of gasket material you can buy. Apply a suitable sealing compound to new gaskets unless otherwise recommended.

To prevent leakage at cylinder head studs and cap screws, apply a suitable sealing compound to the threads entering the block.

With the engine running, thoroughly check the block, both cold and hot, for leakage and correct all leaks found. Small leaks that show up as damp spots often cannot be detected when engine is hot except by rust, corrosion and dye stains from evaporated leakage.

More Causes of Overheating

1) Radiator low on water.

2) Radiator clogged either internally with lime and corrosion, or on the outside with dirt, insects, or some sort of road kill.

3) Ignition spark. If the ignition is retarded or advanced too far, has defective spark plugs, defective condenser or ignition points—anything that causes the engine to misfire and work harder—can cause overheating.

4) Carbon buildup inside of the cylinders. By the way, do not go scratching around on top of the piston after you have removed the cylinder head. The grooves you install will just gather more carbon and start things all over again. Instead, a cure from the old days was to warm the engine completely, then pour small amounts of water down the carburetor with the engine at a fast idle.

LEAKAGE INTO ENGINE FROM WATER JACKET

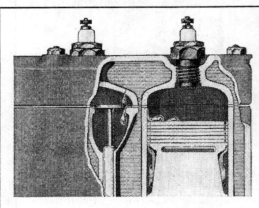
Coolant leaking into engine

Leakage of coolant into the engine through a loose cylinder head joint, or a crack in the cylinder head or block, is a common and serious cause of trouble, both with water and with anti-freeze solution. Whether or not any damage is done depends on the amount and duration of leakage. Appreciable quantities of water and anti-freeze may be removed by crank case ventilation, and do no harm in warm weather, but may cause engine trouble at freezing temperatures.

Water and anti-freeze solutions are, of course, not suitable for engine lubrication, and either mixed with the engine oil in large quantities may form sludge which causes lubrication failure, "sticky" piston rings, valves and valve lifters, and even serious engine damage if driving is continued. In over-head valve engines, outside leakage of coolant from the head joint may run into the crankcase through the push-rod compartment. The "Quick Check" or other pressure tests of the combustion chambers will not detect this type of trouble, and partial disassembly of the upper part of the engine may be necessary to find the leak.

Special attention should *always* be given to the cylinder head joint regardless of whether the cylinder head is aluminum or iron and this joint should be checked regularly to be sure it is always leak-tight. If there is suspicion of head joint leakage, replace the gasket and use gasket sealing compound recommended by the car factory. Authorities state that *stop-leaks cannot be depended on to permanently correct cylinder head joint leakage.*

The cylinder head joint should not be neglected because a car is new. Many have leaking heads and require tightening before delivery. Whenever the cylinder head is removed, a new gasket designed for the particular engine should *always* be installed. Coolant and oil leakage as well as serious overheating can result from an improperly installed gasket. Before replacing head, clean threads in bolt holes and **coat the bolt threads with factory recommended sealing compound.**

EXHAUST GAS LEAKAGE AND AIR SUCTION INTO COOLING SYSTEM

Exhaust gas leaking into
cooling system

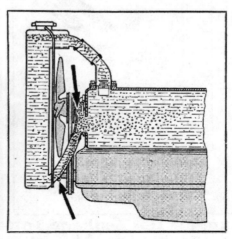

Suction of air into
cooling system

A loose cylinder head joint allows exhaust gas to be blown into the cooling system under explosion pressures as high as 600 pounds, even though the joint is tight enough to prevent liquid leakage into the engine. This exhaust gas can cause serious overflow loss of coolant, and when dissolved in either water or anti-freeze solutions, forms acids which may cause corrosive damage to cooling system metals, as well as rapid rust formation and radiator clogging.

A leak at the water pump, or any point between pump and radiator, will allow air to be sucked into the cooling system when the pump is running. Water pumps may also suck air even though there is no apparent leakage. At high speed the pump actually pulls water down through the radiator core. If there is any leakage in the core, the pump suction may also pull air in through these leaks.

Aeration, or mixing air with water, speeds up rust formation as much as 30 times according to tests, and increases corrosion of all cooling system metals. Clogging and corrosion go hand in hand with water pump leakage and aeration.

Besides speeding up corrosion, air suction into the cooling system may cause serious foaming, overflow loss of coolant and overheating.

Where rusty coolant, severe rust clogging, corrosion or overflow losses are encountered, the cooling system should be checked for exhaust gas leakage, air suction and aeration in top radiator tank.

Simple tests for air suction and exhaust gas leakage, which require no special equipment, are described on the following page.

"QUICK CHECK" TESTS

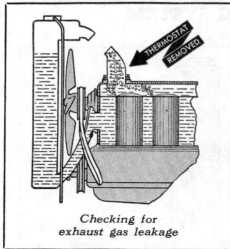

Checking for exhaust gas leakage

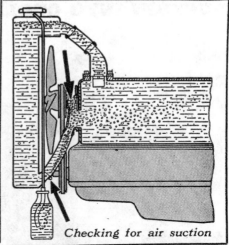

Checking for air suction

Exhaust Gas Leakage Test— Start test with engine cold. Remove fan belt from drive pulley, or disconnect water pump coupling, to prevent pump operation. Drain system until coolant is level with top of engine block *but no lower*. Remove upper radiator hose, thermostat housing, and thermostat. With thermostat housing either removed or replaced, fill block completely by pouring water into the radiator, to remove trapped air.

(1) With engine in neutral gear "gun" it several times, watching for bubbles in water opening while "gunning" and also when engine drops back to "idling," or

(2) jack up rear wheels, run engine at higher speed in high gear, and load it gradually and intermittently by use of foot brake.

(3) On cars with fluid couplings and automatic drives, set hand brake, place selector lever in drive position and intermittently load the engine by gradually depressing the accelerator.

Appearance of bubbles or sudden rise of liquid indicates exhaust gas leakage. Injecting suitable light oil into carburetor while testing sometimes helps to identify exhaust gas leakage by producing smoke in bursting bubbles. Make test quickly before boiling starts since steam bubbles give misleading results.

Air Suction Test—Adjust liquid level in radiator, allowing room for expansion, so as to avoid any overflow loss during test. Be sure radiator cap is on *air tight*. With pressure caps, block open valve, or replace with plain cap. Attach a length of rubber tube to lower end of overflow pipe. All connections must be air tight. Run engine in neutral gear at safe, high speed until dash heat indicator stops rising and remains stationary. Without changing engine speed, put end of rubber tube into bottle of water, avoiding kinks and low bends that might block flow of air, and watch for bubbles in water bottle. In the absence of exhaust gas leakage a continuous stream of bubbles indicates that air is being sucked into the cooling system.

PREVENTION OF ALUMINUM CYLINDER HEAD CORROSION

One cause of the severe corrosion which occasionally occurs in aluminum cylinder heads is the use of water high in chloride salts. The sources of chlorides may include certain types of anti-freeze preparations, cleaning solutions left in the cooling system, and chemical salts sometimes found in the cooling systems of new cars. Also, water supplies in certain areas of the country are high in chlorides.

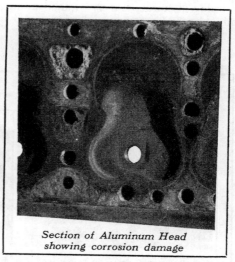

Section of Aluminum Head showing corrosion damage

Another cause of aluminum corrosion we have found is coolant contamination from exhaust gas leakage, which introduces corrosive acids into the coolant through a loose cylinder head. High chloride salt content in water, and exhaust gas leakage also cause serious corrosion of other metals. Suction of air by the water pump through leaks in the system speeds up this corrosion.

Corrosion of aluminum cylinder heads is largely electrolytic, such as is generally found in alloys of other metals, and appears in the form of pitting, usually localized around the water transfer holes. This type of corrosion is accelerated by erosion resulting from high localized coolant velocity.

To obtain satisfactory life from aluminum cylinder heads and to prevent corrosion, use the special cylinder head gasket recommended by the car factory and keep the cylinder head joint and water pump connections leak-tight at all times. Avoid using water of high mineral salt content, as well as anti-freezes, rust inhibitors and stop-leak compounds of questionable merit. Maintain full strength inhibtor protection the year around.

5) Pistons, piston rings, piston pins, and bearings fitted too tightly in a rebuilt engine will cause overheating, as will thick piston rings in shallow grooves.

6) Driving in low gear and racing the engine will cause overheating because the engine is running at high rpm, but not much air is moving through the radiator.

7) Carburetion. If you have been one of those who likes to monkey with the carburetor and you get things too lean, the engine will run hot and will overheat.

8) Wrong weight of lubricating oil. Common sense should tell you not to run straight 40 weight oil in the winter and 10 weight in the summer. Better check your owner's manual.

9) Clogged or collapsed muffler.

10) Frozen radiator. Radiators freeze from the bottom, which cuts off the circulation of frozen water. It's best to thaw out things and install some antifreeze if it is not too late.

11) Fan belt loose, too dumb to mention, but it happens a lot!

12) Finally, trying to outrun your new father-in-law at a shotgun wedding can cause overheating, but that might be the least of your worries.

RUST CLOGGING

FIG. 9. *Rust deposits in water jacket* | FIG. 10. *Rust clogged radiator core*

Although clogging is a fairly common cause of cooling system trouble, it can be avoided entirely by cleaning and rust-proofing. The most common clogging materials are rust, scale and grease, of which rust contributes about 90%. The rust is formed on the iron walls of the engine water jacket. Grease and oil may enter the system through the water pump and cylinder head joint.

Coolant circulation keeps loosening the rust as it forms. Some of it settles in the water jacket (Fig. 9), but fine particles are also carried over into the radiator where they build up a layer of hard scale inside the water tubes .

It usually takes time for this scale to get thick enough to stop circulation (Fig. 10), but the scale keeps cutting down the radiator cooling capacity until finally the engine overheats and boiling starts in the water jacket. This stirs up the rust and dumps it into the radiator

Rusty solutions of anti-freeze or rusty water will eventually cause radiator clogging.

After boiling starts it is only a short time until a load of rust is packed in the tubes of the radiator, stopping circulation. Then further driving is out of question until both the radiator and the engine block are thoroughly cleaned and flushed.

Lime deposits also form rapidly at "hot spots" in the engine. This mineral scale produces an insulating coat on the water side of the cylinder barrels and head, which causes knock and overheating. To avoid excessive formation of water scale deposits, keep the cooling system leak-tight, add as little water as possible and maintain full strength corrosion protection at all times.

Notes

Chapter 8: Engine Fan Belts

The fan belt is what powers the water pump and the mechanical fan on most cooling systems, along with the alternator and power steering on some newer applications. Fan belts are the most often ignored part of the cooling system. After all, the common belief is, if it ain't broke don't fix it! Knowing how a fan belt is designed and constructed will help you better understand how they are designed to work. In the early days of the automobile, engine fans were driven off of the engine using a belt that was made of leather, rubber, or a round rope called hemp rope. In 1917, John G. Gates invented what came to be known as the V-belt, a wedge-shaped rubber belt that fit the shape of a pulley better, and lasted longer than rope or leather belts.

Eventually, rubber compounds were developed and improved to resist winter's brutal cold and summer's scorching heat. These new belts were also expected to resist damage from engine heat, engine oil, coolant leaks, road debris, and the normal things such as dirt and water. These early belts became the basis of the modern V-belt.

Up until the mid-1970s, most V-belts featured a protective fabric cover or band on the outside of the belt. Modern technology, though, has allowed the strength of belts to be improved enough so that the protective cover is no longer necessary.

Quality V-belts are made up of three parts: the overcord, the tensile cord, and the undercord. The overcord is made of rubber compounds and fabric, and protects the tensile cord from dirt and oil. It also gives the cord additional side-to-side support in the pulley.

The tensile cord is the muscle of the belt. Tensile cords are usually made up of twisted polyester that is strong enough to withstand shock, resist stretching, bend easily, and have a long life.

The undercord provides support to the tensile cord and transfers the belt load to the pulley. The undercord has two layers. Directly under the tensile cord is a fiber-loaded stock. Chopped polyester is the best material for this, although some companies use chopped cotton, which is not as strong. Another problem with cotton is that it acts like a wick drawing oil and contaminants into the belt, often causing the belt structure itself to fail.

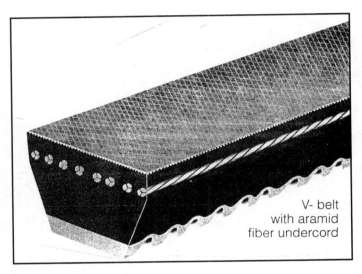

V- belt
with aramid
fiber undercord

The Gates Rubber Co. uses aramid fiber (the stuff used to make bulletproof vests) for the bottom layer (undercord) of its V-belts. Aramid fiber is self-lubricating, heat resistant, runs quiet, and is strong. Most modern V-belts have a notched undercord to accommodate smaller pulley sizes. The notch pattern allows greater flexibility and bend radius.

The three sections that make up a V-belt are held together by strong adhesive materials. First the adhesives and "liquid elastomers" cover the tensile cord. Then a special gum stock is heated, which softens and flows during the vulcanization process filling the empty spaces among the cord, textiles and rubber compounds. (Vulcanization is the process that makes rubber stronger after it is treated with heat and sulfur.) The result is a belt composed of many separate pieces now made into one.

The Important Stuff

Now to finish the belt. The positioning of the tensile cords within the belt can greatly affect the belt's overall performance. If the tensile cord is positioned at the top of the layering process, about thirty percent of the vulcanized material is scrapped after cutting and grinding. These are known as "High Cord Belts."

In contrast, if the cords are positioned in the middle, the cutting process is more efficient; every other belt cut out is just flipped over to fit the wedge shape of the pulley. This creates what is known as "Center Cord Belts." Center cord belts, as a rule, don't last as long as high cord belts. **Remember it is the cord**

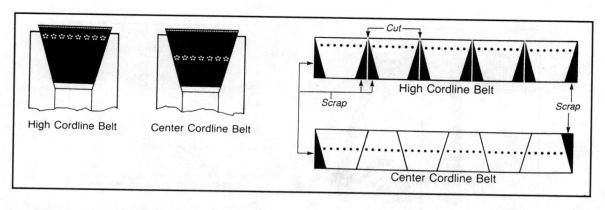

High Cordline Belt   Center Cordline Belt

Cut

High Cordline Belt

Scrap   Scrap

Center Cordline Belt

that gives a belt its strength. High cord belts have approximately forty percent more cords, because the cords are placed in the wider part of the belt.

Beware

Not all high cord belts are better quality than center cord belts. Many cheaply manufactured high cord belts hardly last as long as a quality center cord belt. The attention to details such as the quality of the cord, the angle of the belt and how well it matches the pulley groove, along with the quality of the vulcanization itself, plays a big part in how long the belt will last. If you need the strength of a high cord belt, you are much better off to buy one of good quality from a name brand company.

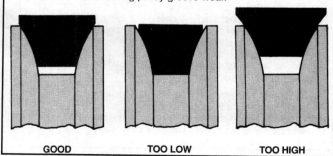

The attention to details such as the quality of the cord, the angle of the belt and how well it matches the pulley groove, along with the quality of the vulcanization itself, plays a big part in how long the belt will last.

The Care and Feeding of Your Belts

Belts are designed to be resilient and flexible, but like anything else exposed to a rough environment they will wear out. Years of exposure to heat, oil, high mileage, and stress does take its toll. (Sounds a little like us, doesn't it?)

One of the first problems that occurs with an older belt is that it begins to slip. A slipping belt doesn't turn the pulley efficiently, and the extra friction created causes the belt itself to overheat, making the problem worse. In addition, the extra heat created can be transferred onto the pulley, then up the pulley shaft where it then melts all of the lubricating grease in the bearings of the accessory, and the accessory fails.

Alternators are a good example of this. Many times the alternator will fail, is replaced, only to have it fail again in a few months. Because the alternator has one of the smallest diameter pulleys of any accessory it spins the fastest and wears out the quickest. A worn alternator pulley can wear out a new belt in just a few thousand miles.

It is easy to see how this problem can go around and around, especially since most replacement alternators do not come with a new pulley.

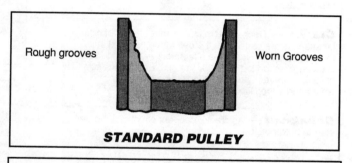

Rough grooves   Worn Grooves

STANDARD PULLEY

How the belt rides in the pulley groove is an important factor affecting a belt's life. The belt should ride slightly above the top of the pulley groove. If the belt rides too high, the edges of the pulley will wear into the belt sides and eventually cut through the cover (or into the exposed internal parts of the belt).

If the belt rides too low it will soon bottom out in the pulley groove. The belt then acts like a flat belt and it loses its wedging grip on the sides of the pulley groove. This will cause the belt to slip, accelerating belt wear, glazing the belt sidewalls and increasing pulley groove wear.

GOOD   TOO LOW   TOO HIGH

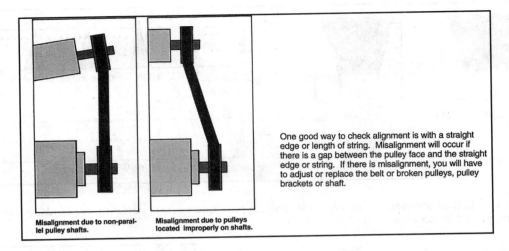

One good way to check alignment is with a straight edge or length of string. Misalignment will occur if there is a gap between the pulley face and the straight edge or string. If there is misalignment, you will have to adjust or replace the belt or broken pulleys, pulley brackets or shaft.

Misalignment due to non-parallel pulley shafts.

Misalignment due to pulleys located improperly on shafts.

Belt alignment is also important! A misaligned pulley will cause noisy belts and can also wear out the bearings in an accessory within a few thousand miles. The new serpentine belts used on today's cars, are especially sensitive to this and do make a lot of noise if they are out of alignment the least little bit.

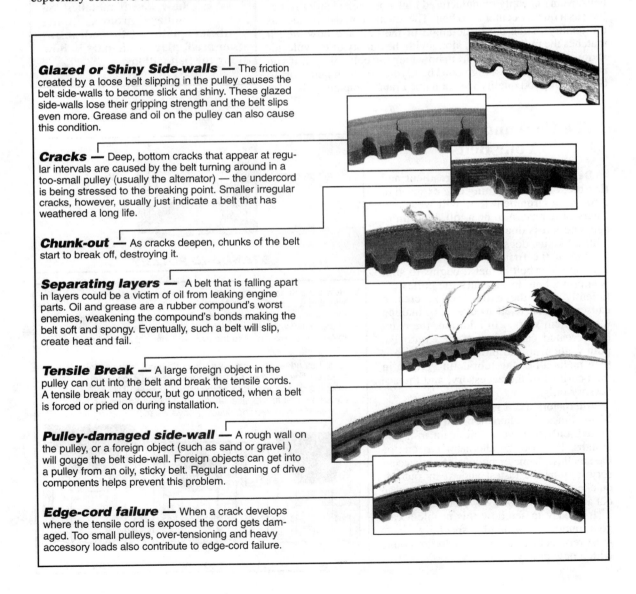

Glazed or Shiny Side-walls — The friction created by a loose belt slipping in the pulley causes the belt side-walls to become slick and shiny. These glazed side-walls lose their gripping strength and the belt slips even more. Grease and oil on the pulley can also cause this condition.

Cracks — Deep, bottom cracks that appear at regular intervals are caused by the belt turning around in a too-small pulley (usually the alternator) — the undercord is being stressed to the breaking point. Smaller irregular cracks, however, usually just indicate a belt that has weathered a long life.

Chunk-out — As cracks deepen, chunks of the belt start to break off, destroying it.

Separating layers — A belt that is falling apart in layers could be a victim of oil from leaking engine parts. Oil and grease are a rubber compound's worst enemies, weakening the compound's bonds making the belt soft and spongy. Eventually, such a belt will slip, create heat and fail.

Tensile Break — A large foreign object in the pulley can cut into the belt and break the tensile cords. A tensile break may occur, but go unnoticed, when a belt is forced or pried on during installation.

Pulley-damaged side-wall — A rough wall on the pulley, or a foreign object (such as sand or gravel) will gouge the belt side-wall. Foreign objects can get into a pulley from an oily, sticky belt. Regular cleaning of drive components helps prevent this problem.

Edge-cord failure — When a crack develops where the tensile cord is exposed the cord gets damaged. Too small pulleys, over-tensioning and heavy accessory loads also contribute to edge-cord failure.

Don't assume that the factory always gets it right. They use lots of different mounting bracket combinations depending on what accessory group is involved, and they themselves have a tough time keeping all of the combinations straight. If you have a noisy belt, check the alignment of the pulleys using a straight edge. I would hate to be the one to tell you, "I told you so."

So What Happened to My Fan Belt?

Sometimes fan belts just wear out from old age or high mileage; that is the ideal way to wear out a belt, but oftentimes fan belts meet a tragic early death. Here are some of the reasons why:

1) **Glazing.** The friction created by a loose fan belt slipping in the pulley will cause the sidewalls of the belt to glaze and take on a glossy appearance. The glazed sidewalls then lose their gripping strength and the belt begins to slip even more. You can guess the rest.

2) **Cracks.** Deep bottom cracks that appear at regular intervals are caused by the belt turning around a too small alternator pulley. The undercord is being stressed to the breaking point. Small irregular cracks simply indicate a belt that has weathered a long life, and needs to be replaced.

3) **Chunk-out.** As cracks deepen, chucks of the belt will break loose and fall out leaving gaps in the belt.

4) **Separating layers**. A belt that comes apart in layers is often a victim of oil leaking from an engine part or accessory. Oil and grease are a belt's worst enemy, but then you already learned that.

5) **Tensile break.** A large foreign object caught in the pulley can cut the belt and break the tensile cords. Oftentimes cuts such as this can go unnoticed, so it is a good idea to inspect your belts on a regular basis.

6) **Pulley-damaged sidewalls.** Rough sides or deep wear grooves on the inside of the pulley can tear up a new belt. If in doubt, check the pulley sidewalls with a straight edge to see if anything is worn excessively.

7) **Edge-cord failure.** When a crack develops where a tensile cord is exposed the cord can easily be damaged. Misaligned pulleys, belts too tight, and heavy accessory loads can all cause edge cord failure.

> **Always replace belts in sets. If you don't, the new belt will carry all of the load and wear out in a short time. Replacing belts about every four years is the rule for vehicles in normal service. A little common sense here—if you put your belts through heck, replace them often. Treat them nice and they will last a long time.**

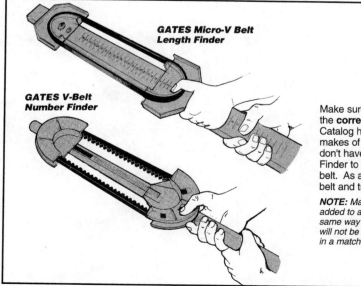

GATES Micro-V Belt Length Finder

GATES V-Belt Number Finder

Make sure the new belt you are putting on the drive is the **correct** size. The Gates Green Stripe Products Catalog has a complete listing of belt sizes for all makes of heavy-duty vehicles and equipment. If you don't have a catalog, use the Gates Belt Number Finder to measure the outside circumference of the old belt. As a last resort, pull a measuring tape around the belt and try to get the most accurate reading you can.

*NOTE: Matched belts **must** be replaced in sets. A new belt added to a set of old belts will not ride the pulleys in the same way the old ones do. As a result, the load of the drive will not be distributed evenly among all the belts. If one belt in a matched set fails, **all** the belts must be replaced.*

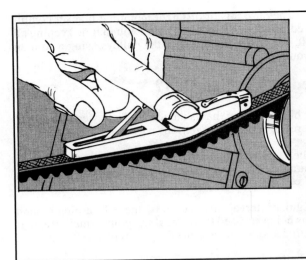

Check belt tension with a tension gauge. The correct tension is usually listed in the vehicle manufacturer's maintenance manual as a range of numbers. Initial tension on a new belt should be 15 pounds higher than the high-end figure recommended in the belt's tension range. Do not tension the belt too tight. An over-stressed belt can fail just as quickly as a slipping one. It also can put unnecessary stress on the accessory. Run the engine 15 to 20 minutes to allow the belt to "seat" into the pulleys, then readjust the tension to the high-end figure on the recommended tension range. **Proper tensioning of the belt is the most important step you can take to extend your belt's service life because it eliminates the problem of slipping — the leading cause of premature belt failure.** Gates Krikit V-Belt tension gauge is pictured here (Part No. 91107). For Micro-V Belts use Krikit II (Part No. 91132). See Gates catalog 31-2020 for tensioning recommendations.

Congratulations

Now that we have covered the two basic types of the cooling system and their parts, you should have a good understanding of how everything works. You should also understand how fan belts and coolant hoses are manufactured, and be able to explain what is atmospheric pressure.

By understanding the basic theory of how older cooling systems work, you should be able to easily figure out some of the odd cooling systems you will encounter, such as those found on antique tractors and heavy equipment. If it is an older vehicle and you don't see a water pump of some sort, and the radiator cap is not pressurized, then the odds are it is a thermo-syphon type of cooling system. (Some John Deere two-cylinder tractors used thermo-syphon cooling systems as late as the early 1950s.) While each design may be a little different, you know the theory of how the system is supposed to work, so it should be easy to troubleshoot common problems.

Notes

65

Chapter 9:
The Pressure Mounts

By the early 1950s, pressurized cooling systems began to be commonplace. The advantage of sealing the system and placing it under pressure was a higher boiling point, which meant that automotive engines could run hotter. This would, in theory, make them more efficient. It also paved the way for higher compression and higher horsepower engines. All of this came about in part because there was now a reliable way of controlling the operating temperature of the engine. Exactly how much difference does a pressurized system make? We already know that a non-pressurized system from the old days had a boiling point of 212 degrees Fahrenheit. **The rule that applies to a pressurized system says that for every pound of pressure in the cooling system, the boiling point of the water will rise three degrees Fahrenheit.**

So it is easy to see there was a definite advantage to developing a pressurized cooling system. Even by starting out with four pound caps as many manufacturers did, they raised the boiling point twelve degrees, which allowed for a hotter thermostat to be used and a higher engine operating temperature. That resulted in a more efficient engine and more horsepower, because the compression in the cylinders could be raised (which created more heat) without the engine coolant boiling over.

Cars today have sixteen pound radiator caps, and thermostats designed to open as high as 195 degrees Fahrenheit. In fact, many new car engines are designed to have a normal operating temperature of 220 degrees—unheard of fifty years ago. NASCAR racing teams have also experimented with some twenty-two- and twenty-six-pound cooling systems. Heat is horsepower, and they are always looking for ways to make an engine more efficient.

But before you run out and buy a sixteen pound cap for your antique car radiator expecting to have great things happen (boy will they), you need to understand a little more about what else is going on here. As you might suspect, things are not as simple as they first appear.

I will get into modern radiators and their construction in an upcoming chapter, but for those of you who can't wait, I will quickly explain what will happen to your antique car's radiator if you were to install a high pressure radiator cap on a cooling system designed as a non-pressurized or low pressure system.

Because of their design and the fact that they were not built for any kind of working pressure, most of the early radiators will come apart at the seams, literally, as the pressure begins to build inside of the radiator. Tube joint leaks were a constant problem with early radiators. In some later radiators built after the 1940s, you can usually get by with installing a five pound pressure cap, which is enough for an overflow recovery system to work. This can be a big benefit. As they say, travel at your own risk and check with an experienced radiator shop before you add much pressure—or you may be sorry.

What will happen to your antique car's radiator if you were to install a high pressure radiator cap on a cooling system designed as a non-pressurized or low pressure system? Because of their design and the fact that they were not built for any kind of working pressure, most of the early radiators will come apart at the seams, literally, as the pressure begins to build inside of the radiator. Tube joint leaks were a constant problem with early radiators. In some later radiators built after the 1940s, you can usually get by with installing a five pound pressure cap, which is enough for an overflow recovery system to work. This can be a big benefit. As they say, travel at your own risk and check with an experienced radiator shop before you add much pressure—or you may be sorry.

Meanwhile, by the late 1950s, most car manufacturers had figured out that a sealed, pressurized cooling system was the way to go. They had also worked on radiator technology enough to keep about twelve pounds of pressure in the system without any problems. So how much did the boiling point rise when a twelve pound radiator cap became the standard?

Remember, to figure this out, you know **there is a rise in the boiling point of three degrees Fahrenheit for every pound of pressure**, so 12 x 3 = 36. We know water boils at 212 degrees Fahrenheit, so if we add thirty-six to that, we now have a cooling system with a boiling point of 248 degrees Fahrenheit. This would mean we could raise the temperature that the thermostat opens to somewhere around 180 degrees, up from the 160 degree thermostats of the old days.

This would make our "heat engine" (as the engineers call it) more efficient, because not only are we running the engine at a higher operating temperature, the compression is also up. Therefore, more horsepower is available, and the engine is putting out less pollution. Internally, the engine is also doing better, because less sludge is being created as a result of the higher operating temperature, which also helps the combustion process to become more efficient.

Oil Changes

Of course motor oils and filters have also changed greatly in the last fifty years. One of the most important advancements was the invention of detergent motor oils that help to collect some of the sludge and contaminant by-products of the combustion process, and suspend them in the oil where they are carried to the oil filter and removed from the system when oil and filter are changed.

The lubricating oils themselves have also gotten much better at their job of lubricating the engine. As the engine operating temperatures began to creep higher and higher, it made it more difficult for the engine lubricating oil to lubricate the internal engine parts under these higher heat conditions. Modern engine parts themselves are also being stressed more than they were years ago.

If you remember back, the SAE (Society of Automotive Engineers) ratings of oil didn't change very often during the 1940s and 1950s—even through the 1960s it was only about every two or three years. But since the 1970s and especially into the 1980s and present decade, the SAE ratings seem to change every six months or so, as well as there being a lot more ratings. We now have turbo rated, diesel rated, small-car rated, high-heat rated, truck and off-road rated, and the list goes on and on.

The point I am trying to make here, is that the quality of engine lubricating oil has improved greatly over what it was in the 1920s and 1930s. The additives are much better quality, the basic oil stock is more refined to yield a product far superior to what we used even just twenty years ago. All of this relates to how efficient our "heat engine" is, and how long a lifespan our engine will have. The automotive engines themselves are also better built with closer tolerances and more accurate machine work, along with better quality materials, all which contribute to a better, longer lasting engine.

As you can see, it was a combined effort by all of the manufacturing groups that has allowed us to have the cooling systems we have today. Now that we have a good working cooling system, and a good lubrication system, we now need to seal the engine to be sure the compression stays in the cylinders, the coolant in the water passages, and the engine oil in the oil passages. Heaven forbid if they should ever come together and get all mixed up!

Chapter 10: Atmospheric Pressure Again

As you might expect, the compression ratio and the physical size of the cylinders themselves will have an effect on the pressure inside of the cylinder during the compression stroke. Another factor that can affect the compression pressure and the horsepower of an engine is the atmospheric pressure. (Something you understand from previous discussion, right?) Just as atmospheric pressure affects the boiling point of water, it also affects the compression pressure and the horsepower of an engine. (**Note: Compression ratio is the "actual" compression ratio as it occurs inside of the cylinders such as an 8:1 ratio and does not refer to the actual pressure inside of the cylinder. Compression ratio is often wrongfully used to refer to the pressure inside of the cylinders.**)

For example, an engine that might run fine and have plenty of power at sea level may likely run rough, lack power, and overheat at a higher altitude. This is because, as we have already learned, the atmospheric pressure is greater at sea level than it is in say, Denver, Colorado, which is some 5,280 feet above sea level.

We also know that as the altitude rises, the atmospheric pressure becomes lower, the density of the air inside the engine cylinders is less, which in turn, means that the compression pressure of the cylinders will also be less. Let's pick on a Model T Ford for instance. At sea level, a Model T Ford has an engine cylinder compression pressure (the pressure inside of the cylinder when the piston is at top dead center) of about 64 pounds per square inch before the ignition spark, and 256 pounds per square inch after ignition, when the fuel has expanded due to combustion.

Now let's take the same Ford car and drive it from sea level up to Denver. What happens to our little Ford car now? Besides having to back up most of the hills due to the gravity fed gasoline tank, the mighty Ford is fast losing power. At Denver, because of the city's 5,280-foot-above-sea-level altitude, the compression pressure is now down to 48.5 pounds per square inch before ignition, and 194 pounds per square inch after ignition.

> We know that as the altitude rises, the atmospheric pressure becomes lower, the density of the air inside the engine cylinders is less, which in turn, means that the compression pressure of the cylinders will also be less. Let's pick on a Model T Ford for instance. At sea level, a Model T Ford has an engine cylinder compression pressure (the pressure inside of the cylinder when the piston is at top dead center) of about 64 pounds per square inch before the ignition spark, and 256 pounds per square inch after ignition, when the fuel has expanded due to combustion.
>
> Now let's take the same Ford car and drive it from sea level up to Denver. What happens to our little Ford car now is that it is fast losing power. At Denver, because of the city's 5,280-foot-above-sea-level altitude, the compression pressure is now down to 48.5 pounds per square inch before ignition, and 194 pounds per square inch after ignition.

Because we have less horsepower available to climb the mountains, our engine is going to work much harder climbing those mountains. This will create more heat, because the engine is now under a greater load. Meanwhile the boiling point of the water in the cooling system is also going to be lower for the same reason.

Do You Think We Might be in Trouble Yet?

But wait, there's more! The thin air also changes the fuel mixture ratio for our Ford engine as well. If the air is less dense, that will make our fuel mixture rich (too much fuel being delivered) so the carburetor will have to be adjusted, so less gas is metered through the carburetor to match the low atmospheric pressure. Our fuel/air mixture needs to stay around the 13:1 ratio—thirteen parts air to one part fuel for the engine to be its most efficient.

Remember, Denver is only 5,280 feet above sea level, so what happens to our Model T Ford at the top of Pike's Peak, which is about 14,000 feet above sea level? The compression pressure will drop down to 30 pounds per square inch, less than half of what it was at sea level. And the after-ignition compression pressure will also fall down to 120 pounds per square inch, a long way from the 256 pounds per square inch we had at sea level.

Insult to Injury

To add insult to injury, the boiling point of water at 14,000 feet above sea level is 185 degrees Fahrenheit. So we are, without question, at a serious disadvantage here. Not only is the atmospheric pressure causing the water in the cooling system to boil at a lower temperature, that same atmospheric pressure is also reducing the horsepower output of our engine, making it work harder and operate at a higher temperature than normal. Is it any wonder the cars of the 1920s and 1930s had a difficult time in the mountains? Remember, engine braking is also less efficient due to the lower compression pressures.

Atmospheric pressure still affects engines today. For example, watch the professional drag race teams, especially the top fuel and funny car racers, as they travel from racetrack to racetrack. Because each track is located at a different altitude, the atmospheric pressure will be different at each location. In addition, the weather and humidity will also have a big effect on the atmospheric pressure, which in turn, can make a big difference in the horsepower output of an engine. So the crew chiefs will check the atmospheric pressure, temperature, and humidity between every run. That way they know exactly how to adjust the fuel mixture for optimum performance. By using too much fuel they can stretch cylinder head bolts and scatter expensive parts down the racetrack. The use of too lean a fuel mixture causes the engine to make less horsepower, allowing the team next-door to take home the prize money.

Summer Nights

Most of us have experienced a time, especially in the warm summer months, when our old car ran much better on the way home at midnight than it did after work at 5 p.m. Did you ever wonder why that was? It was partly due to that atmospheric pressure thing again. At night, the air was denser because the humidity had gone down, which helped. It also helped that the gasoline, which had a tendency to vapor lock during the heat of the day, remained in its liquid form up to the carburetor. This made the gasoline more dense.

By now we have learned that it isn't just the cooling system that is affected by the atmospheric pressure. We have learned that things such as the compression pressure in the cylinders and fuel mixtures are also greatly affected. All of these things together will affect the job the cooling system has to do.

There is one more important part of an engine that we need to talk about—the engine gaskets. While engine gaskets don't seem to have a glamorous role, without them there would be no usable output from the engine and we would all be walking. So stay tuned, as we learn about engine gaskets in the next chapter.

Chapter 11: Engine Gaskets-Sealing The Engine

Hey, I know this is a book about cooling systems and you don't care about engine gaskets or else you would have bought a book on the subject, but I want to touch on the subject briefly because engine gaskets can affect our cooling system and its efficiency.

Engine gaskets have a pretty tough job. First of all, they have to seal the engine from oil leaks. This means making sure the oil follows the correct path throughout the engine block and cylinder heads and doesn't leak or dribble out between the engine surfaces. Aside from making a mess, a leaking gasket could cause parts of the engine not to be lubricated. Eventually, the oil level would drop low enough that the engine lubrication would stop altogether. We know what that means!

The same can be said for the cooling system. The engine gaskets have to seal the coolant passages of the engine block and cylinder heads as well, so the coolant flows through the engine block and cylinder heads without mixing with the oil or leaking into the cylinders. If the fluids are allowed to mix, engine damage will soon result, just as it would with a lack of coolant.

Finally, the engine gaskets are expected to seal the engine cylinders so the compression stays inside of the cylinders, and doesn't leak out into the cooling system, or anywhere else. The reverse can also happen when a cylinder head gasket fails; engine coolant can be drawn into the cylinders during the intake stroke where it dilutes the air:fuel mixture causing poor engine performance and eventual engine damage.

Engine coolant leaking into a cylinder will often appear as white smoke out of the exhaust pipe. You also may find that you have to keep adding coolant to the cooling system on a regular basis even though you can't find any external leaks anywhere. You can follow the steps outlined in your shop manual to determine if a head gasket failure is actually your problem. Then you should replace the failed gasket, but only after finding out what caused the gasket to fail in the first place.

In the Old Days

Engine cylinder head gaskets in the old days were made of soft copper with an asbestos lining on each side. It was common practice and recommended by the gasket manufacturers in the old days to soak cylinder head gaskets in water overnight. This would swell the asbestos gasket material and help the sealing of an engine block or cylinder head that might be slightly warped or uneven.

Equally important today is to follow the gasket manufacturer's installation instructions. After all, who knows better how things are designed to work than the ones who manufactured it? In the absence of instructions, **it is important that the cylinder head be tightened evenly so the gasket will have a chance to seal properly**.

This usually involves tightening the cylinder head bolts in a certain sequence, snugly at first, then going back around sometimes as many as three or four times in a specific sequence before the proper torque reading is achieved. Torque readings are achieved by using a special tool that measures the amount of torque (tightening pressure) required to tighten the cylinder head nuts (which compress the cylinder head gasket between the cylinder head and the engine block), according to the gasket manufacturer's recommendations.

An example would be 110 foot-pounds of torque, which would mean to properly seal the gasket you should apply 110 foot-pounds of torque to each of the cylinder head nuts, following the tightening sequence instructions.

In the old days, the final tightening of the cylinder head gasket was done after the engine had been started and warmed to full engine operating temperature. Because of today's gasket technology, that is seldom necessary. The important thing to remember is that all of the cylinder head nuts should have the same degree of tightness, as this will allow the gasket to seal evenly.

Copper and brass were the gasket material of choice for quality engine gaskets for nearly fifty years. When properly installed, copper or brass gaskets would seldom leak or blow out.

Some of the other types of engine gasket materials used included steel-asbestos (which was made of cadmium-plated steel instead of copper), and graphited asbestos, which were gaskets using only one thin layer of copper or steel and the rest asbestos material. Also used were various combinations of the above.

Cylinder Head Gasket Materials

Cylinder head gasket materials, then as now, must be able to withstand temperatures exceeding 250 degrees, in contrast to most engine gaskets that work in environments of less than 200 degrees. Shellac was often used along with the installation of new gaskets in the old days. However, most manufacturers today recommend that gaskets be installed dry without the shellac. The problem with shellac is that it tends to dry and "set up" in just a short time after the engine has run. This causes the shellac to interfere with the final tightening of the cylinder head bolts. The manufacturers also stress making sure that gasket surfaces are both clean and free of debris.

You should also pay close attention to the instructions that come with the gasket kits. There is usually a top and bottom side of a gasket, even though they may look exactly the same at first glance. Cylinder head gaskets for V-8 engines can also often look the same, but if you read the directions carefully (and usually the gaskets are marked) there is a left and right side, as well as a top and bottom surface to the gasket. If you ignore the directions or don't pay attention, the gaskets themselves may physically fit either way; however, when reversed, the gasket may block a water jacket hole or an oil line hole and cause big problems.

Ford V-8 engines of the late 1960s and early 1970s were often victims of this "reversal." The engine would be overhauled, and then for some "strange" reason it would always seem to run warm after the overhaul. Often blamed on something else, the removal of the cylinder heads revealed the cylinder head gaskets were switched side-to-side or installed upside down. The result was that part of the water jacket holes were blocked shut between the engine block and the cylinder head. Shame! Shame!

There have also been a number of innovations in gasket technology. The following are a few, courtesy of the McCord Gasket Co., which has also been around since the beginning of the automobile.

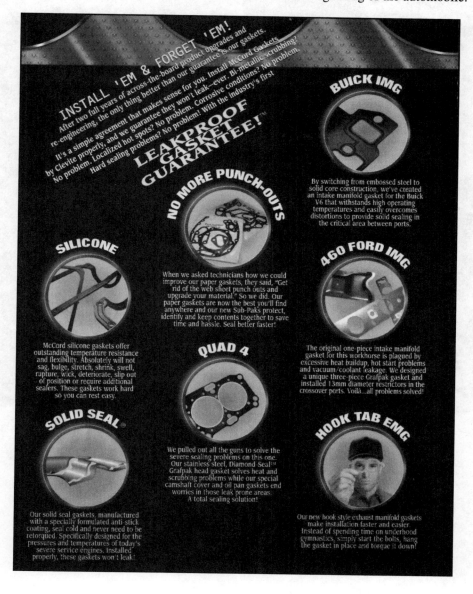

GLOBAL SOURCE FOR IMPORTS

McCord Gaskets by Clevite offers the industry's finest kit gasket program for imports. And since we include components like semi-circular plugs, valve cover grommets, spark plug tube seals, head cover o-rings, oil separator gaskets and oil cap seals, the job can always be finished properly, right out of the box.

GRAFPAK®

Grafpak graphite gaskets provide three times the temperature resistance of conventional gaskets, virtually eliminating the possibility of burn-out. Their cold sealing and no-retorque qualities have made them the preferred gasket for professional engine builders everywhere. You cannot buy a better gasket!

MORE COVERAGE

At AE Clevite Engine Parts, expanded coverage doesn't just mean more gaskets. We are one of few companies to offer a full line of engine parts, and the only one that manufactures over 70% of what it sells. Turn to AE Clevite Engine Parts for all your internal engine, valvetrain and gasket needs.

VITON

McCord Viton® gaskets and valve stem seals offer superior temperature resistance and durability. They are designed to survive in severe service applications, preventing costly and embarrassing comebacks.
Viton is a registered trademark of DuPont Company

THE BEST OF ALL WORLDS

During our re-engineering, we comparison-shopped for sealing products, just like you might. When we found a product or feature that was better, we upgraded our line. When we were superior, we stuck with it or improved. The results are what you find in our new carton, the best of the best!

BEAD SEAL

Our special crush and chemical resistant elastomeric bead concentrates clamping load on the top of the bead sealing surface for a more secure seal that withstands higher pressure. Seal it and forget it!

FIRST IN GRAPHITE

Shhhh, don't tell anyone. We didn't...until now. McCord was first to apply graphite technology to automotive engine sealing and we still lead by a 2-1 advantage over the most popular competitor. As a premiere OE supplier, we will continue to bring you new technology as it develops. There, we've said it!

350 CHEVY OPG

No plastic here! With OE style metal carriers in the side rails and steel torque limiters around each bolt hole, our new molded rubber oil pan gasket for the 350 requires no chemical sealants, eases installation and prevents costly leaks.

Notes

Chapter 12:
The Flathead Ford

The Flathead Ford has, over the last 40 years, acquired a well-known reputation for overheating. Part of its reputation has come about as a result of it also being one of the most popular engines ever built. These engines quickly became popular when they were new, and got even more so as time went on. They made their way into hot rods of all kinds.

Generations of hot rodders have used and abused these engines in everything from midget race cars to jalopy stock cars. Few other engine designs have retained the popularity of the Flathead Ford. Many aftermarket performance companies got their starts building high-performance parts for the Flathead Ford engine.

As a hot rod engine, the compression ratio of the Flathead Ford engine could easily be raised (from the factory 6.0:1 ratio), so more horsepower could be extracted from these engines. However, the stock cooling system (designed for an eighty horsepower, low compression engine) would quickly fall behind.

So along with the popularity of the Flathead Ford came the home remedies to cure the overheating problems. These home remedies (some of which worked and most of which didn't) is the subject of this chapter. I want to explain exactly what worked, what didn't and why, and what works today. It is true the Flathead Ford engines did overheat (in part, due to a less than perfect engine design), but a misunderstanding of the actual problem has led to a mountain of bad home remedies.

Just so you know we are indeed on the right track, let me give you a little food for thought. We all know that many thousands of Flathead Ford engines ended up in roadsters. And we know that if you owned a roadster in those days it wasn't cool, unless you removed the hood and fenders (along with all of the excess sheet metal), and then chopped the windshield. Well guess what! One of the hardest engines to cool is the one in a roadster!

Whoa, no way! With air all around the engine and the hood off? It should be the easiest engine to cool, not the hardest! It is true, open roadster engines are one of the most difficult engines to cool and it is because of one of those silly yet basic rules of physics that states, air will always follow the path of least resistance. (Something many of you may already know from working with exhaust header gaskets.)

Typical Flathead Roadster

Let's look at a typical open roadster. Suppose you are driving that roadster down the highway at 50 miles per hour on a hot summer day. Where do you think the wind hitting the radiator will go? You may be surprised to learn that a good portion of that airflow will hit the front of the radiator (along with a few June bugs) and then flow to either the left, the right, or up over the top of the radiator and up past the windshield, because that is the path of least resistance.

OK, but I have an engine fan and it is supposed to help draw air through the radiator so that should help right?

It is true an engine fan will help draw some air through a radiator, but you have to remember an engine fan is not efficient at highway speeds. (It is difficult for an engine fan to compete with the airflow in front of a radiator at highway speeds.) In this case, we are also concerned with what happens to the air after it is drawn through the radiator. If there are no hood panels (or sheet metal) to direct the airflow, after it passes through the radiator, the air won't stay around the engine compartment for long and you won't get much cooling effect from that airflow.

As we will learn in an upcoming chapter, what happens to the air after it is through the radiator can be just as important as getting the air through the radiator in the first place. For example, one of the tricks we can learn from the design engineers is to create a low pressure area under the hood. A low pressure area performs two functions: First, by creating a vacuum effect, it helps draw the air through the radiator and into the underhood area. Second, a low pressure area can be used to guide the air once it is under the hood.

Research has shown that in many applications (especially in street rods where a large engine is fitted into an early chassis), the exact opposite—a high pressure area—is occurring under the hood. When this happens, the pressure is greater under the hood than it is in front of the radiator. The high pressure actually blocks the air that is trying to flow through the radiator, and the car overheats, even though there is plenty of air under the hood.

In an upcoming chapter I will show you how to check under the hood to see if you have a high pressure area. I will also show you how to make a simple tool to help you identify the changes you need to make in order to create a low pressure area, to help guide the airflow under your hood.

By the way, the parts of the original sheet metal we typically throw away as hot rodders are the inner fender panels. They are ugly and a pain to install, but part of their original purpose was to help guide the air under the hood. In most cases, these inner fender panels were not as critical to the stock applications as they can be to the higher horsepower applications.

Fan Clutches

Also, as a result of what automotive engineers have learned about under hood pressures and airflow, fan clutches were developed. At high engine rpm the fan clutch disengages the engine cooling fan and the engine fan is allowed to coast, so it no longer tries to move air against the airflow coming in through the radiator.

This saves wear and tear on the water pump bearings (which most fans are mounted to) as well as engine horsepower. Can you imagine wasting two or three engine horsepower trying to turn an engine fan against the incoming air blowing through a radiator, and not getting any cooling benefit from it?

The same is true for electric fans. Electric radiator cooling fans work best at idle and low speeds, but are of little help when you are traveling down the highway at sixty-plus miles per hour. Nearly every street rod built today has an electric fan installed on the radiator. And they are a lifesaver when the stuck in heavy traffic. But electric fans can also be a hindrance at highway speeds, especially if the fan is big enough to cover the whole radiator core. Sometimes two smaller fans work better, simply because they draw fewer total amps and block less of the total core area.

> By the way, the parts of the original sheet metal we typically throw away as hot rodders are the inner fender panels. They are ugly and a pain to install, but part of their original purpose was to help guide the air under the hood. In most cases, these inner fender panels were not as critical to the stock applications as they can be to the higher horsepower applications.

Aside from the usual cooling system problems we create ourselves by installing a Flathead Ford in a tight engine compartment, then removing all of the air channeling devices, let's start by looking inside of the engine block and see what's wrong in there. Then we will work our way out to the engine compartment itself.

The Problem

One of the main causes of a Flathead Ford's overheating is caused by engine coolant cavitation. Cavitation occurs when the coolant next to the cylinder (inside of the engine block) gets so hot that the coolant turns to steam. When this happens, a steam pocket forms next to the cylinder, which then prevents additional coolant from reaching the cylinder. Since engine coolant can no longer get next to the cylinder (to draw off the heat of the cylinders), the heat continues to build inside of the engine block. Since Flathead Fords did not have the most efficient coolant passage design, that tends to make this problem worse.

Meanwhile, if the heat buildup is allowed to continue, enough steam vapor pressure can build inside the coolant passages to actually stop, or slow way down, the flow of engine coolant. Then the water pump begins to pump hot steam vapor and not coolant. Anyone for tea?

This is why **it is important when adding coolant to a Flathead Ford cooling system that you make sure there is no air trapped in the system.** Any air trapped will likely create vapor barriers (as if you don't have enough of those already) blocking the coolant flow, which will add to your cooling system woes.

By the way, **dirty engine blocks due to the buildup of rust, scale, and hard water deposits, also cause a lot of overheating problems.** Remember, straight water was the common coolant used in these engines during the summer months, so a heavy rust and scale buildup is common. Usually, that amounts to about forty-five years worth! And because a Flathead Ford engine ran warm most of its life, you can bet that rust and scale are going to be baked on. I have seen Flathead Ford engine blocks with water jacket holes reduced to less than half of their original diameter as a result of rust and scale buildup. You know what hard water does to your kitchen fixtures, so imagine ignoring your kitchen for fifty years. Be sure that when you overhaul a Flathead Ford engine that you get the block absolutely spotless, inside and out.

Also be sure and clean out all of the oil passages. Many times the oil passages inside of these engines are partially plugged with carbon. When these engines ran hot, the engine oils of the day couldn't always handle the excess heat. As a result, the engine oil often burned and was turned into carbon (usually tiny flakes). These flakes were often trapped inside the oil passages. That restricted oil flow, which also contributed to overheating problems. The original Flathead Ford oiling system was a by-pass type, which meant it only filtered about ten percent of the oil at any one time. The oil used during this era was non-detergent oil, which made it even easier for the "nasties" to accumulate inside of the engine block.

The Solutions

Now that you have a little background on the Flathead Ford engines and are aware of some of their common faults, we will learn a little more from three people who have spent most of their lives working on and driving Flathead Ford-powered vehicles. One of the best ways to learn is from somebody who has actually been there, done that, and made it work!

Building a Reliable Flathead Ford Engine

Rex Gardner is an eleven-year veteran of the Great American Race[1] and has logged thousands of miles behind the wheel of Flathead Ford-powered cars. Rex specializes in the early twenty-one stud Flathead Ford engines and has earned a well-deserved reputation for knowing how to build a "Flatmotor" that is both a strong performer and reliable. Rex has agreed to share with us some of his "tricks of the trade" that he uses to build and maintain a reliable Flathead Ford. Thanks, Rex!

This information I am presenting to you deals basically with stock Flathead Ford engines as used by "resto" rods, nostalgia street rods, and those used in cars that are entered in the Great American Race where the engines have to be, for the most part, stock. Many of you may be wondering how I came to be a Flathead Ford expert.

My father began working in a Ford garage when he was twelve years old, so I kind of grew up around flatheads and learned to work on them in part from my father, and in part by my own trial and error. Over the years, I have figured out exactly what works and what doesn't. Driving in the Great American Race is a challenge for me and something I enjoy very much because I can prove to myself how much I really know about a flathead engine and the early Ford cars.

The following is the evolution process I have figured out over the years, and it has worked for me in keeping the operating temperature of a Flathead Ford acceptable. Many of the miles I put on my flathead engine were under Great American Race conditions, such as crossing the desert with daytime temperatures of 120 degrees, climbing Pike's Peak (above 12,000 feet), and hot summer, high humidity Kansas days.

Two things I quickly found out about my 1935 Ford coupe with the 221 cubic inch flathead engine were: first, the engine wasn't strong enough to power the car and maintain highway speeds, especially in the mountains; and, second, the engine compartment didn't allow for adequate airflow to pass through the radiator. The air was "bunching up" in the engine compartment due in part to a lack of an adequate airflow passage. Remember in the old days, you saw a lot of old Fords with the hood sides off in the summer months. That worked, because the warm air in the engine compartment had an escape route.

Let's look at the problems associated with Flathead Ford engines step-by-step. I'll then offer a solution to each problem. Yes, I know some of you will agree and some of you will disagree with my solutions, but I am just telling you what has worked for me.

What Causes the Excess Heat Generated by a Flathead Engine?

Besides the usual things such as the engine being under heavy load, high humidity, warm temperatures, climbing mountains or crossing deserts, the engine design itself is one major cause of excess heat.

One notable design flaw is using one center port to exit the exhaust gases from the two center cylinders, which creates a concentration of heat in one spot. Another design flaw is that all of the exhaust gases exit through the engine block, which heats the engine coolant as the hot exhaust gases travel down the exhaust passages to the outside of the engine. These are known design flaws that we cannot change, but we do need to be aware of them. It is the first step in understanding why a Flathead Ford engine runs warm.

Another factor is the erosion of the engine block after years of corrosion. Let's face it, these early twenty-one stud engine blocks are approaching sixty years of age. Corrosion around the cylinder walls, sludge buildup, and factory sand casting deposits have been eating away at these engine blocks for years. The result is thinner castings around the cylinders, making heat transfer unreliable.

Sonic tests performed on cylinder wall thickness have shown everything from thick to thin, even within the same engine block. My solution is to sleeve all of the cylinders with

---

[1.]The Great American Race is a timed rally event where original pre-1950 cars are driven 4,500 miles across the United States during a fourteen day event. Two people ride in the car, a driver and a navigator. The navigator reads the maps and directions and keeps time. The driver is supposed to watch for road signs and exactly follow driving directions given by the navigator, regardless of the weather conditions. If there are any mechanical problems with the car, it is up to the driver/navigator team to fix the defect(s) using what available tools and spare parts they brought along. It is the preparation beforehand that helps to assure having a reliable car. That means tearing down the car completely to the bare frame, then inspecting and replacing every piece on the car. This includes the engine, drivetrain, cooling system, electrical components, and brakes.

the correct sleeve to accommodate your bore size. In my case, I bore all cylinders to 3-3/16 inches (the maximum for a twenty-one stud engine) using the correct sleeve. This gives me a consistent cylinder wall thickness, plus a modern material for today's piston and ring combinations. Using different bore/stroke combinations, many different engine combinations are possible. My experience has shown that 248, 255, and 262 bore/stroke engine combinations work the best for most applications.

Some later twenty-four stud engines can accommodate bigger bore sizes without the use of sleeves, but if you go that route be sure and sonic check your cylinders to verify their thickness. And when you bore a twenty-one stud engine to sleeve it, don't be alarmed if you bore away most of the original cylinder. This is a fairly difficult process, but an experienced machinist should be able to do it correctly. **Be sure to ask questions before the work begins**.

Now you have a cylinder that is uniform in thickness and can transfer heat properly, plus will retain straight walls for a ring seal. The rest of the block preparation is pretty standard stuff and includes proper cleaning—digging out the lower portions of the block where the sludge and original sand castings are lodged. It will be tough going, but it must be done in order to build an engine that will last and cool properly. After that, block work should include decking the block, line boring, chasing all threads, etc., and doing a complete valve job. After that, the block should be ready.

Radiator—the old original radiator is useless. Opt to at least use the thickest recore you can. Sure, you could use one of the new super-duper aluminum jobs, but we are talking about using original-looking parts for appearance sake. A new four tube core will assure you of maximum volume and you will be able to transfer heat efficiently.

Do not paint the radiator with anything but one light coat of paint; let the core work! Also prepare the radiator neck for a pressure cap of four to seven pounds, then install a coolant recovery tank; this will keep the coolant in the system. Four to seven pounds is about the maximum the water pumps will hold, but this will increase the boiling point of the cooling system.

Water pumps—early Ford water pumps mounted on the cylinder head and were fitted with grease zerks. Truck water pumps were built as heavy-duty sealed-type pumps, so use the truck water pumps on twenty-one stud engines and the equivalent on twenty-four stud engines.

On my 1935 Ford coupe, I also plumbed out of the left-hand water pump into a heater core obtained from a school bus. I mounted the heater core in front of the radiator. The return plumbing connects to the top radiator tank. This gives me an additional 1-1/2 gallons of coolant volume, which made quite a difference in the coolant temperature.

Coolant—I have experimented with all kinds of coolant mixtures and have found that pure water (I also add a pint of water pump lubricant/rust inhibitor to the water) provides the best cooling properties of any solutions I've tried. Antifreeze absorbs heat okay, but the cooling system doesn't allow it to transfer heat properly. Don't forget to reinstall antifreeze in cold weather.

Thermostats—under normal driving conditions thermostats work okay. However, racing in the Great American Race, I cannot risk a stuck thermostat. I have experimented with all kinds of ideas. What works best for me is that I install a "cup-type" engine freeze plug in the radiator hose (I hold it in place with a hose clamp) with a five-eighths inch hole drilled into the center of the freeze plug. Experience will help you determine the correct hole size for your application. This involves a lot of trial and error, but it has worked for me. The size of hole you use may vary, as does the one I use in the left-hand side because of the extra coolant volume going to the heater core. The only downfall to this system is that in cool weather the engine is much slower warming to operating temperature.

Electric Radiator cooling fans—in the Great American Race I use a thermostatically controlled electric fan. This allows engine temperature to warm to operating temperature, then the fan comes on automatically. I have the fan set to turn on when the engine temperature reaches 165 degrees. The Great American Race is run during the summer months across deserts, where daytime temperatures can get brutally hot. The fan is also a tremendous help at slow speeds, such as in-town driving.

Oil Cooler/Filter—another thing that affects engine coolant temperature is oil. I have modified my engine block to accommodate a full-flow oiling system that filters all of the engine oil that passes through the oil pump, except the rear main. This system does a super job of keeping the oil clean and is a big improvement over the stock system.

By having better oil filtering, and better oil, I can take advantage of closer engine tolerances and build a more precise engine. I also use detergent oil because of the improved filtering, although some people will argue you should use only non-detergent oil because that is what was called for originally. I have noticed that engine operating temperature will drop about ten degrees just by using a quality engine oil.

I have torn down Flathead Ford engines after 20,000 miles without finding any sludge buildup inside. That confirms to me that good detergent oil and a full-flow oil filtering system is the correct way to go.

Compression Ratio—the engine is a heat/air pump. To maximize horsepower from the limited cubic inches available, increasing compression ratio is a critical factor. Originally, the stock compression ratio was between 5.5:1 and 6.0:1. This was, in part, due to the quality of the fuel available at the time. Higher compression ratios would have resulted in premature detonation. Today, we have cleaner, more refined fuels, better ignition systems (I convert from the original six- to a twelve-volt electrical system), and more accurate timing. This allows me to increase the compression ratio of the engine without having problems with detonation.

A higher compression ratio will increase the cylinder head temperature, but it will also provide greater useable horsepower. Compression ratios of 7.5:1 up to 8.0:1 seem to work well. I have tried several different bore/stroke combinations and have learned the more cubic inches you achieve, the easier it is to get the compression ratio up. Just keep it about 8.0:1 for best performance. This will lessen the chance of building excess engine temperature.

Timing—original distributors were calibrated (advance initial timing) for compression ratios and the fuels available at the time. Gasoline has greatly improved since then, so timing and the increased compression ratio become a factor in the cooling process. I use the front mount crab-style distributor. One solution is to use a modified stock distributor (one set of points, and no vacuum brake) with an "initial" advance of around eight degrees and a "total" advance up to twenty-eight degrees. Another solution is to use a Mallory (aftermarket brand) total mechanical advance distributor. These distributors work exceptionally well. The bottom line is improved ignition and timing, which results in a better performing and cooler running engine.

My goal is to increase useable horsepower, torque, and durability, while still being able to "keep it cool" and reliable under severe driving conditions. I still continue to experiment with ignition and cooling ideas, as well as being on the lookout for new ideas that might benefit these older engines. The information I have provided you with here is directed at 1932 through 1936 Flathead Ford engines, often referred to as "twenty-one stud engines," so named for the number of studs found on top of each cylinder head.

I hope that what I have provided has been of some benefit to you. At the very least, it will get you started in the right direction and provide you with some proven basic facts and background information, so you will have a better understanding of how fifty-year-old technology was designed to work. That makes understanding a Flathead Ford engine a lot easier.

Rex Gardner

Rex Gardner's 1935 Ford three-window coupe participating in the Great American Race.

The engine bay of Rex Gardner's Ford coupe.

Rebuilding a Flathead Ford Engine

Rex Gardner's photo sequence of rebuilding a Flathead Ford engine begins with fitting piston pins to pistons and honing the engine block's cylinders.

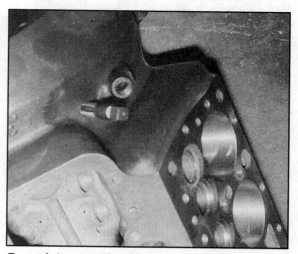

Part of the modifications necessary to convert to a "full-flow" oil system.

Line honing the block is a must for a quality engine rebuild.

The procedure for properly cutting valve seats.

Making sure the deck is "square" is critical.

Cylinder head studs are installed, using Loctite, and tightened to 10-15 inch-pounds.

Cylinder wall finish is also important. Take your time and do it correctly!

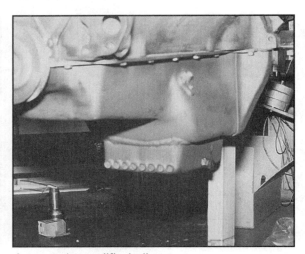
A properly modified oil pan.

Modifying a Mercury crankshaft to fit in an early Flathead Ford engine block.

Resizing the connecting rods is another important step.

For another perspective on Flathead Ford engine cooling, I was referred (quite a number of times) to Dave Lukkari of Apple Valley, California.

The Flathead Ford Engine

Dave Lukkari grew up in California driving and racing Flathead Fords, and gained most of his knowledge through "seat of the pants" experience. Dave has agreed to share with us some of his knowledge and technical advice. And in case you are wondering, yes, Dave (now gray in beard, by his own definition) still owns a number of Flathead Ford-powered cars that he drives daily.

There are three important facts in life to remember: water is the substance of life; heat produces energy; and the temperature gauge in the dash of a Flathead Ford-powered car is the source of much unnecessary worry! Engine operating temperature is, without a doubt, one of the most misunderstood parts of the automobile's operation. I have been studying this subject for many years, and have been lucky enough to have gained much of my knowledge in recent years through the help of my friend Mr. Fred Leydorf[2]. Fred, for many years, was chief engineer in charge of engine development for one of the major U.S. car companies. As an individual, I would have never had access to all of the technical resources or been able to understand in-depth exactly how a cooling system is designed to work without Fred's help.

In our younger days, we spent every penny we had on engine improvements then stuck the old original radiator back in front of the engine. Then when it erupted like "Old Faithful," we cursed the Flathead Ford engine as the problem. Now that many of you, like me, are in your second childhood, let's see what we should have done.

The original old Flathead Ford radiators held about twenty or so quarts of water. Unless you lived in a cold climate, that's all that was ever put in that radiator, just plain water.

Water itself has a pretty high surface tension (you have seen this when water beads up on a waxed surface). Well, the same thing can happen inside of the radiator and engine block, which causes the coolant not to make good contact with the insides of the cooling system.

The better the contact with the metal surfaces inside of the cooling system, the better the heat transfer. Therefore, anything that breaks down the surface tension of the coolant would be a benefit. A (50:50) mixture of antifreeze and water makes a coolant that is economical and easy to obtain. If your tap water is hard or contains lots of minerals, using bottled or distilled water is better.

Proper cleaning of the engine block is important; the phrase "cleanliness is next to godliness" applies here. The water jackets on a Flathead Ford engine are often ignored, but like the rest of the block they need to be as clean as possible. I have seen as much as two quarts of casting sand come out of an engine block. That sand is what was left over from when the engine block was cast at the Ford foundry. That leftover sand acts like an insulation barrier, which makes it more difficult to keep the engine cool. In addition, the cast-iron itself builds up rust that also clogs the cooling system.

The original Ford radiator is another misunderstood component. Most original old radiators had thick fins and wide spacing, and, as a result, didn't transfer heat well. By contrast, a modern radiator core has many thin fins with lots of louvers so the air is able to flow through the radiator and transfer heat more efficiently, which makes this item a good investment.

> Water itself has a pretty high surface tension (you have seen this when water beads up on a waxed surface). Well, the same thing can happen inside of the radiator and engine block, which causes the coolant not to make good contact with the insides of the cooling system. The better the contact with the metal surfaces inside of the cooling system, the better the heat transfer. Therefore, anything that breaks down the surface tension of the coolant would be a benefit. A (50:50) mixture of antifreeze and water makes a coolant that is economical and easy to obtain. If your tap water is hard or contains lots of minerals, using bottled or distilled water is better.

---

[2] I owe a debt of gratitude to Mr. Leydorf for sharing this information with me, and as a way to repay that debt, I am sharing this information with you. The fundamentals explained can be applied to most all liquid-cooled engines, but most of you reading this chapter are concerned with the Flathead Ford engine. They seem to be one of the most difficult engines to keep cool.

The frontal area of the radiator is much more important than the thickness of the radiator. Air often has a hard time passing through a thick radiator. The poor design of the water passages in the Flathead Ford block, along with a less-than-perfect radiator design, together do not lend themselves well to any increase in engine performance.

Controlling the Temperature

Poor temperature control is another one of the biggest causes of Flathead Ford engine overheating. The flow of coolant through the cooling system is an important and somewhat complicated process. If you have a clean radiator and engine block, and a fresh (50:50) mixture of engine coolant, but you still have an engine that continues to run warm, your next reaction may be to remove the thermostats. Wrong move! What is actually happening here is that your coolant is being saturated with heat, and is moving too fast through the radiator to allow the heat to be drawn off. So removing the thermostats will make your problem worse!

One thing to remember is that heat is horsepower, and as long as you are not losing coolant you cannot hurt the engine! An air-cooled engine, for example, can often see temperatures as high as 400 degrees without damage. The limiting factor of a liquid-cooled engine has always been the boiling point of the coolant, so what we are really scared of when we watch the temperature gauge is how close we are to reaching the boiling point of the coolant.

Many new cars run at temperatures around 240 degrees Fahrenheit to reduce emissions and to be able to pass government regulations. The person that brags that his engine never runs over 160 degrees has an engine that is not running efficiently. A higher temperature thermostat would be a big improvement for that person. I like to run 190 or 195 degree thermostats in my Flathead Ford engines. This gives me control of the coolant through the radiator so it has time to transfer the heat into the air.

A coolant recovery system is also a wise investment. The physics of heat is to expand as it gets warmer. The coolant needs to expand and go somewhere as it gets warm. Without a recovery system, the coolant expands and is lost out the overflow. If you try and replace the lost coolant after the system has cooled down, you will find it being pushed out the overflow again, as soon as the coolant is heated to operating temperature. Therefore, a recovery system is the logical solution. When using a recovery system, the system itself must have a tight seal; any air leaks and the recovery system will not work correctly.

Designing the Fan Shroud

A fan shroud can also help direct airflow through the radiator. A simple shroud that fits close to the core and to about half of the fan blade cross section will be a big improvement. All you need is a piece of sheet metal rolled into a circle with a half inch or so of fan blade clearance. A full fan shroud should have a big enough opening on the engine side for the ram air to pass through into the engine compartment without restriction.

I have seen fan shrouds that have actually caused a problem by restricting the increased airflow when it got to the engine compartment, so proper design of your fan shroud is important. Electric fans can also be used, but I prefer engine-driven fans myself. If you are going to use an electric fan, they should be set up to draw air through a radiator like the engine fan would, instead of trying to push the air through the radiator. **Electric fans should be mounted on the upper third of the radiator because that is where the warm coolant enters the radiator, and where you would gain the most benefit**.

According to my engineer friend, Mr. Leydorf, the efficient management of coolant flow through the engine depends a great deal on the design of the water pump. A water pump should be designed to create a fair amount of pressure against the coolant in the block. Because of the less-than-perfect design of the Flathead Ford water pumps (no backing plate on the impellers and a large block cavity), it is difficult for these pumps to build any pressure in the cooling system. The way the Ford water pumps were designed, they act like a big paddle wheel on a riverboat. They move a fair amount of water, but ... the water has no direction or guidance.

348/409 Chevrolet Water Pumps

We had already identified the poor water pump design of the Flathead Ford engine as a problem years ago, but had yet to find a reliable cure. It was with the introduction of Chevrolet's 348/409 engine in the late 1950s that we stumbled onto a solution quite by accident. It seems because of the wide spacing of the outlet on the Chevy 409 water pump, it was a direct replacement for the Ford water pumps! All that we had to do was

A 348/409 automobile water pump.

cut two three-fourths inch plates in the shape of a Ford water pump gasket and the Chevy 348/409 water pump could be installed, and would even clear the late style (1949-1953) Ford timing cover. You also had to make a new drive pulley.

The 348/409's casting holes for the outlet holes matched the Ford exactly. That meant the pump-mounted fan was positioned exactly in the center of the radiator without the use of a remote fan like the Ford originally used. In addition, you only needed one belt to drive the pump and generator. The enclosed impeller of the 348/409 pump was also much more efficient than the two open impeller Ford pumps.

Finally, if you had a tall radiator, you could use the 409 Chevrolet truck water pump to raise the fan about three inches higher and still keep the fan in the center of the radiator. I am not sure who actually figured out the 409 water pump trick, but by the late 1950s and into the early 1960s, most everyone had at least tried it. They were a big improvement and still are.

Our covers for the block (to cover the water pump impeller holes in the block) were not nearly as fancy as they are today, but it is well worth the effort if you want to improve the coolant flow of your Flathead Ford engine. I still run 409 pumps on many of my engines. However, for nostalgia reasons I still sometimes run the stock Ford pumps on my Ardun (overhead valve conversion engine), which, because of its improved head design, does not have the overheating problems typically associated with the Flathead Ford engine.

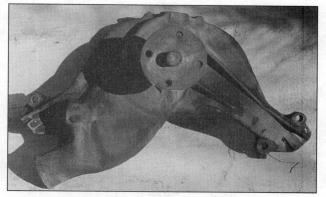
A 348/409 truck water pump.

Coolant Speed

Finally, the coolant speed inside of the engine needs to be controlled to give the radiator enough time to transfer the heat, and spend enough time in the engine block, so the coolant can absorb all of the heat it is capable of. If you ever watch a stream of fast flowing water you will notice that along the bank, the flow of water is pretty slow. In contrast, the water in the middle of the stream is flowing pretty fast. The same thing often happens inside of an engine block. As a result, the trapped coolant becomes saturated with heat, then a steam pocket is formed (even though the coolant in the middle of the engine block is still well below its boiling point), causing inconsistent temperatures in your engine.

Another thing that happens is the impeller speed of the water pumps can be too fast, which causes the water pumps to pump air (a condition known as cavitation) instead of coolant. This was often identified as the problem in the old days, which is why you often got the recommendation to break off or cut off every other impeller blade or drill three-eighths inch holes in every impeller.

While those ideas worked somewhat, it wasn't for the reasons most people think. It was to prevent the coolant from foaming and the water pump from cavitating. But the end results are what count. **If an engine is going to be run at high rpm, such as racing, it might be better to change the pulley sizes (to larger diameter pulleys) to slow down the pumps to the operating rpm they were designed to run.**

An alternate temperature control choice, instead of thermostats, is the use of restrictor washers in place of the thermostats. These take some experimenting with, and usually the holes in the center are smaller than most people would imagine.

Dave Lukkari's 1947 Crosley powered by a turbocharged Ardun Flathead Ford. (The Ardun setup shown was a rare overhead valve conversion kit offer for the flathead engine during the 1950s.)

The engine detail of Dave Lukkari's flathead-powered Crosley. This car has been driven for nine years and over 100,000 miles using the 348/409 water pump conversion.

Dave Lukkari's current ride known as "The Phantom of the Dry Lakes." Note yet another Ardun flathead engine, this time with a vintage supercharger. Wouldn't it be nice to have grown up in his neighborhood?

Flat Head Water Pump Kit

Enjoy the benefits of the proven Chevy water pump design, along with improved cooling and less H.P. loss, all wrapped in a neat, compact package comprised of handcrafted aluminum and steel components. The

Combination AC compressor and alternator mount.

Cornhusker Kit is complete down to the last fastener. It is basically a bolt-on kit, unless you choose the urethane bushed mounting system, which requires welding mounting tabs to a boxed frame. We have four different styles of water pump mounts, early or late style block, stock biscuit, or the optional urethane bushed system which allows the engine to be mounted several inches higher.

Parts included in kit:

1. Pair of CNC milled aluminum pump replacements
2. Steel-sleeved CNC milled aluminum lower crank hub
3. Stainless lower hub retainer, which also centers the pulley
4. Re-manufactured 348-409 Water Pump
5. Aluminum single groove upper and lower pulleys
6. Steel alternator mount
7. Fasteners, gaskets & instructions

My friend Fred Rowe also suggests using a high octane fuel. He claims a drop of up to ten degrees in operating temperature can be gained from this practice. Also the combustion chamber of the Flathead Ford is prone to premature detonation, so quality fuel helps. A slightly rich mixture will also help cool things. Finally, be sure the timing is set correctly, and a free-flowing exhaust is another big help.

Chevy 348/409 water pump installed on a Flathead Ford using the Cornhusker installation kit.

Chevy/Flathead Ford water pump kit.

Most people who think they have an overheating problem do not. If your cooling system isn't losing coolant there is no problem. If your temperature gauge makes you nervous, use a little black magic and cover the gauge with electrical tape and enjoy your motoring pleasures.

Dave Lukkari

When addressing the cooling problems of the Flathead Ford, in addition to Rex Gardner and Dave Lukkari, the name of Paul Kosma of Kosma Design and Fabrication, located in Walls, Mississippi, also came up on a regular basis.

Yet More Flathead Advice

By now you have figured out that there is no cut and dried "one fix cures all" solution to cooling the Flathead Ford. We now have the chance to learn from Paul Kosma, another veteran who has forty years of experience in dealing with these problems.

My name is Paul Kosma; my friends call me "Koz." I have had a love affair with the Flathead Ford engine for most of my fifty-three years. It started when I was in grade school, growing up in Lisbon, Connecticut. Every morning while waiting for the school bus, a black 1932 Ford sedan would come flying down our hill and let off the gas right in front of our house. It was the most beautiful sound I had ever heard. Later on, I got to see my first Flathead Ford engine. It belonged to a guy named Charlie Brown and featured two Stromberg 97s, finned aluminum heads, and Smitty mufflers. I remember this car like it was yesterday. I had no idea then how much the sound of a flathead would affect me for the rest of my life.

Today, I run a 1930 Ford roadster with an 8BA engine. I bought this car in 1973 when I returned to Memphis, Tennessee, after four years in the Army. It has been my test bed for new ideas, and has always been flathead powered. Cooling a Flathead Ford has always been a challenge and mine is no exception. Here are some of the tricks I have learned over the years:

Let's start with the engine block. With five inches of exhaust passage on each of the four corners and Siamese chambers in the center, the engine design itself is not the most efficient design. Because straight water was used as coolant in the summer months in the old days, rust tends to accumulate in the water jacket areas. This restricts the water flow, creating hot spots and makes cooling the engine more difficult.

Cleaning the engine block is absolutely necessary! Stick a sandblaster and/or a high pressure washer in every hole in the block to make sure it is clean. I know you have already heard this before, but do it because it is important.

Next is cylinder wall thickness. Cylinder walls vibrate from the explosion going on inside of the cylinder; the thinner the walls the more the vibration. When this happens, the vibration pushes the coolant away from the cylinder walls allowing a layer of air to form around the wall surface. Engine coolant is then unable to cool the surface. Steam begins to form and turn into air bubbles, overriding the pressure cap and causing the cooling system to begin losing coolant.

The harder you push the engine the worse things get. **Flathead Fords have a "sweet spot" around 2200 rpm where you can cruise on a 95 degree day without much problem. If you bump up the rpm to 2500, however, the engine tends to run warm and you will begin to loose coolant. So the secret is to keep the engine rpm down.** Flatheads like tall gears, so using an overdrive transmission really helps your cause.

Another suggestion I have is don't overbore the cylinders. Flathead cast-iron is soft. Also, I like to install a center exhaust divider. It will help lower your cooling temperature as well as improve the exhaust note. Cleaning any slag or sharp edges from the exhaust ports will also help exhaust flow. Do not use stock or light-pressure valve springs because they cannot squeeze out the carbon and keep the valve seats clean. A good seal is a must! Isky part number 185G valve springs are good for the street.

Head gaskets—my favorite is the Fel-Pro brand part number 1055 and number 1056 copper for the 8BA engines. If you run aluminum heads, you must relieve the block. The compression ratio on aluminum heads always takes into consideration the block relief. Always use head studs and never head bolts. Bolts are hard on the block threads, and remember the block cast-iron is soft. You will also get a much better clamping pressure and will be able to maintain better torque with studs. Use Fel-Pro gray bolt prep part number "graz" on all of the threads. I torque my aluminum heads to 55 foot-pounds cold.

Keep your ignition timing at a total of twenty degrees advance, ten degrees initial, and five degrees in the distributor. Distributor degrees are always doubled equaling twenty degrees. Timing is important. If your timing is too far advanced your engine will run warm.

Spark plugs—I run Champion #L82C plugs in my flathead engine with Edelbrock heads, which I have relieved on the inside of the combustion chamber so the plug fits flush. Do *not* screw a new spark plug into aluminum threads. Keep an old cast-iron head handy and screw in the new plug and crush the gasket in the cast-iron head first. It will save wear and tear on your aluminum cylinder heads. The important thing to remember is always be careful with the threads in aluminum heads because they can be easily damaged.

If possible, do not run an electric fan on the front of the radiator. Instead use a six blade metal fan. If you have to run an electric fan, I recommend a Walker Max Air part number MA-16 from Walker Radiator Co. located in Memphis, Tennessee. This fan works well, but does draw a lot of amps so be sure to use ten gauge wire and a thirty amp relay in the installation. Also, remember a puller fan is better than a pusher fan because the pusher fan has a tendency to block the flow of fresh air through the radiator when traveling at highway speeds.

Radiators—always buy the best you can afford, and remember the thicker the radiator, the harder it will be to pull air through it. I have run a three-inch thick core from Walker Radiator Co., and had good results.

I also suggest you run the lightest pressure radiator cap you can with no fluid loss when hot. By the way, while we are on the subject of hot, how hot is too hot? I run a 180-degree thermostat in my flathead engine and it does not run well until it reaches that temperature. After the fuel mixture is set correctly, it likes 180-200 degrees best.

If your temperature gauge reads over 210 degrees and you have rapid coolant loss out of the overflow pipe, shut the engine down immediately. This is how the valve warping and head cracking occurs. The secret is preventing coolant loss; if you are in traffic and the temperature climbs, but you are not loosing coolant, chances are things are okay.

Water is the best disperser of heat there is. Water does have a tendency to push away from the cylinder walls and starts to vaporize at 212 degrees. **A high pressure radiator cap will keep the coolant in the engine, but it is hard on the original radiators and often causes leaks over time**.

Antifreeze doesn't cool any better, it just raises the boiling point and keeps the rust and corrosion from forming in the system. Speaking of rust, J.C. Whitney sells a zinc anode part number 74VC7496U that will help keep your system clean and happy for years.

In my present cooling system, I run one gallon of Peak antifreeze and two twelve-ounce bottles of Red Line Water Wetter along with a five pound pressure cap. I also use an overflow tank to catch any coolant. This system seems to work well for me.

All of this brings me to the last item on my list, the subject of Evans NPG Coolant. I ran the Evans NPG Coolant in my flathead engine for about two years. When I first called Steve Pressley at Evans Cooling about wanting to try his product in my flathead engine, he was helpful and answered all of my questions. I installed the coolant and have had

Paul Kosma's 1930 Model A Ford roadster.

The roadster ready for the salt. Paul Kosma has driven this car on the salt flats of Bonneville, Utah, with great success. In 1977, he set the XX/STR class record of 137 mph driving this car, a record that stood for the next eight years.

The attention to detail is evident in Paul Kosma's work.

A reliable flathead engine for the street.

good results. The advantages I could see were the high boiling point and being able to use it in a non-pressurized system. I also liked the elimination of the "hot spots" and the non-corrosive properties due to the lack of water in the coolant.

One of the problems I had was getting used to the temperature gauge reading 200 degrees and above, although I never lost any coolant or had any hint of boil-over. The Evans coolant likes to be pumped fast and it is thick, just like uncut antifreeze. Flathead water pumps are not the most efficient and many street rod radiators are built using small diameter tubes to promote good air circulation around the tubes. I never had any problems whatsoever with the Evans coolant.

Paul Kosma

Summary

Okay, if you have gotten this far along, you should have a good understanding of how we got to where we are today. You should know the basic parts of a cooling system, understand atmospheric pressure and how that affects a cooling system, and be able to figure out the boiling point of water if given the pressure of the cooling system and the elevation of the location.

All of this will become important as we get into the more modern cooling systems. Like everything else today, cooling systems are much more complicated than they were forty years ago. But before you can begin to make sense out of today's cooling systems, you needed to understand how we got to this point in the first place.

In the upcoming chapters we will get into the modern cooling systems of the 1980s and 1990s and examine how antifreeze/coolant has changed since the 1960s. We will also learn about synthetic antifreeze and the theory behind how it works and compares to conventional antifreeze.

We will also get into racing applications, where we will learn about performance cooling systems such as those used in NASCAR racing. By studying how these high performance systems are designed, and how each race team approaches cooling problems, we can learn a great deal about how to approach and solve our own problems.

Notes

Chapter 13: Things You Need to Know About Engine Oil

I know you may think engine oil doesn't have much to do with a cooling system, but the engine oil is responsible for absorbing and removing about ten percent of the heat generated by the engine. In the old days (1920s-1930s), engine oil was made of mostly mineral oil. That combined with the poor bearing materials, and the lack of filtering (both oil and air), usually resulted in engines that didn't have a long service life.

One of the first things that happened as cars became popular was the establishment of some sort of guidelines for the classification of motor oil. The purpose was to ensure that no matter what brand of oil you purchased, you knew it was refined to some sort of standard. Oil standards were developed beginning in 1911 by the Society of Automotive Engineers (SAE). In those days, oil was rated or "graded" based on viscosity (the resistance to flow) or how well the oil flowed at a specific temperature.

It took until 1947 to establish the API ratings that are common today. American Petroleum Institute (API) first established ratings or specifications for three different grades of engine oil: Regular, Premium, and Heavy-Duty. Five years later, another certification rating system was established, the ESCS or Engine Service Classification System. This new rating system further identified and separated the different formulations of oils based on application and became the standard for the next twenty years or so.

In 1970, a more strict and accurate rating system using laboratory testing was developed. It was based, in part, on actual random sampling of the oil being sold at the retail level. Today, the current oil rating system is a combination of all three societies working together (API, SAE, and ASTM, the American Society for Testing Materials) along with the Motor Vehicle Manufacturers Association. These groups have developed engine oil service ratings that range from SA, which is almost pure mineral oil, to SJ, which is the top rating (which also meets the International Lubricant Standardization and Approval Committee or GF-2 standard) and is considered the "good stuff."

The Society

The SAE is responsible for the viscosity rating tests, and have two established ratings: one for winter as in 5W, 10W, and 20W, and another for the rest of the seasons such as SAE 20, 30, 40, and 50. The winter grades are tested at zero degrees Fahrenheit, while the others are tested at 210 degrees Fahrenheit.

The multi-viscosity oils that are common today have what is known as a high viscosity index, which means their resistance to flow changes easily, according to the temperature. For instance, 5W-30 motor oil meets the 5W standard at zero degrees Fahrenheit, and the SAE 30 standard at 210 degrees Fahrenheit. This means the oil is able to flow well enough to provide engine lubrication at zero degrees, while still providing the lubricating film protection needed at high engine temperatures. The quality of the lubricating oil, through better filtering of both air and oil, has gone a long way towards extending the service life of the engine.

In addition, modern engine oils have acquired a number of additives to further help the cause. Detergents and dispersers are blended into the oil and help to pick up dirt and foreign materials. Viscosity improvers are added to reduce the rate of thickness during the temperature change to cold weather. Extreme pressure agents are also added to increase film strength and keep the oil from being squeezed out of load bearing joints under pressure. Pour point depressants are added to make the engine lubricant easier to pour out of a can or container at low temperatures. Defoamants are added to control frothing and foaming. Anti-oxidants are added to help prevent overheated oil from thickening and forming tar and varnish (we really could have used that when the Flathead Fords were new), along with friction modifiers to help reduce internal friction.

As you can see, modern engine oil is a lot more complicated than the old straight weight mineral oil used during the 1920s and 1930s. As a result, engines are able to run at higher operating temperatures without failure, and have a much longer service life. The reduced friction also helps improve engine performance without creating excessive heat. It is plain to see how the engine oil can affect the job the cooling system has to do.

Chapter 14:
Modern Antifreeze and Coolant

The "official" definition of antifreeze is often said to be "a liquid that prevents freezing when mixed with water in an automotive cooling system." But much has changed since that description was written many years ago. Modern antifreeze does much more. It provides year-round corrosion protection to the cooling system, it prevents freeze-ups in winter, boil overs in the summer, especially in cars with air conditioning, all of this while not damaging the cooling system itself. That is quite a job description.

In addition, ethylene glycol-based antifreeze is relatively low in cost, is chemically stable, does not have an unpleasant odor, and does not adversely affect automotive finishes. Unlike the old days, when antifreeze was mostly used as winter freeze protection, modern antifreeze has become a year-round solution. Modern antifreeze has become a complex product containing additives designed to solve many different and complex problems.

Beginning in the 1980s, automotive engines became much more efficient. As a result, the operating temperatures of automotive engines became much higher. Also the use of lightweight materials (such as aluminum and plastics) in the cooling system further complicated matters. Finally, the total volume of coolant in the cooling system was reduced, which meant that the remaining coolant was being circulated faster and was being exposed to higher temperatures.

It is because of these changes that modern antifreeze solutions had to be reformulated. The new job description for antifreeze looks something like this:

* be an effective heat exchange fluid

* capable of providing both freeze and boil over protection

* capable of protecting metals against corrosion

* be compatible with plastics and elastomers

* chemically stable at both low and high temperatures

* compatible with hard water

* low foaming

* be acceptable to the environment and have and be an acceptable toxic risk

Heat Exchange

The ability of a coolant to transport heat away from a heat producing surface (such as a cylinder liner) is important and is measured using straight water as a comparison (because plain water is the best disperser of heat). The working temperature of the water used during this test is 59 degrees Fahrenheit. Engineers use this test and resulting data as a way to establish the efficiency of a given coolant mixture, at drawing heat away from a hot surface.

The thermal conductivity of a coolant is also important, and is measured as the amount of time it takes for a given amount of heat to be transferred through a surface of a given size and thickness. This test will establish how efficient the coolant is at transferring the heat, after it has been absorbed.

The heat exchange capacity of a mixture of ethylene glycol (EG) and water is reduced with an increased concentration of EG. Water is without question the best heat exchange fluid available, but some freeze protection is also necessary. So a compromise must be made between the freeze protection and the heat exchange efficiency of the coolant.

The viscosity or thickness of the fluid also makes a difference in how well a given fluid is able to transfer heat. The lower the viscosity, the more efficient the heat transfer will be.

Freeze Protection

Because of its low cost and good heat exchange properties, water was used in the old days as the primary engine coolant. However, because of its freezing point, water was mixed with an antifreeze solution in the winter months to prevent damage to the engine block and radiator. When water freezes it expands about nine percent, enough to crack an engine block or damage a radiator.

In contrast, ethylene glycol does not become a solid when it freezes, but instead forms ice crystals. The liquid portion of the solution becomes more concentrated, which, in turn, lowers the freezing point still further. A further decrease in temperature will cause more ice crystals to form, until a thick ice slush begins to develop. It is the slushing that allows the ethylene glycol to continue to flow even as it expands.

While a mixture of an EG solution pretty much eliminates the freezing worries, other winter-related problems sometimes appear. They include overheating, boiling, and engine damage, if the "slush" becomes too thick and can no longer circulate through the cooling system. Therefore, coolant/freeze protection ratings are based on the lowest temperature at which an EG and water-based coolant solution can provide freeze protection and still properly circulate through a cooling system.

Typically, freeze protection ratings are based on the surrounding climate and lowest anticipated temperature, and will range between minus four degrees Fahrenheit and minus forty degrees Fahrenheit. To provide that range of freeze protection the concentration of EG ranges between 33 and 50 percent.

Boiling Protection — As engine efficiency is increased (partly by increasing the engine operating temperature), more heat must be released into the cooling system. Additional cooling can be provided by increasing the cooling system pressure, and by allowing the coolant to circulate at a higher maximum temperature. The higher boiling point (as a result of the higher cooling system pressure) helps reduce evaporation losses, water pump cavitation (caused by flash boiling on the intake side of the water pump), and after boil caused by heat soak from a warm engine.Additive Technology

Straight solutions of EG and water by themselves are corrosive to the metals inside of the cooling system. As a result, some sort of corrosion inhibitor package needs to be added to the coolant solution. These inhibitors must be compatible with plastics and elastomers (used as engine cooling system components) and should not form insoluble salts when diluted with hard water.

Corrosion in an engine cooling system will not only deteriorate metal components but will also produce insoluble corrosion compounds that will tend to block radiator passageways, and thermostat valves, while also blocking heat transfer by building deposits on heat exchange surfaces.

The metals in a cooling system that need to be protected fall into four main categories:

(1) iron, steel, and gray cast iron

(2) aluminum alloys in cast and wrought forms

(3) copper and brass

(4) lead-based solders

Gray cast iron has been the traditional material for cylinder blocks, heads and liners, but is slowly being replaced by aluminum alloys that are lighter and have better thermal conductivity. Copper or brass automotive radiators are also being replaced by aluminum radiators with crossflow plastic tanks. Steel cast iron and copper alloys are also being used in more progressive designs of component parts such as water pump impellers and thermostats.

These changes in cooling system materials mean that several different kinds of inhibitors are now required in a balanced formation to protect the aluminum, steel cast iron, copper solder, brass, and copper materials found in a modern cooling system. Modern engine cooling systems often develop unique corrosion problems not found in cooling systems thirty years ago. These problems include pitting of the radiator tubes, crevice corrosion in cylinder head packing, depletion of corrosion-inhibiting products, cavitation in water pumps and cylinder liners, and high temperature corrosion in cylinder heads.

Inhibitors

Some of the traditional inhibitors used in antifreeze include borates, phosphates, benzoates, nitrates, silicates, mercaptobenzothiazole and tolytriazole. In addition to direct inhibition, alkali metal borates and phosphates provide extended metal protection by means of a buffering action and alkaline reserve. These inhibitors maintain the coolant in an alkaline condition by neutralizing the acid products that may cause a deterioration of the coolant. They also protect the coolant from contamination as a result of defects such as a leaking cylinder head gasket.

These inhibitors must be present in strong enough concentration to provide complete metal surface protection. The concentration of the inhibitors depends on the operating conditions, hardness of the water used, and the length of time the engine runs at operating temperature. Corrosion protection is one of the reasons for maintaining the concentration of ethylene glycol to between 40 and 50 percent year-round.

Because inhibitors are depleted (wear out) over time through interaction with metals and other substances in the system, the coolant must be replaced periodically. Hence, the long time rule that you should replace the coolant in your cooling system at least every three years. Something else you may not realize is that often times **when a radiator becomes clogged it is not always from hard water deposits, but just as often from depleted coolant inhibitors,** so pay attention and change your coolant!

Hard water compatibility has been a major concern when dealing with inhibitors. Phosphate additives are difficult to stabilize in when hard water is used. Common problems with hard water include the formation of insoluble calcium phosphates. Europe, along with many other foreign countries, has hard water problems and therefore formulates its antifreeze without the use of phosphates.

As we learned earlier, the life of an engine coolant depends, in part, on the continued effectiveness of its corrosion inhibitor package. Some inhibitors such as nitrates and silicates are consumed quite rapidly in service. The phosphates and trizoles are consumed at moderate rates while the borates and organic acid salts have slow depletion rates.

> **Many of the additives and inhibitors found in conventional antifreeze are designed to "plate" or coat the metal surfaces of a cooling system, to prevent the formation of rust and corrosion on the metal surfaces. The problem with plating is that while it does protect the metal surfaces of the cooling system from corrosion, it also reduces the ability of the metal to transfer heat. This is another one of those compromise situations, where you have to give up something to get something else. In this case, you are giving up some of the heat transfer ability in order to protect the metal surfaces from rust and corrosion.**

Many of the additives and inhibitors found in conventional antifreeze are designed to "plate" or coat the metal surfaces of a cooling system, to prevent the formation of rust and corrosion on the metal surfaces. The problem with plating is that while it does protect the metal surfaces of the cooling system from corrosion, it also reduces the ability of the metal to transfer heat. This is another one of those compromise situations, where you have to give up something to get something else. In this case, you are giving up some of the heat transfer ability in order to protect the metal surfaces from rust and corrosion.

Supplemental coolant additive packages (referred to as SCAs) are sometimes used to boost the useful life of the engine coolant, by replacing the inhibitors that are quickly depleted. Most of the SCA additives are designed for the Heavy-Duty Fleet Market where large tracks average over 100,000 miles in a year compared to the average private vehicle that averages about 15,000 miles a year.

The SCA in fleet coolants are added by releasing the additives through a screw-on-type filter canister, or as a liquid additive package added at specified mileage intervals. A simple test kit is used to determine the condition of the coolant. The main concern in fleet coolants is the presence of the nitrate inhibitor that protects the engine cylinder liners from cavitation.

Fleet Coolants

Another problem in fleet coolants is too much SCA being used. Many people wrongfully believe that if some is good, more is better. With SCAs that is not true. To much nitrate, for instance, can cause corrosion of the solder used to hold the radiator and heater core together. To much silicate will result in a gel formation that will begin plugging the radiator and SCA coolant filters. A partially plugged radiator will cause the engine operating temperature to climb, which could eventually lead to engine failure.

To give you an idea how difficult it can be to solve cooling system-related problems, the following photo pages show examples of heavy-duty cooling system problems and the steps involved in solving those problems.

Heavy-Duty Coolants. The first major change.

In the 1970s, heavy-duty engines went through significant design changes. It was a time when horsepower increased, while engine weight was greatly reduced. With these changes, greater power and better fuel economy were gained. However, the changes also caused a major problem with cylinder liner vibration. Because of this vibration, many cylinder liners became so damaged by cavitation and pitting that soluble-oil coolants could leak into the engine and cause significant and expensive damage. It soon became apparent that new coolants had to be developed for these newly designed heavy-duty engines.

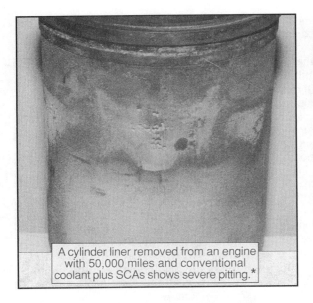

A cylinder liner removed from an engine with 50,000 miles and conventional coolant plus SCAs shows severe pitting.*

Thermostat from a CAT 3176 engine with 70,000 miles showing the silicate deposits left behind with conventional coolant and SCAs.*

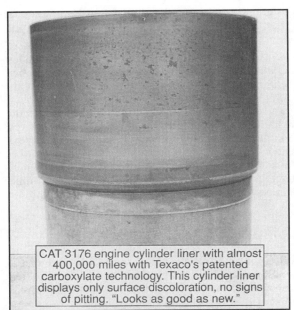

CAT 3176 engine cylinder liner with almost 400,000 miles with Texaco's patented carboxylate technology. This cylinder liner displays only surface discoloration, no signs of pitting. "Looks as good as new."

CAT 3176 engine thermostat with almost 400,000 miles using Texaco's patented carboxylate technology. Clean, no deposits.

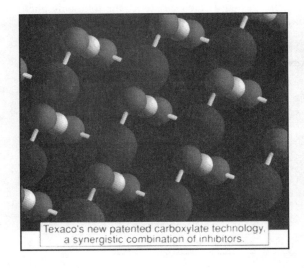

Texaco's new patented carboxylate technology, a synergistic combination of inhibitors.

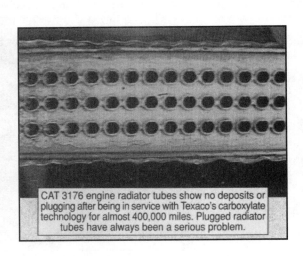

CAT 3176 engine radiator tubes show no deposits or plugging after being in service with Texaco's carboxylate technology for almost 400,000 miles. Plugged radiator tubes have always been a serious problem.

Detroit Diesel 149 engine, radiator tubes in mining service, with over 6,000 hours. No deposits or plugging evident.

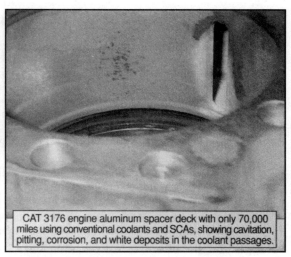

CAT 3176 engine aluminum spacer deck with only 70,000 miles using conventional coolants and SCAs, showing cavitation, pitting, corrosion, and white deposits in the coolant passages.

CAT 3176 engine cylinder liner with almost 400,000 miles and Texaco's patented carboxylate technology. The left side is exposed to coolant and the right dark portion of the liner is exposed to motor oil. This cylinder liner displays only surface discoloration, no rust or pitting is present.

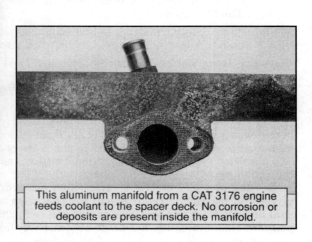

This aluminum manifold from a CAT 3176 engine feeds coolant to the spacer deck. No corrosion or deposits are present inside the manifold.

CAT 3176 engine aluminum spacer deck shows no sign of pitting, corrosion or deposits. This engine has almost 400,000 miles with Texaco's carboxylate technology coolant.

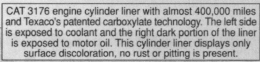

Brass Temperature Sensor

CAT 3176 engine thermostat, housing and brass temperature sensor all clean of deposits and corrosion. All were in service for almost 400,000 miles with Texaco carboxylate technology coolant.

Antifoamants

Excessive foaming either in regular service or during refilling of the system must be avoided. Foam that accumulates in a cooling system as a result of air entrapment will reduce the coolant's ability to transfer heat. Certain higher alcohols and silicone polymers are used in modern coolants to help suppress foaming. These substances lower the surface tension of the liquid to allow the bubbles to break and dissipate.

Dyes -- A dye is added to engine coolant to help identify it from other automotive fluids. The dye must remain stable during the life of the coolant and should not be harmful to vehicle paint finishes.

Propylene Glycol

There has been a lot of controversy in recent years concerning antifreeze and the environment. With the introduction of propylene glycol-based antifreeze coolants the controversy has expanded further. The following are the actual facts concerning ethylene glycol (EG) vs. propylene glycol (PG) solutions:

(1) EG is toxic (to humans and animals) while PG is essentially non-toxic. However, being toxic to humans and being toxic to the environment are two completely different things.

(2) Both types of coolants, EG and PG, are 100 percent biodegradable to carbon dioxide and water. They are both better for the environment than most other man-made chemicals. In fact, EG-based coolants are actually better for the environment because EG uses 30 percent less biological oxygen to biodegrade than PG-based coolants. EG-based coolants also biodegrade at a faster rate than PG-based coolants.

(3) In engine cooling systems, EG-based coolants are slightly better at providing freeze protection. EG-based coolants are also slightly better in viscosity and heat transfer, than PG-based coolants.

(4) EG-based coolants are usually between 50 and 75 percent less expensive than PG-based antifreeze.

Hazardous Waste Concerns

As part of the Clean Air Act of 1990 ethylene glycol and 46 other substances were added to the list of hazardous air pollutants. These newly listed substances by definition (of being classified a hazardous substance) were automatically assigned a rating of one pound. This meant that any spill of one pound or greater of a classified substance within a 24-hour period, meant a report was to be filed with the Environmental Protection Agency (EPA).

In May of 1995, the EPA reclassified ethylene glycol and raised the requirement for reporting a spill or leak from the previous one pound to 5,000 pounds. This means that EG-based coolants are, for the most part, no longer considered an environmental hazard. This came as a great relief to many EG customers, especially airlines and airports that use EG-based solutions to de-ice airplanes and runways.

Other Uses of EG

Ethylene glycol is common to more things than just antifreeze/coolant. Its number one use is in the manufacture of polyester, the second most popular use is antifreeze, followed by the manufacture of plastic two-liter beverage bottles. Ethylene glycol is also used in the manufacture of adhesives, and in the manufacture of cork, tobacco, vinyl floor tiles, printing inks, and nitroglycerin, as well as many other common consumer products.

Extended Life Coolants

The newest development in engine coolants is the extended life coolant. Texaco is being used as an example simply because it is one of the most popular brands currently available.

First we need to clarify the fact that there are actually two extended life coolants manufactured by Texaco. One is for the light-duty automotive market

TEXACO EXTENDER

Cooling System Capacity		Approximate amount at 300,000 miles of on-road use (three years or 6,000 hours of off-road use)
Gallons	Liters	Quantity
6 - 8	22 - 30	0.5 quart
8 - 13	30 - 49	1 quart
13 - 22	49 - 83	1.5 quarts
22 - 30	83 - 114	2 quarts
30 - 41	114 - 155	3 quarts
41 - 52	155 - 197	4 quarts
52 - 64	197 - 243	5 quarts

and is known simply as Havoline Extended Life Coolant (this is factory fill in all General Motors vehicles built since 1995 and is also marketed by General Motors under the DEX-Cool name).

The other coolant formula is known as Texaco Extended Life Coolant and is designed for use in the heavy-duty market. Texaco Extended Life Coolant contains additional additives that provide protection (against the pitting of wet sleeve cylinders) in diesel engines, for 600,000 miles or 12,000 hours of service, without any additional SCA being added.

Both types of Texaco's Extended Life Antifreeze are manufactured from an ethylene glycol base and use a patented carboxylate-based rust inhibitor package that totally eliminates the need for silicates, phosphates, borates, nitrates, and related additives normally found in conventional engine coolants. Havoline Extended Life Coolant for automotive use meets European requirements for phosphate free coolant, as well as Japanese requirements for silicate free coolants.

For automotive use the Havoline Extended Life Coolant has a service life of five years or 150,000 miles. Additional benefits include effective long-term protection for aluminum, brass, cast iron, steel, solder, and copper. Also extended water pump seal life is possible because of fewer dissolved solids in the coolant. Also, there is no silicate dropout or gel formation during use or storage.

With a 50:50 mix of water and antifreeze, freeze protection is provided to minus 34 degrees Fahrenheit, and boil over protection to 265 degrees Fahrenheit using a 15-pound radiator cap. While it can be done, **it is strongly recommended that conventional EG-based coolants not be mixed with the extended life coolants. Doing so will dilute the special additives package that is a part of the extended life coolants.**

Checking Freeze Protection

Because Texaco's Extended Life Coolant is EG-based, it can be checked using a conventional hydrometer (the cheap floating ball antifreeze tester we all have). Test strips such as those used by many truck fleets will also work with this new coolant. **All EG-based coolants, regardless of type, can be checked using a conventional hydrometer.**

PG-based antifreeze/coolants do require a different "hydrometer" calibrated to PG's specific gravity. While you can mix the two types of coolants together, and they will physically work together, it will be difficult (if not impossible) for you to measure the freeze protection because of the two different specific gravities of the coolants. If in doubt, read the label on the container before you add any coolant to be sure you are adding the same type of coolant.

A refractometer is starting to replace the hydrometer as a way to test the freeze point of engine coolants. The main advantage is its accuracy and the fact that most are also able to check both EG- and PG-based coolants.

One final thing — Texaco advertises its new extended life coolants are ideal for vehicles with air conditioning, while also providing excellent year-round protection. So, what is the air conditioning benefit? Simple. The new extended life coolants keep the entire cooling system free of scale and corrosion while not forming a "coating" (known as plating) on the metal surfaces, which can restrict the transfer of heat. In addition, there is no dropout of the inhibitors and additives, which allows the cooling system to work at peak efficiency throughout its lifetime.

Modern cooling systems have a small margin of error. Anything that affects the cooling system's ability to transfer heat, can cause overheating and eventual engine failure. It is important to keep a modern cooling system in good working order.

Summary

The information on the previous pages will not make you a chemical engineer by any means, but I wanted you to understand a little more about how antifreeze is manufactured, what the additives are supposed to do, and why inhibitors are also necessary. You also need to know the difference between an automotive cooling system and the one found in an over the road truck. Finally, you should have gained a better understanding of how extended life antifreeze/coolant differs from conventional antifreeze.

Thanks to Texaco Lubricants Co. and Rich Armstrong for providing the background and technical information on antifreeze/coolant.

Accuracy of Measurement

By the way, I mentioned earlier about refractometers, and how they were much more accurate than a hydrometer for checking the concentration of EG or PG in an engine coolant solution. For help in understanding the importance of accuracy in measuring engine coolant I called on Mike Reimer of the Leica Corp. Mike did a great job of answering my questions so I could, in turn, explain this to you. Like many of you, I did not realize that temperature could affect the accuracy of a hydrometer so much. Now that we know, we have no excuse but to do it right.

In many professional shops a "refractometer" is used to measure the freeze point of the coolant solution, because a refractometer is much more accurate than a hydrometer. One of the biggest problems that affects the accuracy of a hydrometer is temperature. Other problems are caused by air bubbles and dirt/rust particles.

There are three basic designs of hydrometers: the floating disks, the floating needle, and the floating balls. While different in design, all three work based on the same principle, and that is the more balls that float the higher the specific gravity, and the more freeze protection you think you have.

One other thing to keep in mind is that a hydrometer needs to be calibrated to the coolant solution you are testing. Because of the difference in specific gravity you cannot use an EG-calibrated hydrometer to check a PG coolant solution, and you cannot check EG coolant using PG-calibrated hydrometer. And, as we learned before, if you mix EG and PG coolant solutions together, well, there is nothing that can check that!

Temperature is the variable that causes the most problems. As the temperature rises, the specific gravity of the coolant decreases. Most hydrometers are calibrated to be accurate at 60 degrees Fahrenheit. But how many of us check our antifreeze when it's exactly 60 degrees outside? Usually it's about 35 degrees Fahrenheit—with the threat of a hard freeze before morning—that makes you stumble out and check the seven or eight vehicles in the yard. So what difference does the temperature make anyway?

Would it surprise you to learn that hydrometers can be off as much as 23 degrees Fahrenheit? Most of that is due to their lack of temperature compensation. While that may not be a problem if you live in Red Lizard, New Mexico, it could be a big problem if you live in Frostbite, Montana. Because of the temperature, you may get a false reading from your hydrometer, which leads you to think you have much better freeze protection than you actually have. A cracked engine block could prove you and your hydrometer were wrong.

The government has already figured this out, and that is why the military uses a temperature compensated refractometer to ensure accurate measurement of the coolant concentrations in all military vehicles. (Can you imagine phoning the enemy and calling for a time out because we don't have the right amount of antifreeze in our trucks!) Most all large fleet trucking companies also use a temperature compensating re-

> Temperature is the variable that causes the most problems. As the temperature rises, the specific gravity of the coolant decreases. Most hydrometers are calibrated to be accurate at 60 degrees Fahrenheit. But how many of us check our antifreeze when it is exactly 60 degrees outside? Usually it is about 35 degrees Fahrenheit—with the threat of a hard freeze before morning—that makes you stumble out and check the seven or eight vehicles in the yard.

fractometer to measure coolant concentrations as do most all NASCAR teams. In addition, many modern cars are computer controlled and the emissions devices are designed to work within a certain engine operating temperature. An improper coolant mixture can cause the operating temperature to be too hot or too cold, sending the poor computer into orbit trying to adjust for an improper engine operating temperature.

The thing to keep in mind is that temperature compensation is important to a refractometer as well. **If you are going to buy a refractometer, be sure the one you buy has the ability to compensate for the temperature**, otherwise you have not bettered your equipment much. Which brings us to our next question....

How Does A Refractometer Actually Work?

A refractometer works based on the speed of light as it moves through the air. Using water as an example, water is said to have a reflective index of 1.3, which means light travels through water 1.3 times slower than it does through air. So, what you are really measuring when you are using a refractometer is how much a beam of light can be slowed when it passes through, in our case engine coolant.

A refractometer measures only soluble solids, and completely ignores suspended matter such as flakes of rust and scale. Air bubbles also do not affect a refractometer like it does a hydrometer. This is where a refractometer gets part of its increased accuracy. It is able to ignore most of the things that trip up a hydrometer.

It is well known that nearly all materials expand when heated. They also become less dense. Light will be slowed less as temperature goes up. Therefore the refractive index will decrease. For a solid this thermal effect is minor, but for liquids the change in density is quite substantial. That is why it is important to have a way to compensate for the temperature changes.

To better understand how a refractometer works, imagine driving down the highway and you accidentally drop the right front wheel off the asphalt, onto the soft shoulder. The wheel is slowed by the increased friction. Meanwhile, the left wheel continues to travel at the same rate as before. As a result, the left wheel advances faster than the right wheel and the car is forced to the right. (And you, likely, will end up in the ditch because you were not paying attention!) It is the difference in the speed of the wheels that forced the car to the right and into the ditch.

A refractometer works based on the same principle. Using water as a standard, we know water has a refractive index of 1.3 and a solution of EG and water will have a different reading because of the difference in density of the EG. The water will still be 1.3 while the EG, because of its density (it is thicker), will reduce the speed of light more than the plain water. The difference between the two measurements becomes the refractive index of the EG and water solution. That measurement can then be used to tell you the exact concentration of EG in the water.

A refractometer is calibrated to 68 degrees. But unlike most hydrometers, a refractometer can be calibrated to adjust for a change in temperature. Most quality refractometers will work in a range between 0 and 104 degrees Fahrenheit, and should check up to a 70 percent concentration of EG and water. Its accuracy should be within plus or minus two degrees—even at the extreme ends of the scale. It is because of this accuracy that refractometers are often used.

The other good thing about a quality refractometer is that most will have a dual scale, and therefore are able to check both EG and PG coolant solutions. **In addition, most refractometers can also be used to check the specific gravity of a battery, so you can determine its state of charge**. The pictures on the following pages show some of the features of a quality refractometer as well as some of the features you should look for.

101

LEICA Duo-Chek Engine Coolant & Battery Tester

New sample cover increases the image brightness and contrast

Redesigned all-glass eyepiece - features a large depth of field for easy reading

Impact resistant body is rugged and waterproof

Includes coolant transfer pipet and battery fluid dipstick

Direct-read scale shadowline indicating reading

Model DC70

Model DC60

Accurately Measures All Engine Coolants Including Automotive, Heavy-Duty and Environmentally Safe Coolants

Quickly and Accurately Determine Freeze Protection of Engine Coolants and Battery Charge Level

Leica Duo-Chek Engine Coolant/Battery Tester (refractometer) offers an accurate, fast and easy-to-use method for testing engine coolant freeze point, glycol concentration and battery charge condition. It provides automatic temperature compensation for immediate, accurate direct readings of ethylene glycol or environmentally safe propylene glycol coolants with only a few drops of sample.

Standard Features

- Automatic temperature compensation—correct readings at any temperature. Responds much faster than older models.
- Portable—no batteries or power cord
- Waterproof design—eliminates the possibility of condensation on the optics
- Brighter, direct read scale—readings provided in concentration or freeze point protection
- Quality optics - The large depth of field eyepiece is easy to read even when wearing eyeglasses
- Rugged design - Drop tests indicate the Leica Duo-Chek maintains calibration when repeatedly dropped from 36" height
- Manufactured in the United States

Trust Your Engine to the Accuracy of a Leica Duo-Chek

Accuracy is important to be sure the coolant provides adequate freeze-up and boil-over protection. Accurate coolant concentration also means the coolant viscosity and heat transfer properties are correct. The proper coolant/water mix means worry-free, trouble-free cooling system operation and prevents engine damage from cavitation corrosion, a problem which can occur when the coolant/water ratio is too high. Compare the Leica Duo-Chek with a field test hydrometer which meets ASTM standards:

	LEICA Duo-Chek	Hydrometer
Precision	±1°F (ASTM D 3321)	±8°F (ASTM D 1124)
Measures "Environmentally Safe" Propylene Glycol Coolants	Yes	No
Automatically Correct readings for temperature effects	Yes	No
Measure Coolant and Battery Charge level with one instrument	Yes	No

Temperature Compensation Makes the Difference

Automatic temperature compensation makes it unnecessary to measure temperature and apply a correction factor when taking readings. Without temperature compensation or correction readings can be very inaccurate. The chart shows the difference between a temperature compensated instrument and a non-temperature compensated instrument.

Freeze Protection Readings at Various Temperatures
50% Ethylene Glycol based engine coolant

[Bar chart: Y-axis "Freeze Protection °F" from 0 to -60; X-axis "Ambient Temperature °F" at 90°, 68°, 48°, 32°]

- LEICA DC70 Duo-Chek hand-held engine coolant refractometer
- Non-temperature compensated competitive coolant refractometer

**Cutaway view showing DC70/60 optics and temperature compensation mechanism.
As temperature changes the bi-metal strip moves, changing the position of the optical wedge.
This automatically applies the temperature compensation.**

[Diagram labels: Sample Cover, Impact Resistant Housing, Prism, Optical Wedge, **Bi-Metal Strip**, Lens, Calibration Adjustment, Scale, Lenses, Eyepiece, Eyeguard]

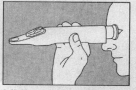
Technical Specifications

LEICA Duo-Chek is available in two models to measure freeze point protection: Model DC70 measures degrees Fahrenheit and Model DC60 measures degrees Centigrade.

	Model DC70	Model DC60
Catalog No.	7584L	7564L
Specific Gravity Scale Division	1.100-1.400 0.01	1.100-1.400 0.01
AntiFreeze Protection		
Ethylene Glycol	+32° to -60°F	0°C to -48°C
Propylene Glycol	+32° to -60°F	0°C to -48°C
Scale Division	5°F	3°C
Coolant Concentration Scale		
Ethylene Glycol	0 - 70%	0 - 70%
Propylene Glycol	0 - 63%	0 - 61%
Refractive Index Range	1.3330-1.4048	1.3330-1.4048
Temperature Compensation Range	0° to 104°F	-18° to 40°C
Calibration Liquid	Distilled Water	Distilled Water
Accuracy	±1.0°F	±0.55°C
Application	Check engine coolant and battery condition	Check engine coolant and battery condition

Notes

Chapter 15: But Wait, There is More

Jack Evans

Just when you thought you knew all there was to know about antifreeze/coolants, along comes Jack Evans of Evans Cooling Systems. Jack has spent over twenty years doing in-depth cooling system research, and has developed a unique hi-tech coolant that has some truly amazing properties. For starters, how about a boiling temperature of 370 degrees Fahrenheit at sea level, and freeze protection to minus 70 degrees Fahrenheit! Having such an extreme range of protection is amazing enough, but in addition, this coolant does it without any water, and with low (4.0 pounds per square inch), or in some applications no pressure at all in the cooling system. In addition, Evans NPG is essentially non-toxic!

Jack Evans is foremost a designer and builder of high efficiency OEM (original equipment manufacturer) and race car engines. Jack has spent many years developing ideas that have led to the increased efficiency of race car engines. His ultimate goal is to make race cars run faster. Jack began by focusing on ways to prevent damaging levels of detonation and pre-ignition knock. His research led him to the conclusion that the coolant in the engine was the limiting factor, so Jack begin doing extensive research. After more than twenty years, Jack has developed a highly efficient cooling system package.

Racing engines especially, but all types of engines can benefit from Jack's research. He has learned that most engines are capable of operating at much higher efficiencies, but that the limiting factor has always been the water-based cooling system. A low boiling point and excessive vapor (steam bubble) generation has caused localized coolant boiling, vapor blanketing (where steam bubbles build up and attach themselves to metal surfaces, preventing coolant from reaching the hot metal around the combustion domes) and hot spots (steam bubbles collecting in an area and blocking the flow of coolant). These problems have been around for years.

The extra heat in the cylinder area (caused by steam bubbles blocking coolant flow to the critical hot spots), can often heat the cylinder area enough to cause the fuel mixture inside of the cylinder to ignite early, before the normal ignition firing of the spark plug. This is what is known as pre-ignition. A common occurrence in racing engines, pre-ignition can occur in most any engine and can result in piston damage, cracked cylinder heads, engine bearing damage, and blown head gaskets.

Research Results

In all engines, hot metal (such as the cylinder heads) coming in contact with coolant can cause localized boiling, called "nucleate" boiling, at critical temperature locations inside of an engine. When this happens, the coolant is turned into vapor as it absorbs the extreme engine heat. This vaporized coolant is then ideally carried to the radiator where it is then recondensed (turned back) into a liquid once again. That is how it is supposed to work—in theory, anyway.

An ethylene glycol and water (EGW) type coolant usually recondenses back to a liquid inside of the radiator. Because the vapor produced in a 50:50 mix of EGW is more than 98 percent water vapor, the ethylene glycol does not "boil-out" with the water, so the vaporized coolant cannot recondense until the temperature of the coolant drops below the boiling point of the water at the system pressure. In other words, the coolant will not turn back into a liquid until the temperature of the heated coolant falls below the boiling point of the cooling system vapor. In most cooling systems, the only place that can happen is in the radiator.

Under heavy load and high stress conditions such as racing, the engine coolant often becomes so saturated with heat that it is unable to recondense the vapor inside of the radiator. So the heated vapor is just recycled, while the heat in the cooling system continues to build and form still more vapor bubbles. **This is exactly what happened to our Model T Ford engine at the higher elevations; the coolant system just was not able to keep up.**

As a result of this nucleate boiling, a layer of steam vapor begins to form on the surface of the hot metals (places such as the cylinder head jacket surfaces). The steam vapor continues to build to a point where it completely covers a "hot spot" area (this is known as surface boiling). Meanwhile, the size of the steam pocket continues to increase, until we have what is referred to as a "hot spot." These hot spots are one of the common causes of engine detonation and pre-ignition.

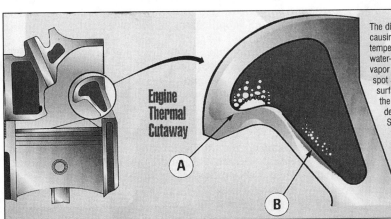

The diagram at left shows the loss of Nucleate Boiling causing a vapor blanket to be formed **(A)** as the metal temperature has exceeded the thermal capacity of a water-based coolant. A hot spot develops because the vapor blanket keeps the coolant from contacting the hot spot and increased detonation results. The very high surface tension of the water-generated steam promotes the formation of the vapor blanket and eventually destructive levels of pre-ignition (knock) occur. Sustained Nucleate Boiling reveals continuous heat transfer through the uninterrupted liquid-to-metal contact of the NPG Coolant **(B)**. The relatively low surface tension of NPG Coolant aids in the breaking away of vapor and the movement of coolant across the hot spots, controlling surface vapor, and resulting in lower metal temperatures at the hot spot in each cylinder.

Research shows that when either EGW coolant or 100 percent water coolant can no longer be recondensed (turned back into a liquid) in the radiator, the coolant temperature would continue to rise above 220 degrees Fahrenheit. **Once the coolant reaches 220 degrees Fahrenheit, the water pump begins to cavitate** (pump vapor instead of coolant), which further reduces the flow of coolant through the system. This, in turn, causes the coolant temperature to rise still higher. This results in still more cavitation and the loss of coolant through the pressure vents.

In examining the formation of coolant vapor it became apparent that the water in the coolant mixture was the main cause of the high amount of vapor production. This, in turn, was helping to create the hot spots. So it was the overheated water vapor mixed with the engine coolant that was identified as the major cause of the overheating problems. Water was also part of the reason for the development of pressurized cooling systems, **(as we have already learned)**, the pressurized cooling system became necessary as a way to raise the cooling system's water boiling point beyond 212 degrees Fahrenheit.

Further research also showed that it was the water in the coolant that was causing the additives added to EGW coolants (to prevent corrosion) to become depleted over time, making it necessary to replace the coolant. Water is a well-known cause of the corrosion and is the cause, in part, of other serious damage to metal parts inside the cooling system. It has also been found to be, in part, responsible for the high concentrations of lead and other metals being found in the coolant.

In addition, most people do not realize how toxic EG really is. It is alarming to note, for instance, that swallowing one ounce of EG coolant can kill a 50-pound child. EG causes kidney failure, and is one of the most common causes of pet animal deaths. A vehicle parked in a driveway may drip EG coolant, where an animal will then stop and lick the coolant (because it tastes sweet) become sick and often die.

In developing a replacement coolant, one thing became clear: Eliminate the water! By doing that, a number of common problems were being addressed, including: toxicity/waste, environmental concerns, cavitation, internal corrosion, heavy metal deposits, additive depletion, development of hot spots, and, finally, overheating.

That was quite an idealistic menu. But, after years of extensive research, Jack Evans came up with what he calls Evans NPG or **Non-Aqueous Propylene Glycol** coolant. Because of the specific heat and conductive heat transfer differences between the Evans NPG and conventional EGW (ethylene glycol and water) based coolants, original research showed it might be necessary to increase the coolant flow rate through the cooling system by twenty-seven percent when using NPG, over that of EGW, to be able to remove the same amount of heat from the engine.

In real life applications where the EGW coolants were producing large amounts of vapor, often times the NPG was producing the same or greater heat rejection with the same coolant flow as the EGW coolants. Since there is no water in the Evans NPG coolant system to cause cavitation at the water pumps, the equal heat transfer rate was easily matched. It was further determined that increasing the flow rate of the Evans NPG coolant could provide even better cooling of the engine.

How This is Possible

The size of the vapor bubbles that form on the hot metal surfaces can directly affect the size of the vapor barrier that develops on the metal surface. Nucleate boiling produces bubbles of different sizes, depending on the coolant's liquid characteristics (this is referred to as "surface tension"). If you lower the surface tension of a coolant, smaller vapor bubbles should form as opposed to larger ones. Evans NPG has a much lower surface tension than a mixture of 50:50 EGW.

Another fluid characteristic that works in favor of decreasing vapor bubble size is the difference in "vapor pressure" (the amount of pressure needed to retain vapor within a liquid). **The vapor pressure of water is 100 times higher than that of Evans NPG.** In addition, the more turbulent flow of the Evans NPG coolant tends to produce shear forces that break down the larger bubbles into smaller bubbles on the metal surfaces. All of this works in favor of the Evans NPG coolant.

Heat of Vaporization

Still another characteristic that helps to determine the amount of vapor generated in changing a liquid to a gas is called "heat of vaporization." **When heat is transferred from a hot surface, it does so according to a measurement referred to as heat of vaporization.** Evans NPG has a heat of vaporization rating of 12,500 as compared to conventional EGW coolants that have a heat of vaporization rating of 9,720. Therefore, the Evans NPG coolant (when compared to 50:50 mixture of EGW) generates less vapor by volume (when equal amounts of heat are being removed from the coolant). Evans NPG will also displace less coolant from a hot surface than will an EGW coolant, given the same amount of heat transferred.

Hot Spots

It would stand to reason that if the vapor bubbles could be condensed back to a liquid more rapidly, there should be less vapor trapped inside of the cooling system. Less vapor in the cooling system should mean higher metal to liquid contact and a cooler running engine.

Compared to Evans NPG, water from an EGW coolant condenses water at a much slower rate, and at best, usually not until it reaches the radiator. In contrast, the temperature of the Evans NPG in the cooling system is well below the boiling point of the coolant itself, so the vapor is being returned to liquid while still in the engine block and cylinder heads—long before it gets to the radiator. The smaller bubbles created by the Evans NPG coolant also help to return the vapor to a liquid much sooner.

Remember, there is no water in Evans NPG coolant, so the corrosion problems associated with water are gone. **Because the Evans NPG coolant works either as a non-pressure coolant or a low-pressure coolant, it is ideal for antique and classic cars, as well as for modern racing applications**. Any of you Flathead Ford guys listening? While Evans NPG is more expensive to buy up front, the long term benefits will more than return your investment.

Evans NPG vs. PG: What's the Difference?

It would be easy to believe that all propylene coolants are alike except for a few different additives, but that isn't so. The Evans NPG coolant is made up of a special blend of additives that do not require water as the carrier. In contrast, most 50:50 PGW-type coolants (i.e.: Sierra) use water to suspend additives such as phosphates and borates, which are unstable without the water carrier. The reason these additives are necessary in the first place is to prevent the system pH from turning acidic, which causes corrosion and also erodes the metals in the cooling system.

We learned about the importance of the pH balance to a cooling system in the first part of this book. We know that a 50:50 mixture of EGW (ethylene glycol and water) has a pH of about 12 with the additives included. PGW (propylene glycol and water) has a pH of about 14 with the additives, and the Evans NPG coolant has a pH of just 6 with its additive package.

Normally, when looking at pH numbers of a coolant, 7 is considered neutral. Anything above 7 is alkaline or to the base side (usually good) while anything below 7 is to the acidic or acid side. But remember, there is no water in Evans NPG so the corrosion, hard water scale, and related problems associated with water simply do not exist with Evans NPG coolant. No additives are necessary with the NPG because there is no water to cause the deterioration of the pH balance.

It is important to remember that it is the water and the usable amounts of suspended oxygen in the water that are the major cause of the engine coolant turning acidic in the first place. So by removing the water and the suspended oxygen, the rate and formation of the "uglies" is greatly reduced.

> **It is important to remember that it is the water and the usable amounts of suspended oxygen in the water that are the major cause of the engine coolant turning acidic in the first place. So by removing the water and the suspended oxygen, the rate and formation of the "uglies" is greatly reduced.**

Typically EG and water-based PG coolants start out with a pH above 12, so as the additives deteriorate over time, the coolant does not turn acidic too quickly. "Reserve alkalinity" is the official term for this. In contrast, because the Evans NPG coolant does not use water, it has no need for reserve alkalinity.

In Case You Are Wondering

Yes, there has been a patent issued—actually three separate ones—for the Evans NPG coolant. (Patent numbers 4,550,694, 4,630,572, and 5,031,579 for you Internet-types who like to look things up.) Along with those patents, there are additional patents pending for the additives formula used in NPG, as well as the design of the Evans closed cooling system and other related cooling system products developed by Evans Cooling. Okay, the theory sounds good, but has anybody really used this stuff in real life?

Real Life Usage

That's exactly what I wanted to know, when I first found out about the Evans coolant. I read all of the information I could find on the product, then called Evans Cooling and talked at great length with Steve Pressley, vice-president and general manager of engineering at Evans Cooling Systems. Steve was helpful and took my skeptical nature in stride. He also forwarded some of Jack Evan's research results as it applies to racing engines. That helped put things into perspective.

Test Results

We know that water is to blame for the large amounts of steam created in a cooling system under heavy load. In fact, the only way water is actually able to release large amounts of heat is through some kind of boiling action. Ideally you should use the nucleate boiling point of the engine coolant as the control point for determining the maximum temperature the engine metals should be allowed to reach. If the metals in the engine exceed the nucleate boiling point of the engine coolant, the engine coolant starts to boil excessively (going from nucleate to film boiling), and the effort to control the coolant temperature fails.

Evans Cooling selected propylene as a basis for its engine coolant for several reasons:

1) It has a low surface tension, which means the bubbles will break away from a metal surface fairly quickly.

2) Propylene also has a lower tendency to mix with or be drawn to other nucleate sights—which could then form still larger vapor bubbles.

So it is these traits of propylene that allow it to actually knock off the small nucleate bubbles from the hot metal surfaces. This results in the coolant having a higher thermal efficiency at its boiling point than water does at its boiling point.

The "terminal molar" heat of a fluid (its ability to draw heat from a metal surface) is measured in BTUs (British thermal units). Water has a terminal molar rating of approximately 9,400 units. In contrast, propylene has a rating of nearly 15,000 units. As a result, propylene is able to transfer heat much more efficiently. This is a step in the right direction towards solving cooling system problems.

The temperature inside of a cooling system needs to drop at least twenty degrees below the boiling point of the coolant itself before the heated coolant will begin to change back from a vapor to a liquid. Under extreme conditions, the engine coolant (EGW) temperatures were found to be dropping only 12 to 14 degrees at the radiator, not enough (under high load conditions) to return the engine coolant back to a liquid. As a result, the nucleate boiling increased, which raised the engine coolant temperatures still higher, resulting in a "surface boiling condition."

Engine Detonation

Engine detonation normally occurs five to ten degrees after top dead center (TDC). One of the ways used to control engine efficiency is to control the detonation point. When unwanted detonation begins to occur, it creates additional unwanted heat, while at the same time, creating a secondary flame front that ignites the fuel mixture in the cylinder ahead of schedule, causing yet still more detonation.

When the engine nucleate temperatures get high enough, engine detonation begins to occur before TDC (this is known as pre-ignition). With pre-ignition comes the damaging engine knock. Pre-ignition causes massive amounts of heat to begin building in the cylinder. From there it is only a matter of a short time before a piston breaks, the cylinder head cracks, the engine bearings are hammered out, or if you're really lucky, just the head gasket itself gives up.

So the lesson learned here is that by controlling the hot spots inside of the engine block and cylinder head, you will be able to keep the engine within detonation limits, all of the time. Even high compression engines that typically run hotter can still be controlled using this technology. The ability to control hot spots, stay at or below the nucleate boiling temperature, and scrub away the bubbles is part of the key technology associated with the Evans NPG cooling system.

Heat Soak

During one of our telephone conversations, Steve Pressley relayed to me how much horsepower some racing engines will lose during an event. Many circle track cars or dirt racers can lose up to fifteen percent of their horsepower during the last half of the races because of heat soak and detonation inside of the engine. This "heat soak" affects engine volumetric efficiency, fuel mixtures, and the density of the fuel, as well as the point when detonation begins to occur. Reducing the engine timing advance or adding extra fuel can stop engine detonation, but will also reduce the horsepower output of the engine.

I explained earlier about the properties of propylene and how its low heat transfer properties were overcome as a result of its efficiency at high temperatures in a standard engine cooling system, but my original concern was racing applications.

One of the important things that Jack learned was that getting the heat out of an engine is based on three basic things: the coolant flow, the specific heat, and the characteristics of the coolant itself. By increasing the rate of the coolant flow, Jack discovered he could get back a lot of the heat transfer rate that the Evans NPG coolant had lost.

Coolant Flow Rate

Further research showed that by increasing the coolant flow rate by thirty percent, the heat transfer rate of the Evans NPG coolant could be made equal to that of conventional coolants, in the period where EGW or water-based engine coolants work best (which is just before vapor is produced). After the point of vaporization, the Evans NPG coolant outperforms conventional water-based engine coolants by a wide margin.

So for racing applications, Evans Cooling builds special high-volume coolant pumps to increase the flow of coolant through the engine. With the increased coolant flow comes the need for specially designed radiators. If you were to try and increase the flow of coolant thirty percent through a conventional radiator, you would create a tremendous amount of pressure inside the top inlet tanks and have restricted flow through the radiator. Therefore, Evans Cooling has also designed and builds special high flow nearly zero differential pressure radiators. These radiators are made of aluminum and have excellent heat transfer ability, and are specially designed for high volumes of coolant flow. While unnecessary for many conventional applications, the specially designed Evans Cooling water pumps, radiators, and accessories are a must for racing and high-performance applications.

Pressure Difference

The pressure difference between the engine block and the radiator is also important. If you have good coolant flow through the engine block with the help of a high-volume coolant pump but the radiator is not able to accept the increased flow, then there will be pressure buildup in the radiator, causing a restriction in the coolant flow. That is what Jack Evans is talking about when he says he builds "low pressure drop radiators." What he is saying is that the pressure in the engine block and radiator are nearly equal, which means there is no restriction of coolant flow even when using a high-volume coolant pump.

Jack's research also refutes the longtime belief in racing that if you run an engine hotter than 200 degrees Fahrenheit, you begin to lose horsepower. This is often true with a water-based engine coolant. As advanced detonation lets pre-ignition set in, it creates a reverse sonic wave-pulse that travels back up the intake manifold. This wave effect will often negatively affect the tuning of the intake runners and the breathing of the engine.

In reality, a hot engine should not lose horsepower as long as you do not affect its breathing. Jack explains, "With our system we can run hotter engine temperatures and not lose horsepower. We have experienced a slight drop in volumetric efficiency, however, we don't have any dramatic detonation movement back to TDC, and no problems at all with pre-ignition. As a result, the cylinders breathe better, stay more fuel efficient, and the burn time in the cylinder is increased. As a result, the engine makes more power with a higher operating temperature."

Evans NPG vs. PG Again!

As you might expect, the Evans NPG coolant is quite different than conventional PGW coolants. One of the biggest differences is in the additives package. PG coolants that mix with water still have to deal with the acid pH so these coolants will still contain phosphates and borates (just like EG coolants) to get their pH up into the twelve to fourteen range. Evans NPG coolant, on the other hand, has no problems with acid or cooling system corrosion because no water is used. The pH ratings of the Evans coolant is six, quite a difference to begin with, and a pH the Evans coolant will maintain over time without additional maintenance being required.

The additives in a conventional EG coolant require the buffering of the water to keep them from separating. If these additives are allowed to separate from the EG coolant, they will often plug the radiator. In addition, they are known to have an abrasive affect on the water pump, pump seal, impeller, heater and radiator core (which is why some water pumps do not last long in certain applications, especially if the coolant is not replaced along with the water pump). This is also the reason conventional EGW coolant should be replaced every two to four years to keep the pH level in check.

The Evans NPG coolant is formulated to use no water. The difference is in the patented additive package. Another concern when developing the Evans NPG was the natural absorption of water into the coolant from the atmosphere. What Jack learned was that the vapor point of water is so high as compared to NPG that at underhood temperatures above 90 degrees, the water actually will evaporate out of the coolant (stored in the overflow reservoir), instead of being absorbed into the coolant.

Because the boiling point of Evans NPG coolant is also high (370 degrees), it is easy for the NPG system to stay well below the condensation point of NPG. An engine operating at 200 degrees Fahrenheit is still 170 degrees below the boiling point of NPG.

Higher Coolant Temperatures

Now comes the hard-to-believe part, as Jack explains the theory behind running higher coolant temperatures as a way to increase efficiency and develop horsepower in racing engines. Follow along closely—this is really interesting!

Horsepower causes heat, this we have known for years. Because water boils at 212 degrees Fahrenheit, the unwritten rule was that you needed to keep your coolant temperature below 200 degrees. That was the old theory. **With the Evans NPG cooling system, coolant temperatures in the range of 230 to 260 degrees are acceptable. Now I know that takes a giant leap of faith to ignore what we have been told about coolants all of these years.**

In test programs for Chevrolet, Evans Cooling has operated small-block Chevrolet engines with 16:1 compression ratios, at continuous operating temperatures of 300 degrees for entire races with no coolant- or pre-ignition-related problems.

Think of Evans NPG as insurance. Using dirt racing cars as an example, when their radiators get plugged with mud, they have to make unscheduled pit stops in order to unplug the radiator or risk engine damage from overheating. Sometimes something as simple as a piece of paper sucked from the track will flatten out across the front of the radiator. The engine temperature quickly climbs to 240-260 degrees. That is a dangerous temperature with an EGW or 100 percent water-based coolant system, but it's not a problem with the Evans NPG coolant system.

The average racing engine has a compression ratio of 12:1. Engine coolant temperatures of around 200 up to 250 degrees Fahrenheit are quite acceptable using the Evans NPG coolant system. Using a conventional EGW or a 100 percent water-based coolant means you are constantly trying to get coolant temperatures down into the 180 degree range, which means you will have to increase the airflow to the radiator. In order to do that, you will have to give up some aerodynamic advantages, which will slow your car. So the extra horsepower created extra heat. In turn, you made the radiator opening bigger to flow more air to keep the engine cool, which slows your car. How much did you really gain by increasing the horsepower while still using an EGW or water-based cooling system? Not much!

By using the Evans NPG cooling system you are able to run a much higher coolant temperature, with increased horsepower, as well as a smaller radiator frontal area. Raising the compression ratio (if allowed by the rules) to as high as 16:1, while running a leaner fuel mixture has also proven to be possible using an Evans NPG cooling system.

The advantage of Evans NPG coolant in a racing application is that you are now able to run much hotter, nearly 50 usable degrees hotter (or more if needed), which allows you to develop more horsepower while still being able to control the extra heat you are creating. In entry level racing classes such as Street Stock where the rules say you can't increase the horsepower by changing either compression or carburetion, you can reduce the airflow to the radiator to gain an aerodynamic performance advantage.

What About Oil Temperature and the Evans Cooling System?

One of the questions I had is: *"What happens to the oil temperature when your engine temperature is increased by fifty degrees?"* I know modern engine oils are better than they were even just twenty years ago, but fifty degrees better?

Evans NPG Cooling has worked closely with Detroit's automakers, namely Chevrolet, whose engineers now say modern engine oil operating temperatures should be around 220-240 degrees Fahrenheit (if they are not, you are giving away horsepower). Chevrolet's research has shown that modern non-synthetic engine oils begin to have a reduced lifespan above 260 degrees Fahrenheit. Research has also shown that running a modern engine at below 180 degrees is hard on the engine bearings, because the oil is too thick to lubricate well. (Machining tolerances are much closer than they were years ago.) In addition to the engine bearings, the engineers also say the engine oil pump is working harder and the rings have a more difficult time if the oil is thicker. As a result, the heavier oil's pushing steals horsepower from the engine.

Water Pump Design and Its Effect on Cooling

As we talked about earlier, **we know the Evans NPG coolant does not have the heat transfer rate that conventional EG and water-based coolants do. In most low-horsepower applications this is not usually a problem because of the increased efficiency of the Evans NPG at higher coolant temperatures. However, in high-performance and racing applications, the heat transfer rate becomes extremely important. The Evans NPG coolant system has been designed with that in mind.**

Jack Evans explains further: "In the beginning, we took stock water pumps and turned them faster to get the increased flow we needed. Some pumps ended up being turned at twice their normal rate. We got the flow we wanted but the pump bearings, accessory drives, and belts started to fail. We were spinning the pumps way too fast. So we decided to design and make our own pumps.

"A centrifugal pump's efficiency is most affected by its physical diameter. When we designed our pumps, we opened up the pumping area diameter, and designed the impeller with big blades to move a greater volume of coolant. Using a small-block Chevrolet racing engine as an example, at 7000 rpm coolant pump speed, we like to see coolant flow of around 90 gallons per hour compared to stock OEM pumps, which are good for about 60-65 gallons per hour. We designed our water pumps to give us the volume we need and still spin at a normal rate.

"We also increased the size of the inlets and outlets of our coolant pumps, and increased the physical size of the pump housing itself. As an example, the small-block Chevrolet water pump housing was increased from the factory (3.75 inch) size to the same as the big-block (4.5 inch). We also moved the cover mounting bolt bosses (bolt holes in the housing) out of the way of the coolant flow. In addition, we added bosses to both legs so they can be drilled and tapped for external lines. Finally, we added an air bleed to the top of the pump to be able to purge the air out of the impeller cavity of the pump. Once the pump is full of coolant it will stay full, eliminating the problem of cavitation and trapped air."

Next Comes the Low Pressure Drop Radiator

The other unique thing about the Evans NPG coolant system is the design of its radiator. When I found out the Evans coolant system was based on a non-pressurized cooling system, I immediately thought of all the antique vehicles built before 1950 and their non-pressurized cooling systems. Would this NPG cooling system work for antique and classic cars as well? Let's find out as Jack Evans explains further:

"In order to get a large volume of coolant flow and not lose horsepower we were concerned about pressure drops across the radiator. Since we get a lot of flow from the water pump, we do not want to create pressure at the inlet of the radiator. In order to minimize the inlet pressure, we have to maximize the cross-sectional area of the radiator tubes, to allow more coolant flow."

Jack also discovered that one of the properties of the Evans NPG is that it had a tendency to flow down the center of the radiator tube (this is known as laminar flow). "When this happens," Jack explains, "the coolant in the center of the radiator tube doesn't touch the outside walls, resulting in a loss of heat ex-

Coolant Pumps

- Competition Units Feature Larger Diameter, Computer Designed Impellers
- Highest GPM Flow In The Industry
- Impeller Cavity Air Bleed Standard
- Designed To Optimize NPG Coolant
- External Line Bosses Standard On S/B & B/B Chevrolet Competition Units
- Heavy-Duty Roller Bearings & Seals
- CNC Steel Billet Fan Hub With Locking Set Screw
- Compatible With Water Systems

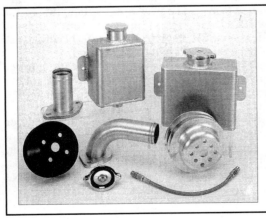

Pulleys And Accessories

- Specialized Diameters To Optimize NPG Coolant
- High Strength 6061 T-6 Alloy
- Race Applications Black Hard Coated
- CNC Machined For Accuracy
- .090 Wall Expansion Tanks
- Large 1 3/4" Chevrolet S/B and B/B Coolant Outlets
- AN-3 Constant Air Bleed Lines
- Precision Quality Throughout

change. The cross-sectional tube width becomes important. Further research showed that if a high aspect ratio tube (such as a 1-1/4 inch tube) was used it would cause the coolant inside of the tube to tumble and roll (turbulate). This mixed the coolant well and helped with the transfer of heat."

Jack also became conscious of the airflow through a radiator. He states, "Evans Cooling now builds radiators with different 'fins-per-inch' arrangements (depending on the application) in order to maximize the air through the radiator. (To do this you need to find the balance between the fins-per-inch, in relationship to the deeper core depth of the wider tube.) This way you will get the additional heat exchange without creating additional drag. Every time there is an excessive amount of fins, they cause air drag."

Racing Secrets

"NASCAR teams have also figured this out, as they use a different radiator for each track (as well as for qualifying). Teams base their selection, in part, on the length of the straightaways, and the radius of the curves, all of which affects the airflow through the radiator, and the ability of the radiator to transfer heat.

"The radiator Evans Cooling has designed for its low-pressure drop radiator cooling system is also vented. The filler cap is a screw-on, zero-pressure cap, with the vent built into the neck. It is important not to have any pressure buildup in the radiator, which could reduce or restrict the coolant flow through the system. Evans Cooling Systems also has available radiators with conventional (pressure cap) necks, as well as radiators with no necks at all.

"Heat of vaporization testing shows that Evans NPG coolant can extract twenty-five percent more heat (at the point of boiling) than water. Evans NPG coolant is also less likely to vaporize. Remember it is the liquids that cool hot metal, the vapor does not. Therefore, **when vapors do form, it is important that they change back to a liquid quickly. The lower the vapor pressure, the easier it is for the vapors to change back. The low vapor pressure of the Evans NPG coolant means it can change engine coolant vapors back to a liquid fifty times faster than water.**

"The surface tension of a liquid should also be low, because you want the liquid to break away from the hot surface and mix with the incoming coolant flow. **Evans NPG has half the surface tension of water**. Water has a tendency to cling to a hot surface, which will increase its temperature and cause the formation of vapor. In contrast, Evans NPG coolant recondenses (changes back to a liquid) quickly and will easily mix in with the incoming coolant.

"In summary, what I have learned from all of this cooling research is that our biggest coolant enemy is vapor. What I have done by creating the Evans NPG coolant is to improve the liquid contact with the engine. This improves cooling because there is more liquid coolant touching the hot metal surfaces at all times, which draws away the heat allowing the control of engine heat to be more efficient."

Inside Information on High-Flow Coolant Pumps

As the trend continues to increase the flow of coolant through the cooling system by increasing the flow rate of the water pump, you need to understand how high-flow water pumps are designed to work and how they are tested. Just as with electric cooling fans, it is how close to real life applications they are tested that determines how accurate the test results will be.

First, let's look at the four basic designs of the water pump impeller, which is the heart of the water pump as well as having the biggest effect on the pump's efficiency. Prior to the 1970s, most water pump impellers were made of cast-iron and were known as the closed-blade design. Then about the mid-1970s, in the interest of saving money, the original equipment manufacturers

Modern stamped steel impeller design.

Various impeller designs.

Closed blade impeller design. (Early GM cast-iron)

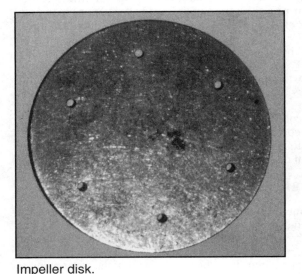

Impeller disk.

(OEM) began switching to stamped steel water pump impellers. These new stamped steel impellers were much cheaper to build (over a dollar per impeller cheaper in some cases) and were known as the open-blade design. They were simply a water pump impeller with no backing plate. While it was true the new-design impellers were less efficient, for most stock applications the design worked okay.

From a high-performance standpoint, though, the "new and improved" water pump impellers were not better. In fact, because of their design they proved to be much worse. The new coolant pumps actually circulated less gallons per hour than did the previous design. However, it has taken us as hot rodders a few years to first, understand exactly what was going on and second, how to fix it. We have a tendency to assume that if a new design comes along, that it is an improvement over the old design, but that is *not* always so.

This helps to explain why so much cooling system research has been done in the last few years, especially by NASCAR teams. In their unending quest for more horsepower, every part is checked for efficiency. Sometimes it is easier to make better use of existing horsepower than to try and find more.

One of the design improvements made to the modern open-blade impellers is that a large disk is being added to the area behind the stamped steel impeller. This increases the efficiency of the water pump by preventing the coolant from flowing over the back edge of the impeller.

Another design being introduced is the curved, slanted-blade impeller design, also known as the "scroll design," which resembles an engine turbocharger propeller blade. **An Evans "scroll" impeller, because of its increased diameter and efficient design, provides a much higher flow rate at lower engine rpm and creates less drag at higher rpm.**

Now that you are aware of the differences in impeller designs, and the theory behind how each is designed to work, high-flow coolant pumps should be easier to understand.

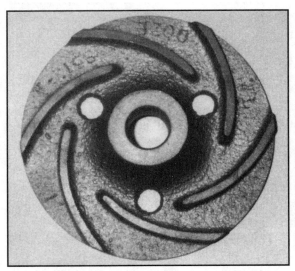

SHO Mustang high-performance impeller.

Evans scroll design impeller.

Water Pump Testing

The final thing you need to know is how the pumps are tested and where the coolant flow ratings come from. So here goes! (By the way, this is my research not Jack's.)

One way of testing a pump is by the free-flow method. This is just as it sounds and is based on the amount of coolant, in gallons per hour, the pump can physically flow without any restrictions on either the inlet or outlet side of the pump. This is like running an engine on a dynamometer with no power steering or air conditioning or other accessories installed. While this will give you some idea of what the pump is capable of, it should not be your only test.

Actual Application

Another test should include installing the pump on the actual application it is designed for, and then measuring the coolant flow through the pump in a real life application. It is interesting to learn that some pumps may flow as high as ninety gallons per hour in a free-flow test, but be reduced to seventy gallons per minute when connected to an actual cooling system. The radiator, thermostat, and all the related parts that make up the cooling system can all affect the outcome; some cooling systems are simply more efficient than others. Also, if the pump is turned at a higher rpm than stock, such as a racing or performance application, the coolant flow can be reduced even further as cavitation begins. **An actual engine coolant flow test is one of the most accurate tests, if done correctly.** Together with the free-flow test, you will know exactly what the pump is capable of and how efficient it is in a real life application.

Marketing Test

Next is what I call the marketing test. We, of course, know that as cavitation begins the pressure inside of the cooling system begins to drop as the coolant turns into vapor. If the radiator cap is rated at sixteen pounds, that is the working pressure of the coolant until the coolant turns to vapor as a result of cavitation (among other things). Then guess what happens to the pressure in the system? Correct, it drops to sometimes less than half of what it was originally. You know what that does to the gallons per minute rating of the pump? It also falls along with the pressure!

But suppose you manually re-pressurized the cooling system back to what it was originally during this test? Think what kind of gallons per minute flow rating you could achieve then. Maybe higher than you got on the free-flow test, and the results would have been taken during an actual flow test. So if you were selling your pump by the gallons per minute numbers, which test would you use?

My goal here is to first, make you aware of the different impeller designs and the theories behind them, and second, make you aware of how pumps are tested and where the rating numbers come from. Like anything else, if you understand how it works, you then know what questions to ask to get the right answers. (Our thanks to Jack Evans for sharing his research information with us.)

Summary

In summary, yes, the Evans Cooling system would be ideal for antique and classic vehicle cooling systems as well as modern vehicles of all types. **Because the Evans coolant works in a non-pressurized cooling system it would be great for antique and classic cars that are driven on a daily basis as well as cars that are in long-term storage. (Remember, there is no water to cause deterioration of the cooling system.) Museum cars could also benefit from the Evans cooling as well because the pH is maintained throughout the life of the coolant without any additives.**

Because most vintage and collector car engines have relatively low compression as compared to the modern racing applications, no changes to the original cooling system are normally required when converting to the Evans cooling system. Check the installation guide or call Evans Cooling for more details (phone number in Appendix B).

Automaker Testing

By now, it should become apparent that the Evans coolant should be ideal for most any application. But I also was curious: Had any of the "Big Three" (Chrysler, Ford and GM) automakers ever tested this Evans coolant in a real life modern application? So I placed another call to Steve Pressley at Evans cooling and asked. His reply was, "Yes, they have and not only the 'Big Three.' There have been literally hundreds of independent tests completed since 1983 by all sorts of independent testing labs, along with a number of real life applications. If you want to see a partial listing of the tests check out our web site (www.evanscooling.com).

"I will also send you a few samples," Pressley added, which he promptly did. One of the best examples he sent was a test that GM did in its "Hot Tunnel" (where a number of weather conditions can be simulated) using a then new 1986 Corvette equipped with aluminum heads and the heavy-duty cooling package. The test compared an EG-based coolant to the Evans coolant. What follows are the results of that test.

INTRODUCTION

A production 1986 Corvette equipped with aluminum heads and the heavy duty cooling package was tested in the CPC Engineering Hot Tunnel to determine the afterboil protection of 50/50 Ethylene glycol/Water and Propylene Glycol.

CONCLUSIONS

With the vehicle turned off after reaching a radiator inlet coolant temperature of 260 deg F, the following performance differences were seen (refer to Figure 1 also):

1. Rad. inlet temps with EG/Water increased while temps with PG decreased.

2. EG/Water goes into afterboil and expels over 30% of the system capacity out the radiator cap, filling the reservoir bottle and dumping 3.8L of coolant on the ground

   Amount expelled out rad. cap =   5.6L
   Reservoir capacity above hot
      line =   1.8L

   Amount dumped on ground =   3.8L

   (Total system capacity = 13.8L)

   PG does not boil and expands less than 10% of the system capacity into the overflow bottle.

After the vehicle has been turned off for 3 minutes and then restarted and idled, the following performance differences were seen:

1. Rad. inlet temps with EG/Water increased dramatically (approaching 280 deg F) while temps with PG decreased (approaching 240 deg F).

2. EG/Water in the overflow bottle does not return back to the system (because the cooling system contains large amounts of vapor). PG, however, does return back into the system (because the cooling system contains liquid instead of vapor).

Therefore, if the coolant temperature warning light comes on and the vehicle is stopped briefly, a vehicle having PG can be safely restarted and driven away; but a vehicle having 50/50 EG/water would expel enough coolant to completely fill the reservoir bottle and also dump 3.8L of coolant on the ground. Such a vehicle would have to remain stopped for a long period of time to allow the system to cool down completely and return a maximum of 4.6L (total capacity of reservoir bottle) back to the cooling system, thus leaving the cooling system low by 0.96L and with an empty reservoir bottle.

DISCUSSION

Vehicle# P6Y137 was tested in the CPC Engineering Hot Tunnel at standard test conditions (100 deg F ambient and 40% humidity). The vehicle was equipped with aluminum cylinder heads, V01 radiator, pusher fan, and 3.07 axle ratio. EG/Water was evaluated using the production cooling system. PG was evaluated by also using the production cooling system but with a zero pressure radiator cap. It should be noted that this is not an optimal system for PG An optimal system for PG would have higher flowrates and would minimize cylinder head coolant pressures. Nevertheless, evaluating PG with the production system and a zero pressure radiator cap provides a relative comparison.

A 50 MPH 7.2% grade in second gear was the test point used to attain a radiator inlet coolant temperature of 260 deg F. Once the test point was reached, the vehicle was then stopped and the engine turned off. After a soak period of 3 minutes, the engine was then restarted and idled.

Figure 1 compares the radiator inlet coolant temperatures for EG/Water versus PG. During the 3 minute soak period, EG/Water had higher temperatures than PG. After the engine was restarted, coolant temperatures for EG/Water increased dramatically whereas temperatures for PG decreased and remained in control.

The test results clearly show the advantage of PG over EG/Water in a situation where EG/Water goes into afterboil.

Mark D. Nemesh
HVA/C, Engine Cooling
Advanced Technology

Jim K. Petersen
HVA/C, Engine Cooling
Advanced Technology

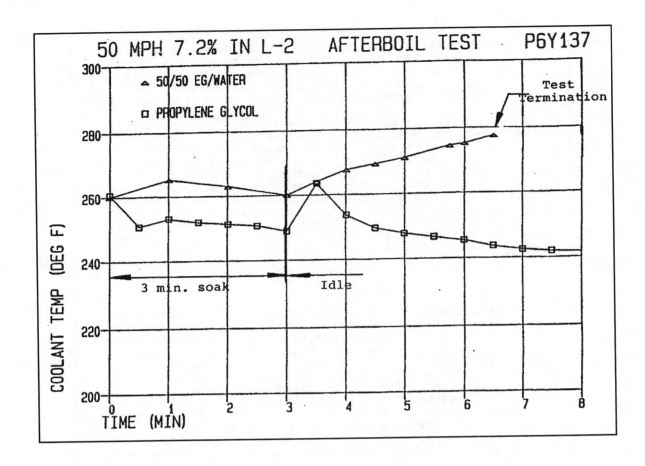

Okay, by now we know the theory behind Evans NPG coolant, how it is designed to work, and have seen actual test results. Our next step is to see how difficult it is to actually convert to this new type of cooling system.

Conversion Process to Evans NPG Coolant

Because many of you have an interest in this new Evans NPG coolant for use in antique and classic cars, we should begin by looking at what is involved in converting an original non-pressurized cooling system to the Evans NPG coolant system. What follows is from the Evans NPG Technical Reference and Installation Manual.

Advice from Evans Cooling

Never mix conventional water-based antifreeze/coolants with any Evans NPG coolant. Possible engine damage could result. Water is considered an impurity, and therefore, is harmful to the system.

Although the design of the latest Evans cooling technology prevents the escape of coolant vapor from the non-pressurized venting system, boiling can still occur within the engine. The design of the system permits boiling to occur but condenses all coolant vapor within the cooling jacket of the engine, preventing the loss of coolant as is common with traditional water-based coolants.

Storage of Evans NPG Coolant

Tests have proven the life expectancy of Evans NPG coolant to be a minimum of 100,000 miles. Since the NPG coolant naturally absorbs moisture from the atmosphere, if it becomes necessary to drain the NPG for any reason, it should be kept in an airtight container. When placing a vehicle in long-term storage, it is also recommended that you fill the radiator to the top of the radiator neck with Evans coolant. This will keep out air, and let the NPG coolant protect the metal during storage. When you wish to operate the vehicle again, remove enough coolant to allow for normal expansion (usually referred to as the "cold fill" level of your cooling system).

Removing Old Coolant

The complete removal of all EGW (ethylene glycol and water) coolant from the original cooling system is essential to the successful conversion to the Evans NPG system. **Just one ounce of water left over from the old solution will produce sixteen liters of steam!**

Begin by draining the expansion tank, if there is one. Next, open the radiator drain cock and begin removing the old antifreeze from the radiator. Then remove the lower radiator hose and open the engine block drain petcocks. Remove the heater hose connections at the engine block and drain all coolants. When finished, gently blow air through the heater core to be sure the entire unit is free from EGW coolant.

When the engine block is completely drained, circulate air throughout the radiator and engine block to remove any remaining water. Next, flush the engine block and radiator with a PG-based coolant, such as Sierra, but use *no* water, only the Sierra solution. After the engine and radiator have been flushed with the PG coolant and all water has been removed from the system, remove the remaining PG coolant. It is now time to add the Evans NPG coolant.

After adding the correct amount of Evans NPG coolant (remember, no water), you need to perform the following steps to purge the remaining water from the system. It is common for a small amount of water residue to remain in the cooling system despite your best efforts.

Step One

First, drain your expansion tank if you have one, and remove the inlet line. Using a piece of additional hose, temporarily connect the separated portion of the hose to a high point (such as under the raised hood) and let the remainder fall to the ground. Next, cover the front of the radiator to block the flow of air. Start the engine and warm it to approximately 250 degrees Fahrenheit at idle speed. **NOTE:** According to the Evans technical manual, 250 degrees is a safe coolant temperature with the Evans NPG coolant system, and the engine will not be damaged. Race engines developing 600 horsepower have been tested to 300 degrees Fahrenheit with no damage.

If your vehicle does not have a temperature gauge that reaches 250 degrees Fahrenheit, you can use a oven-type probe thermometer. The best method is to loosen a hose clamp, slide the temperature probe under the radiator hose so the probe end reaches into the coolant, then re-tighten the hose clamp. **CAUTION:** Water may vent rapidly from the vent line as steam, so be sure no one is standing nearby. There is a chance they could be burned by the escaping steam. If there is only a trace amount of water remaining in the system, idling the engine at 250 degrees should cause only water vapor (steam) to escape and not coolant.

If steam (water vapor) does appear, continue engine idling. Maintain 250 degrees by removing and applying the radiator cover as necessary. Continue until venting stops. Then remove the radiator cover and allow the engine to cool.

Should violent venting occur (steam with a visible amount of liquid coolant), this indicates a large volume of water is still in the system. The engine should be turned off each time this occurs and allowed to cool. The radiator should then be refilled to the top with NPG coolant and the process repeated. Water is adequately removed from the system when the coolant remains quiet (no boiling or venting) at idle, and the temperature is 250 degrees.

After Water Is Removed

After you have all of the water removed from the system, shut off the engine and allow it to cool completely. When the engine has cooled, refill the radiator to within one or two inches of the top of the filler neck. Install the radiator cap and warm the engine to normal operating temperature. During the warm-up, let the coolant passing out the vent hose empty into the original Evans coolant jug. When the engine has reached full operating temperature, shut it off and reconnect the original overflow vent hose to the radiator. Seal the Evans coolant jug and store for future use.

Next, after the engine has cooled, use a tape measure to check how far down from the top of the radiator fill neck the Evans NPG coolant is. This is your new "cold fill" coolant level. When the vehicle warms to full operating temperature the NPG coolant will expand and rise to completely fill the radiator, sealing the system from moisture.

The Evans NPG cooling system described above is known as a stage one kit and is recommended for the basic low-compression stock applications such as antique and classic cars, and vehicles to the 1960s. Evans NPG coolant has been proven to work well with thermo-syphon-type cooling systems.

For more advanced applications, the Evans cooling system kits are available for race car as well as high-performance street rod engines. In addition to their custom-designed water pumps and radiators, Evans Cooling Systems also builds its own thermostats and pulleys. The installation instructions are basically the same, with the recommended addition of the Evans cooling products to increase the flow of coolant through the system. Check out Evans' sales brochure and technical manual for more details.

Troubleshooting

As with most everything we do in life, there are times when things don't follow the rules and cooling systems are no exception. Evans Cooling Systems provides the following troubleshooting guide in its technical manual. Not only does this make you aware of some of the problems before they occur, it also gives you further insight into how the system works and reacts to different applications. The following are Evans' troubleshooting guidelines:

1. Sudden Loss of Coolant: In the event of a sudden loss of coolant, never add water to the system. If coolant loss occurs, adding a PG-based (propylene glycol and water) 50:50 coolant such as Sierra will work until you get home and the system can be drained and the NPG replaced. Remember, *never* add water to the Evans NPG coolant. The mixed, emergency coolant should be replaced with pure Evans NPG coolant no later than 30 days after the incident.

2. Coolant Temperature Spikes in Cold Weather: During periods of extreme cold weather, some engines have a tendency to run at elevated temperatures close to 250 degrees Fahrenheit at idle then return to normal when the vehicle is underway. In most cases, this is caused by an unusually large bypass circuit in the thermostat housing, which allows the coolant to bypass the radiator through the open circuit at slow pump speeds. Although not a serious problem, it often can be corrected by replacing the OEM thermostat and with an Evans-designed thermostat.

3. Expansion Tank Does Not Return Coolant to Engine: When this happens it is usually a result of a vacuum leak somewhere in the system, or the radiator cap was removed "hot" and not closed again during engine cool down. Since vacuum draw on the coolant in the expansion (overflow) tank is the only way for the coolant to be drawn back into the system, any air leak, no matter how small, will cause the engine to draw air instead of the coolant. If you find you have to keep adding coolant to the radiator after each cool down, even though there is coolant in the expansion tank (and the level keeps rising after each run), that is proof that you do, indeed, have a leak that must be found. Check all clamps and vent hoses, or attach a vacuum tester to the vent line at the tank connection to locate the leak.

4. Engine Runs Hot at all Speeds and Loads: This problem can usually be traced to an air-locked water pump. Be sure the coolant installation directions were followed properly, and the air was removed from the system as per instructions given in the Evans technical manual. In some applications, the problem can be traced to a water pump with not enough coolant capacity, or a radiator that is unable to accept the increased coolant flow. An upgrade to an Evans-designed radiator and coolant pump is then recommended.

5. Coolant Temperature vs. Metal Temperature: With the changeover to the Evans NPG coolant, it is important to keep in mind that **the real function of the temperature gauge is to keep track of the actual engine coolant temperature, and not the temperature of the metal engine surfaces.** Temperature readings with the Evans NPG coolant installed may, at times, differ slightly from the readings obtained with conventional EGW coolants. Slightly higher coolant temperatures are normal for engines with increased compression ratios and power output, and operated at increased speed or loads with the Evans NPG coolant installed.

6. Safety Precautions: As with most glycol-based engine coolants (including EG and PG), Evans NPG coolant vapor will ignite (at about 240 degrees Fahrenheit) and burn when exposed to open flame or hot engine parts (such as exhaust headers). Caution must be exercised when handling warm coolant. **It is always a good idea to wear eye protection when working around liquids.**

Evans NPG coolant is non-hazardous to humans and animals. However, in some instances when traces of ethylene glycol coolant (which remain in an engine after a conversion) are mixed with the Evans NPG coolant, the Evans NPG coolant becomes contaminated with the EG residue. This is considered a hazardous material. The disposal of used EG coolants should be done following the standard procedures for hazardous waste materials. Used Evans NPG coolant that is free of contamination is non-toxic and is not considered a hazardous material.

Now You Know

The information about the Evans Cooling System was provided to give you an idea of what the system is about, how it is designed to work, and what steps are involved in installing the system. From there, you should be able to determine if the Evans system can be of benefit to you. If you decide to call an Evans Cooling System representative and ask for more specific information about your application, you at least now know enough to ask the right questions. That is the first step to finding out exactly what you need to know to make an informed buying decision and is, in part, the purpose of reading this book in the first place, isn't it?

Notes

Chapter 16:
Coolant System Additives

Besides the Evans Cooling System approach to engine overheating that we learned about in the last chapter, there are other ideas and products on the market that you need to be aware of. The two products featured here are by no means the only two of their kind on the market (there are lots more); these are two of the most popular additives on the market. My goal is to make you aware of some of the different types of cooling system products available and how they are designed to work. You can then determine if this type of product could be of benefit to you, and if so you can then seek out more information.

40 Below Engine Coolant Additive

"40 Below" is an engine coolant additive marketed by Pro-Blend Motorsport Products. 40 Below comes packaged in a 30-ounce can and is designed to lower the operating temperature of the engine coolant up to 40 degrees. 40 Below is also designed to "cool" the engine coolant nearly twice as fast as a conventional 50:50 antifreeze solution. What follows is the company's explanation of how 40 Below works.

Pro-Blend pioneered and developed the science of "metal preferential characteristics." In other words, the science of chemically reversing the direction of water and making it prefer to seek and cling to hot metal. 40 Below engine coolant additive works by bonding to all of the metal surfaces it contacts. This bonding action is motivated by heat and pressure. The bonding takes place microscopically—you cannot see it, feel it, or measure it, and it will not build on itself.

Once the 40 Below additive is bonded in place, it takes control of the water and totally dominates its actions and reactions. The hotter the engine and radiator get, the harder the water in the coolant works to stay in contact with all of the hot metal surfaces.

After 40 Below is added to a cooling system, it immediately coats all internal metal surfaces, and causes a virtual flood of coolant to constantly embrace the new coating, resulting in dramatically improved heat transfer. This, in turn, lowers the vehicle operating temperature, creating a more stable and efficient cooling environment.

In contrast, without 40 Below in the cooling system, as the engine and radiator begin to heat up, a small amount of hot retreating coolant desperately tries to leave the point of contact. The result is inadequate heat transfer from the hot metal to the coolant, which causes excessive operating temperatures, frequent boil-overs, and potential engine failure.

WHY WOULD MY ENGINE RUN HOT?

IT MAY BE ONE OR MORE OF THE FOLLOWING

1. A Lean Air/Fuel Ratio. (Also Check Fuel Pump And Filters).

2. Too Much Timing/Retarded Timing/Advance Curve Malfunction.

3. Clogged Radiator/Collapsed Hose (Restricted Water Flow)

4. Clogged Engine (Restricted Water Flow)

5. Stuck Thermostat/Incorrect Thermostat.

6. Bad Water Pump

7. Incorrect Water Pump Speed (Too Slow/Too Fast).

8. Radiator Too Thick.

9. Wrong Pressure Cap.

10. No Shroud Around Fan. Improper Fan Positioning Within Shroud.

11. Bad Fan Design-Stock Factory Type Usually Works Best.

12. High Volume Or Hi Pressure Oil Pump.

13. Electric Fan (Pullers / Pushers) Blocking Air Flow.

14. Too Much Anti-Freeze.

15. Wrong Type Anti-Freeze

16. FLOW TEST: Begin With Cool Engine. Remove Radiator Cap. Start Engine. Bring Engine Up To Operating Temperature So That The Thermostat Opens. Increase Engine Speed To 2000 RPM. If Water Gushes Out Of Radiator There Is A Flow Restriction In The System. This Must Be Corrected For Proper Cooling.

17. Wrong Spark Plugs (ie. Heat Range).

18. Wrong Gasoline Type (Try 89 Or 92 Octane).

19. Clogged Catalytic Converter.

20. Clogged Injector System.

21. Exhaust Getting Into The Water Due To A Cracked Head Or Blown Head Gasket. Have Your Local Radiator Shop Test Your System For Carbon Dioxide.

Installing 40 Below Engine Coolant Additive

Now that we understand the basic theory behind 40 Below, and how it is designed to work, let's take a look at installing 40 Below into the cooling system.

Most vehicle cooling systems hold between 3.5 and 4.0 gallons of liquid. A 50:50 mix of water and antifreeze is common to most coolant systems. Although the 40 Below coolant additive is compatible with antifreeze, antifreeze has a tendency to absorb heat and hold it. This prevents the 40 Below additive from working at its maximum efficiency. Therefore, it is recommended that you remove all of the antifreeze from the cooling system, when installing the 40 Below coolant additive.

1) Remove all of the antifreeze/coolant from the cooling system by draining the radiator and flushing the engine block.

2) Install a new thermostat rated between 160 and 180 degrees, if possible.

3) Begin to fill the cooling system with fresh water. Fill the radiator until it is about half full, then take two cans of 40 Below engine coolant additive and shake well. Pour the contents of both cans into a bucket. Into the bucket add one-half gallon of antifreeze and one-half gallon of water.

4) Mix the contents of the bucket well, then pour contents into the radiator.

5) Start the engine and continue to fill radiator with water. Leave the engine running. Heat will build, causing the engine thermostat to open. Continue to fill radiator until system is completely full and no air pockets exist.

Replace the radiator cap, close the engine hood and go for at least a 30 minute drive to allow the 40 Below engine additive to properly circulate through the system.

CAUTION: Do not use any form of radiator block sealer, stop leak or any other type of additive in the cooling system along with the 40 Below additive. **It is also recommended that you do not use any synthetic or environmental PG-type antifreezes with this product.** During the winter months it is suggested that you add the necessary amount of antifreeze needed to protect your cooling system from freezing.

Summary

By now, you have a good idea how the 40 Below coolant additive is designed to work and what is involved in converting your cooling system to be able to use this additive. If you are interested in this product and want more information, you will find the contact address and telephone number in Appendix B. Now let's look at yet another approach to solving engine overheating.

Red Line Water Wetter Super Coolant

Super Cool Water Wetter is a cooling system additive developed by Red Line Synthetic Oil Corp. It is designed to reduce cooling system temperatures up to 30 degrees. This product can

Red Line Water Wetter Test Results

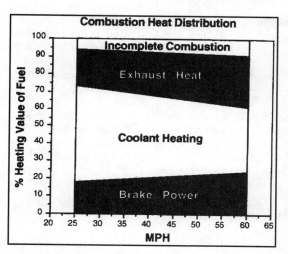

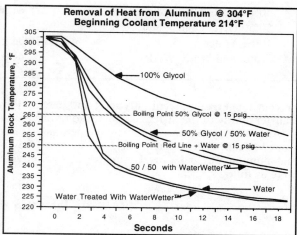

be used along with plain water as corrosion protection in racing engines. It can be added to new or used antifreeze to improve the heat transfer of the engine coolant. It is also designed to provide corrosion protection for aluminum, cast iron, copper, brass and bronze systems.

How Red Line Water Wetter Super Coolant is Designed to Work

Red Line Water Wetter is designed to provide improved metal wetting and excellent corrosion inhibition when added to plain water or glycol coolant. Proper cooling system maintenance is important to replenish the corrosion system inhibitors, which deplete over time. Aluminum radiators, common to modern cooling systems, have a high corrosion potential, even higher than zinc which is widely used as a sacrificial anode. The only property that allows aluminum to be used in cooling systems is that it will form a protective film under certain conditions, which will prevent the uncontrolled corrosive attack of acids or bases on the cooling system.

Red Line Water Wetter will provide the proper corrosion inhibition for all common cooling system metals, including aluminum, cast-iron, steel, copper, brass and lead. In addition, Red Line Water Wetter improves heat transfer, doubles the wetting ability of water, reduces cylinder head temperatures, and prevents rust, corrosion, and electrolysis.

Heat Transfer

Red Line Water Wetter can reduce cooling system temperatures even when compared to glycol solutions or plain water. Water has excellent heat transfer properties in its liquid state, but high surface tension makes it difficult to release water vapor from a metal surface. **Under heavy load conditions, much of the heat in the cylinder head is transferred by localized boiling at hot spots, even if the bulk of the cooling solution is below the boiling point. Red Line's Water Wetter reduces the surface tension of water by a factor of two, which means much smaller vapor bubbles will be formed.**

Vapor bubbles on a metal surface create an insulating layer that impedes heat transfer. Releasing these vapor bubbles from the metal surface can improve heat transfer properties in this area by as much as fifteen percent.

As an example, an aluminum bar heated to 304 degrees Fahrenheit is cooled using different coolants at 214 degrees Fahrenheit under 15 pounds of pressure (to simulate actual engine coolant conditions) to identify the different cooling properties of liquids.

This comparison represents lowering of the coolant temperature in a system from 304 degrees Fahrenheit down to 214 degrees Fahrenheit (the boiling point of water in the system under 15 pounds per square inch system pressure).

Time Required	
Red Line Water Wetter only	3.2 seconds
Red Line Water Wetter and water mix	3.7 seconds
Red Line Water Wetter in 50:50 antifreeze mix	10.2 seconds
Glycol coolant only	21.0 seconds

Cooling System Fluid	Stabilized Temperature (F)
50% Glycol/50% Water	228 degrees
50:50 Glycol and Water Wetter	220 degrees
100% Water	220 degrees
Water and Water Wetter	202 degrees

The following are the results of that test:

In summary, the coolants when compared to the base 3.2 second time using only Red Line Water Wetter: when Water Wetter was mixed with water required 15 percent longer, a mixture of 50:50 antifreeze and Water Wetter took 220 percent longer, and glycol only took 550 percent longer. These tests were done to demonstrate the heat transfer ability of the different coolant solutions as compared to Red Line's Water Wetter solution.

Another way to measure coolant temperatures is through the use of an engine dynamometer. Test results from Malcom Garrett Racing Engines using a Chevrolet 350 cubic inch V-8 engine with cast-iron block and aluminum cylinder heads, running at 7200 engine rpm for three hours (using 160 degree thermostat) were as follows:

Coolant Effects on Performance

Performance Properties of Coolants			
	Water + Red Line	50% Glycol	70% Glycol
Increase in Cylinder Head Temperature	Baseline	+45°F	+65°F
Increase in Octane (RON) Requirement	Baseline	+3.5	+5.0
Change in Spark Timing for Trace Knock	Baseline	-5.2°	-7.5°
Change in Torque	Baseline	-2.1%	-3.1%

Under moderate load conditions, for every percent of glycol in the engine coolant it will raise cylinder head temperature by one degree. An example of this is a solution containing fifty percent glycol will raise the cylinder head temperature by fifty degrees. **This increase in temperature will raise the octane required for trace knock levels by nearly 3.5 octane numbers.**

One thing that needs to be understood is the effect of the higher combustion temperatures on pre-ignition and detonation. **The higher the combustion chamber temperature, the higher the octane rating of the fuel must be, to prevent pre-ignition and detonation.** Since the octane rating of the available fuel is limited, the spark timing must be retarded to compensate for the increased temperature. Retarding the spark will, in turn, affect the amount of peak torque available from the engine.

Higher engine temperatures also reduce the density of the incoming fuel mixture. This, in turn, reduces the engine's torque output even further. It is because of these factors that it becomes important—especially in racing applications—to control the coolant temperature inside of the engine.

Boiling Point Elevation

Red Line Water Wetter does not significantly increase the boiling point of water, however, increasing the cooling system pressure will raise the boiling point. The boiling point of water, treated with Water Wetter in a cooling system using a 15-pound radiator cap, will be 250 degrees Fahrenheit compared to 212 degrees for water only, and 265 degrees for a 50:50 glycol and water solution.

Because Red Line Water Wetter doubles the radiator's ability to transfer heat, boil-over using the Red Line Water Wetter solution is not a problem as long as the engine is circulating coolant through the cylinder heads and the engine fan is circulating air. Sudden shutdown after hard driving may cause boil-over.

Freezing Point Depression

Red Line Water Wetter does not significantly reduce the freezing point of water. If the vehicle will see freezing temperatures, an antifreeze must be used. Even in the summertime, the use of air conditioning can blow freezing air through a heater core and cause freezing, unless a mixture of at least 20 percent antifreeze is used.

Corrosion Protection

Modern automotive engines now use aluminum for cylinder heads, radiators, water pump housings, and nearly all hose fittings. These engines require much greater corrosion protection than their cast-iron coun-

Comparison of Corrosion Inhibition Properties			
PROPERTY	RED LINE	SPEC	COOLANT A
pH	8.5	7.5 - 11	9.8
Boiling Point @ 15 psig	250°F		265°F (50%)
Freezing Point	31°F	-35°F(50%)	-35°F
Foaming Height, ml	5	150	50
Color	Pink	green/blue	green
Ash, %	0.5	5, max	1
Surface Tension @ 100°C, Dynes/cm2	28.3	58.9 (water)	
Simulated Service Test, Weight Loss, mg/specimen			
Copper	4	20 max	11
Solder (low-lead)	0	60	1
Solder (high-lead)	9	---	---
Brass	4	20	11
Steel	1	20	6
Cast Iron	1	20	12
Aluminum	+1	60	0

terparts. Aluminum is such an electroactive metal that it requires an impenetrable corrosion inhibitor film in order to prevent rapid corrosion. The acid neutralization capability of the coolant used is important. Coolant that has been left sitting inside of a cooling system for several years has probably become acidic from the oxidation of the glycol to acids. Keeping the concentration of glycol in an aluminum cooling system below fifty percent will also help stability.

Red Line Water Wetter also provides excellent protection from cavitation erosion in the water pump and cylinder head. Localized boiling in the cylinder forms vapor bubbles that collapse when they come in contact with cooler liquids. This collapse creates tremendous shock waves that remove the inhibitor film from the aluminum surfaces. This can cause catastrophic erosion of the aluminum if the inhibitor does not reform quickly.

Another problem created by cavitation erosion is the aluminum deposits left over from the erosion. They collect in the lower radiator temperature tubes causing poor heat transfer. Red Line Water Wetter prevents this corrosion through effective film formation and smaller vapor bubble formation, which tend to have a less violent collapse.

Finally, foam control is equally important since entrained air will cause cavitation erosion due to the collapse of the foam bubbles. Red Line Water Wetter provides excellent control of foaming with water alone and also glycol solutions.

Most coolant additives on the market provide only protection for iron and perhaps moderate protection for aluminum. The milky soluble oil-types can actually impede heat transfer by wetting the metal surface with oil. This can swell and soften rubber coolant hoses causing them to fail.

Red Line Water Wetter Super Coolant Installation Instructions

One twelve-ounce bottle of Red Line Water Wetter Super Coolant treats twelve-sixteen quarts of water, or a 50:50 solution of ethylene glycol antifreeze or propylene glycol antifreeze solutions. In smaller cooling systems, use is four-five caps per quart. Red Line Water Wetter can be added directly through the cooling system fill cap into the radiator or into the overflow recovery tank.

For best protection of aluminum radiators, Red Line Water Wetter should be replenished or replaced every 15,000 miles. The anti-scaling ingredients in Red Line Water Wetter will work with ordinary tap water, however, using distilled or deionized water will accomplish some additional scale removal in the cylinder head area.

Plain water with or without Red Line Water Wetter should not be used in cooling systems containing magnesium, only EG antifreeze solutions should be used with Red Line Water Wetter. For maximum protection use the most water and the least amount of antifreeze possible to prevent freezing in your climate.

Summary

Okay, by now you should have a good understanding of how engine coolant additives are designed to work. If you decide to use them or not is up to you. I wanted to present you with some of the technical information provided by the manufacturers so you can understand what is involved if you decide to use them. You can call the companies involved for more information by using the contact numbers found in Appendix B in the back of this book.

Notes

Chapter 17:
Fans, Radiator Caps, Thermostats and Testing Devices

We already know, in theory, what a radiator cap is and what job it is supposed to do. Back in the old days, a radiator cap wasn't much to be concerned with. As long as you had one and it worked you didn't much care, but like everything else today, the job a radiator cap does has become important, and is a part of what determines how well your cooling system is able to do its job.

In the old days, because the cooling systems were low-pressure systems, losing a pound or two of pressure from a leaking cap wasn't the end of the world. Today, with most cooling systems being pressurized to 16 pounds or greater, the operating temperature of the engine being over 200 degrees Fahrenheit and controlled by a computer, losing radiator pressure because of a faulty radiator cap can be a serious problem. The cooling system depends on the pressure held by the radiator cap to raise the boiling point of the coolant and to allow higher operating temperatures.

Just for reference, most radiator pressure caps actually work in a range of pressure. For example: a cap rated at 4 pounds actually has a working range of between 3-5 pounds, a 7-pound cap has a working range of between 6-8 pounds, 10-pound cap 9-11 pounds, 14-pound cap 12-16 pounds, 16-pound cap 14-18 pounds, and 18-pound cap 16-20 pounds, and 20-pound cap 18-22 pounds.

Okay, suppose your cooling system radiator was built for a maximum pressure of 12 pounds. What is the highest rated pressure radiator cap you should use? Correct, a 10-pound cap that has a maximum pressure range of 11 pounds. The next cap available is a 14-pound rated cap with a range of between 12 and 16 pounds. File this information away in a safe place, as it will come in handy when we design and build our own cooling system from scratch in an upcoming chapter.

Thermostats

Thermostats have also changed in recent years, in part, as a result of the higher operating temperatures of modern engines. For instance, most thermostats were rated at 160 or 180 degrees even into the late

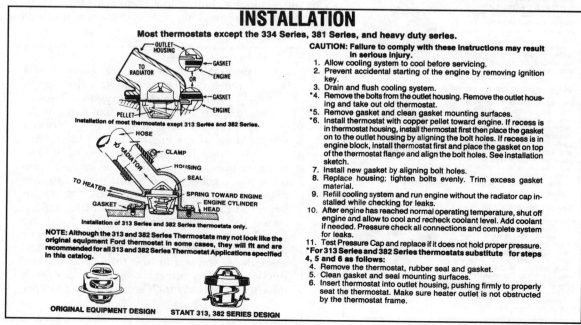

INSTALLATION

Most thermostats except the 334 Series, 381 Series, and heavy duty series.

Installation of most thermostats exept 313 Series and 382 Series.

Installation of 313 Series and 382 Series thermostats only.

NOTE: Although the 313 and 382 Series Thermostats may not look like the original equipment Ford thermostat in some cases, they will fit and are recommended for all 313 and 382 Series Thermostat Applications specified in this catalog.

ORIGINAL EQUIPMENT DESIGN   STANT 313, 382 SERIES DESIGN

CAUTION: Failure to comply with these instructions may result in serious injury.
1. Allow cooling system to cool before servicing.
2. Prevent accidental starting of the engine by removing ignition key.
3. Drain and flush cooling system.
*4. Remove the bolts from the outlet housing. Remove the outlet housing and take out old thermostat.
*5. Remove gasket and clean gasket mounting surfaces.
*6. Install thermostat with copper pellet toward engine. If recess is in thermostat housing, install thermostat first then place the gasket on to the outlet housing by aligning the bolt holes. If recess is in engine block, install thermostat first and place the gasket on top of the thermostat flange and align the bolt holes. See installation sketch.
7. Install new gasket by aligning bolt holes.
8. Replace housing; tighten bolts evenly. Trim excess gasket material.
9. Refill cooling system and run engine without the radiator cap installed while checking for leaks.
10. After engine has reached normal operating temperature, shut off engine and allow to cool and recheck coolant level. Add coolant if needed. Pressure check all connections and complete system for leaks.
11. Test Pressure Cap and replace if it does not hold proper pressure.
*For 313 Series and 382 Series thermostats substitute for steps 4, 5 and 6 as follows:
4. Remove the thermostat, rubber seal and gasket.
5. Clean gasket and seal mounting surfaces.
6. Insert thermostat into outlet housing, pushing firmly to properly seat the thermostat. Make sure heater outlet is not obstructed by the thermostat frame.

1960s. Radiator cap pressures have continued to climb from the four-pound caps of the 1950s to the twelve-pound caps of the late 1960s, all the way to sixteen- and eighteen-pound caps of the 1980s and 1990s. As this happened, the accuracy of both the thermostat and the radiator cap became more important. In today's cars, there is often just ten or fifteen degrees separating the normal operating temperature of the engine and disaster from overheating.

You should also be aware that there is more than one thermostat design used, even today. The reverse poppet design has been the most popular since at least the 1950s, but there are other designs used, some for industrial and heavy-duty applications.

Checking the Cooling System

To take some of the guesswork out of finding a cooling system defect such as the source of that annoying antifreeze leak staining your driveway, there is a simple device that can pressurize your cooling system to simulate its actual working conditions. This makes the job of finding leaks much easier, because you are not having to work around a warm engine. A pressure tester (officially called a cooling system cap and pressure tester) will also help you check components such as the radiator cap to be sure it is working correctly, as well as holding the correct amount of pressure it is designed for.

Especially with modern cooling systems, it is important that the system maintain working pressure. This directly affects the boiling point of the coolant and, in turn, the operating temperature of the engine. It also affects the computer loop in most modern cars. As the working pressure of cooling systems continues to climb, it gets more difficult to hold in that pressure.

Just a couple of pounds leaking out here and there can cause overheating. Oftentimes, the cooling system pressure leaks are found at places such as loose hose clamps or pinholes in a coolant hose, and *not* in the common places you would first think to look. And many times they appear only under pressure, making them that much more

> **Especially with modern cooling systems, it is important that the system maintain working pressure. This directly affects the boiling point of the coolant and, in turn, the operating temperature of the engine. It also affects the computer loop in most modern cars. As the working pressure of cooling systems continues to climb, it gets more difficult to hold in that pressure. Just a couple of pounds leaking out here and there can cause overheating. Oftentimes, the cooling system pressure leaks are found at places such as loose hose clamps or pinholes in a coolant hose, and not in the common places you would first think to look. And many times they appear only under pressure, making them that much more difficult to find.**

INSTALLATION
334 Series Thermostats

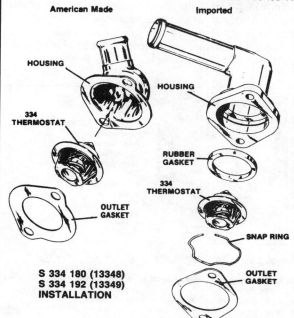

American Made

Imported

HOUSING

HOUSING

334
THERMOSTAT

RUBBER
GASKET

334
THERMOSTAT

OUTLET
GASKET

SNAP RING

OUTLET
GASKET

S 334 180 (13348)
S 334 192 (13349)
INSTALLATION

American-made Vehicles
CAUTION: Failure to comply with these instructions may result in serious injury.

1. Allow cooling system to cool before servicing.
2. Prevent accidental starting of the engine by removing the ignition key.
3. Drain and flush cooling system.
*4. Unbolt thermostat housing. Remove old thermostat which may have to be turned counterclockwise until locking pressure is released and it can be withdrawn from housing.
*5. Remove old gasket and clean gasket mounting surfaces.
*6. Install new thermostat into water outlet housing with copper pellet toward engine.
7. Align gasket with bolt holes.
8. Replace housing; tighten evenly.
9. Refill cooling system and run engine without the radiator cap installed while checking for leaks.
10. After engine has reached normal operating temperature, shut off engine and allow to cool and recheck coolant level. Add coolant if needed. Pressure check all connections and complete system for leaks.
11. Test Pressure Cap and replace if it does not hold proper pressure.

Imported Vehicles
*For 334 Series thermostats, imported vehicles, substitute for steps 4, 5 and 6 as follows:

4. Unbolt water outlet housing. Remove snap ring, thermostat and rubber gasket.
5. Remove old gasket and clean gasket and rubber gasket mounting surfaces.
6. Install new thermostat into water outlet housing with new rubber gasket pressed firmly down over thermostat to flange. (Note: Rubber gasket MUST be installed on thermostat before thermostat is placed in housing.) Reinstall snap ring.

INSTALLATION
381 Series Thermostats

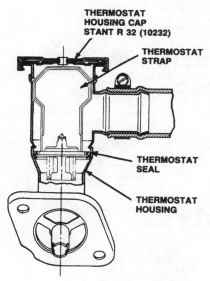

THERMOSTAT
HOUSING CAP
STANT R 32 (10232)

THERMOSTAT
STRAP

THERMOSTAT
SEAL

THERMOSTAT
HOUSING

NOTE: The thermostat housing cap and thermostat must be removed to add coolant.

1. Allow cooling system to cool before servicing.
2. Prevent accidental starting of the engine by removing ignition key.
3. Do not attempt to remove thermostat housing cap when engine is hot.
4. After engine cools turn thermostat housing cap slowly counterclockwise to remove. If there is any indication of pressure, stop immediately.
5. Remove thermostat by grasping thermostat strap and pulling upward.
6. Before installation of new thermostat, re-check coolant level and add if necessary. Make sure the thermostat sealing seat in housing is clean and free of any solid material which will cause leakage.
7. To install new thermostat, lower thermostat into housing, using strap as handle. (No excessive force is needed.)
8. Replace thermostat housing cap by turning clockwise. If cap fails to seal filler neck and leaks coolant, replace the cap.

difficult to find. These pressure testers are available at your local full-line auto parts store so if your neighbor doesn't have one, go ahead and buy one. Then he can borrow yours!

Heater Control Valves

Heater control valves are something that became popular in the late 1950s and early 1960s. These valves usually mount in the heater hose or on the engine manifold. Their main job is to provide greater cooling efficiency by shutting off the flow of warm coolant to the heater core, which reduces the volume of warm coolant circulating through the system in the summertime. They also make the job the air conditioner has to do easier because no warm coolant is circulating through the heater core (inside of the vehicle) where the air conditioner is trying its best (you hope) to cool the inside of the vehicle.

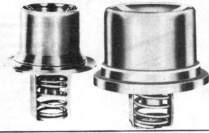

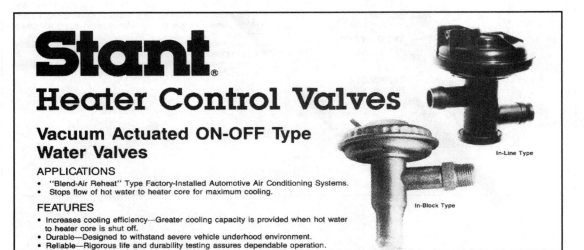

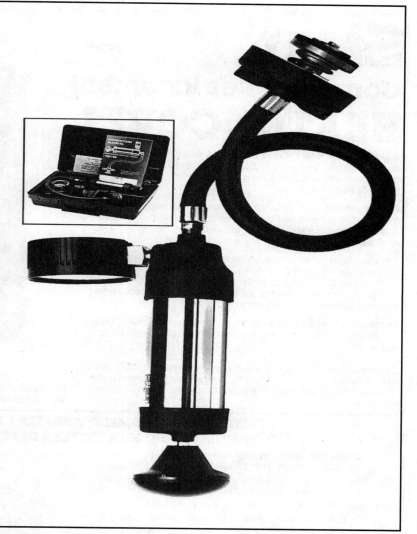

The ST 255 (12255) cooling system and cap pressure tester. Use it anywhere a radiator cap fits to find leaks in cooling systems.

The Stant ST 255 (12255) pressure tester is the quick, accurate way to tell instantly if a cooling system or radiator cap is defective. There's no guesswork. You can see exactly where repair or replacement is needed—and so can your customers, which makes for easier parts and repair job sales and greater profits.

The ST 255 (12255) has a flexible 14" hose that connects the radiator adapter to the tester body. The color-coded 2" diameter dial is easy to read.

The Stant ST 255 (12255) pressure tester comes in its own plastic carrying case with one 255 9 (12559) spacer to drop in 1" deep filler necks for testing, one 255 2 (12552) cap adapter to check 3/4" deep caps, and an easy-to-understand instruction manual that makes testing quick and easy to do.

Some heater control valves work manually via a cable from the dash, some work via vacuum, but they all have the same basic job. And you are right, there are a zillion different styles (take a look in an illustrated parts book sometime). Who knows why—maybe that is the department where design engineers start out. Our main concern is knowing what job these valves are supposed to do.

In many cases you will see heater hoses on older cars (of the 1940s and 1950s) where someone has installed a manual shut-off valve. This type of valve looks like something from a plumbing supply house. Well, that is most likely where that valve came from, and while it doesn't look pretty, it will work to shut off the flow of warm coolant to the heater in the summertime—which means it functions the same as a modern heater control valve.

Heater Cores

Just a note about heater cores and their construction. Most modern heater cores are still made of copper and brass. The things that have improved over the years are the tube designs and the core arrangement. Also, improvements in fin design and construction have helped to make heater cores more efficient. In addition, like their radiator counterparts, you can check a heater core for leaks. To do that you need what is called a vacuum chamber tester and heater core adapter kit (as pictured). The process for checking a heater core works much like that used to check a radiator (and you thought you learned all of that for nothing).

Stant.
Complete Replacement
HEATER CORES

Stant Complete Heater Cores feature innovations like louvered fin design, high efficiency core and extra strength tube support. These design elements add up to a top quality aftermarket heater with optimum fit and performance.

Our heaters are manufactured from the highest quality materials available. All our inlet and outlet tubes are made of 100% copper, and our tanks and water channels are made from the highest quality brass.

The story does not end there. Using space age technology we now offer you our "Polished Core Finish." Finally an aftermarket replacement Heater Core that is every bit as good as it looks. Our special "Polished Core Finish" means you can have the best of both worlds; superior performance and good looks.

Our Heater Cores are packed for shipping with special foam packaging designed to offer the greatest product protection for you and your customer.

Our quality control standards are the toughest in the business, with accountability every step of the way. Every Stant Complete Heater Core we ship must live up to the highest standards in the industry... our own!

It's all part of our continuing effort to bring you the best aftermarket Complete Heater Core in the world.

TESTING STANT COMPLETE HEATER CORES
USING THE 260 8 (12608) TESTER ADAPTER KIT

OPERATING INSTRUCTIONS FOR 260 8 (12608) HEATER CORE TESTER ADAPTER KIT

Note: This adapter kit should be used in conjunction with Stant Vacuum Chamber Tester No. SVT 260 (12260).

This heater core testing kit contains one each of the following:

    1 rubber adapter that fits ¾", ⅝", or ½" diameter tubes.

    1 aluminum adapter for vacuum pump hose and larger rubber adapter.

    3 caps sizes ¾" (red), ⅝" (black), and ½" (yellow) diameter to seal tubes on heater cores.

Method of testing heater cores in vehicle or out

  A) Testing in vehicle.

    1) Remove heater hoses (normally two) from tubes, let coolant drain from core as much as possible.

    2) Place proper sized cap on either of two tubes on core. Push on as far as it will go and air tight.

    3) Force larger black rubber adapter on remaining tube. It should fit tight.

    4) Fit blunt end of aluminum adapter into vacuum hose on tester.

    5) Insert cone shaped adapter into black rubber adapter which is now on heater core.

    6) Pull on vacuum tester handle gently until 10-12 in. Hg. (25 CmHg) is shown on gauge. Let stand for approximately two minutes. If no drop in vacuum is shown, core is satisfactory.

    CAUTION:
    If heater core has coolant in it, **do not** pump fast or go beyond 13 in. Hg. as coolant will be drawn into pump tube. If coolant is drawn into pump, disassemble barrel, check valve and clean with air hose or dry rag.

  B) Testing new or old heater cores out of vehicles and dry:

    1) Same procedure as above except vacuum may be as high as 18 to 20 in. Hg.

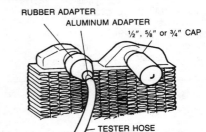

RUBBER ADAPTER
ALUMINUM ADAPTER
½", ⅝" or ¾" CAP
TESTER HOSE

TESTING ASSEMBLY ON CORE

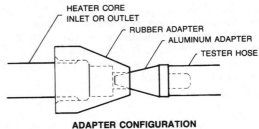

HEATER CORE
INLET OR OUTLET
RUBBER ADAPTER
ALUMINUM ADAPTER
TESTER HOSE

ADAPTER CONFIGURATION FOR TEST

WARNING: HEATER CORE TESTING OF THIS TYPE SHOULD BE DONE WHEN THE SYSTEM IS NOT WARM TO THE TOUCH TO AVOID ANY POSSIBILITY OF PERSONAL INJURY. ALWAYS WEAR EYE PROTECTION WHEN CONDUCTING TESTING.

Fan Clutches

Remember way back in the beginning of this book we talked about fan clutches? We learned that they control the rpm of the engine fan based on the rpm of the engine as well as the amount of air flowing through the radiator at highway speeds. We also said that a fan clutch could save engine horsepower by not working against the air flowing through the radiator at highway speeds.

Well, you know all of that is true. Fan clutches are one of the most efficient cooling accessories you can install to overcome a heating problem. So let's learn more about them.

There are two basic types of fan clutches: non-thermal and thermal. A non-thermal fan clutch operates in response to engine rpm. At low road speeds (rpm), the clutch drives the fan when air movement is needed. At high road speeds, the non-thermal fan clutch slows the fan when normal airflow through the radiator is enough to cool the engine.

In contrast, thermostatically controlled fan clutches adjust the fan speed in response to the operating temperature. This results in quieter operation as well as horsepower and fuel savings. Fan clutches are stan-

Stant FAN CLUTCHES, FAN BLADES, SPACER KITS

DOMESTIC FAN CLUTCHES

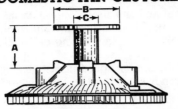

IMPORT FAN CLUTCHES

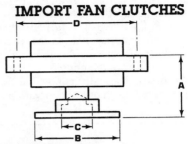

FAN CLUTCH DIMENSIONAL CHART
NEW PART NUMBERS FOLLOW OLD PART NUMBERS.

DIM "A" (in.) Shaft Length	DIM "B" (in.) Shaft Hub Dia.	DIM "C" (in.) Pilot Bore	NON-THERMAL Part No.	THERMAL Part No.
STANDARD ROTATION FAN CLUTCHES (CW)				
1.400	2.35	0.630	FC 12 (55012)	FC 512 (55512)
1.400	2.35	0.750	FC 38 (55038)	FC 538 (55538)
1.400	2.55	0.630	— —	FC 549 (55549)
1.900[1]	2.55[1]	0.630[1]	— —	FC 513[1] (55513)
1.400	2.55	0.630	— —	FC 545 (55545)
1.400	2.55	0.750	— —	FC 554 (55554)
1.800	2.35	0.630	FC 11 (55011)	FC 511 (55511)
1.800	2.55	0.630	FC 26 (55026)	FC 526 (55526)
1.800	2.55	0.750	— —	FC 552 (55552)
2.000	2.55	0.630	FC 43 (55043)	FC 543 (55543)
2.000	2.55	0.750	FC 37 (55037)	FC 537 (55537)
2.500[1]	2.35[1]	0.630[1]	— —	FC 510 (55510)
REVERSE ROTATION FAN CLUTCHES (CCW)				
1.400	2.55	0.630	FC 49 (55049)	FC 649 (55649)
1.400	2.35	0.750	— —	FC 654 (55654)
1.400	2.35	0.630	— —	FC 642 (55642)
1.400	2.35	0.630	— —	FC 645 (55645)
1.800	2.55	0.630	— —	FC 646 (55646)
1.800	2.35	0.630	— —	FC 653 (55653)
1.800	2.55	0.630	FC 26 (55026)	FC 626 (55626)
2.000	2.47	0.630	FC 43 (55043)	FC 643 (55643)

[1]Refer to Import Clutch Drawing.

DIM "A" (in.)	DIM "B" (in.)	DIM "C" (in.)	DIM "D" (in.)	NON-THERMAL Part No.	THERMAL Part No.
IMPORT FAN CLUTCHES					
1.92	2.205	1.40 Coned	4.409	— —	FC 580 (55580)
1.92	2.362	1.25 C'Bore	5.276	— —	FC 582 (55582)
2.12	1.965	1.00 C'Bore	5.276	— —	FC 588 (55588)
2.12	2.441	1.95 Coned	4.803	— —	FC 581 (55581)
2.12	2.375	1.25 C'Bore	4.094	FC 84 (55084)	— —
2.42	1.734	0.630	4.803	— —	FC 586 (55586)
2.42	2.117	0.630	4.803	— —	FC 587 (55587)
2.42	2.435	1.80 C'Bore	5.367	— —	FC 585 (55585)
— —	— —	— —	4.094	FC 83[2] (55083)[2]	— —
— —	— —	— —	5.276	— —	FC 589[2] (55589)[2]

[2]Water pump/fan clutch assembly.

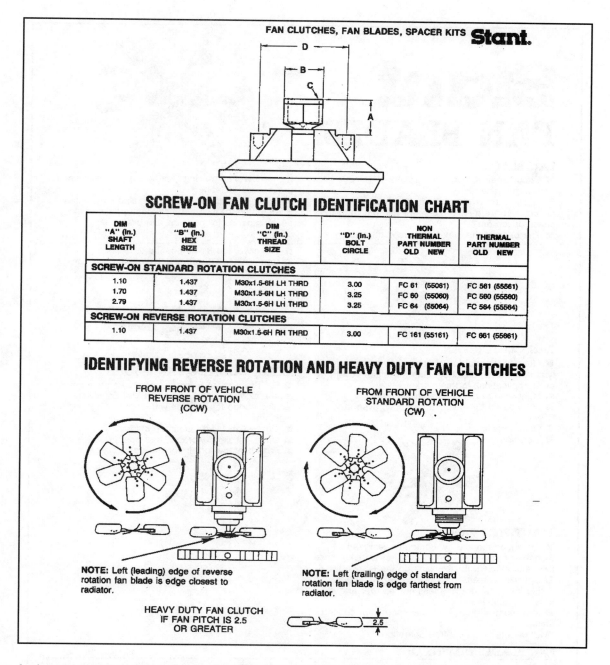

SCREW-ON FAN CLUTCH IDENTIFICATION CHART

DIM "A" (In.) SHAFT LENGTH	DIM "B" (In.) HEX SIZE	DIM "C" (In.) THREAD SIZE	"D" (In.) BOLT CIRCLE	NON THERMAL PART NUMBER OLD NEW	THERMAL PART NUMBER OLD NEW
SCREW-ON STANDARD ROTATION CLUTCHES					
1.10	1.437	M30x1.5-6H LH THRD	3.00	FC 61 (55061)	FC 561 (55561)
1.70	1.437	M30x1.5-6H LH THRD	3.25	FC 60 (55060)	FC 560 (55560)
2.79	1.437	M30x1.5-6H LH THRD	3.25	FC 64 (55064)	FC 564 (55564)
SCREW-ON REVERSE ROTATION CLUTCHES					
1.10	1.437	M30x1.5-6H RH THRD	3.00	FC 161 (55161)	FC 661 (55661)

IDENTIFYING REVERSE ROTATION AND HEAVY DUTY FAN CLUTCHES

FROM FRONT OF VEHICLE REVERSE ROTATION (CCW)

FROM FRONT OF VEHICLE STANDARD ROTATION (CW)

NOTE: Left (leading) edge of reverse rotation fan blade is edge closest to radiator.

NOTE: Left (trailing) edge of standard rotation fan blade is edge farthest from radiator.

HEAVY DUTY FAN CLUTCH IF FAN PITCH IS 2.5 OR GREATER

dard on most all vehicles since the mid-1960s. They have proven themselves as a simple, efficient way to help draw air through the radiator when needed, while also saving horsepower and extending water pump bearing life by not trying to do battle with the incoming air at highway speeds.

Clutch fans are also available as a cooling system accessory. The accompanying information shows the different types of universal fan clutches available and what measurements you need to take with you when shopping for a fan clutch.

Fan Blades

Depending on the degree of overheating problem you are experiencing, maybe a more efficient fan blade is in order. Especially in applications prior to the 1940s many fan blade assemblies had only two blades and a poor pitch. (Pitch is the angle of the fan blade, and the sharper that angle the more air that is moved, in theory anyway.) Because the original fan blades themselves were not efficient, increasing the horsepower is not going to help the cooling system do a better job. What may have been "good enough" for a stock 80-horsepower engine is woefully inadequate in a 100-plus-horsepower racing application.

Stant.
FAN BLADES

FAN BLADES
■ Circulate air through the radiator to remove heat from the engine.
■ Flexible fan blades are used without a fan clutch, and are a less expensive alternative to the clutch-driven fan.
■ The pitch of the Flex Fan blades changes at higher speeds, drawing less horsepower and improving gas mileage.
■ Extra Cooling Fan blades are also used without a fan clutch to maintain maximum airflow at all engine speeds for engines with overheating problems.
■ Full coverage for all popular vehicles.
■ Can replace OE fan clutch system (with Fan Spacer Kit).

FAN CLUTCH FAN
■ Fits non-thermal fan clutches and thermostatically controlled fan clutches. One fan blade covers most applications in this market.
■ Lightweight rigid aluminum blades.
■ Engineered for maximum air flow, even at low RPMs.
■ Quiet, efficient.
■ Vibration-free.

EXTRA COOLING FAN BLADES
■ For use without a fan clutch. Direct drive maintains maximum air flow at all RPMs. Especially recommended for engines with overheating problems.
■ Lightweight rigid aluminum blades.
■ Quiet, efficient, vibration-free operation.
■ Full coverage for all popular applications.

STANT FLEX FANS
■ Advanced metallurgy, computer-designed technology and engineering excellence make these the most efficient flexible fans on the market today.
■ Special stainless steel blades flex as engine RPMs increase, drawing less horsepower and improving gas mileage.
■ Maximum air flow at slower speeds for cooling efficiency.
■ Ultra-quiet vibration-free operation.

FAN BLADES DIMENSIONS

	Part No. OLD NEW	Dim. A	Dim. B	Dim. C	Dim. D		Part No. OLD NEW	Dim. A	Dim. B	Dim. C	Dim. D
FAN CLUTCH FAN	UF 618 55718	2-3/8" 2-5/8"	3"—3-1/4"	2-1/4"	18"	EXTRA COOLING FANS	CF 615 55615	.625	1-3/4"—2-1/4"	1-7/8"	15"
							CF 617 55617	.625	1-3/4"—2-1/4"	1-7/8"	17"
							CF 618 55618	.625	1-3/4"—2-1/4"	1-7/8"	18"
FLEX FANS	FF 615 55265	.625	1-3/4"—2-1/4"	2"	15"	IMPORT/ COMPACT CAR FANS	IF 2 55002	.625	1-3/4"—2-1/4"	1-7/16"	14"
	FF 617 55267	.625	1-3/4"—2-1/4"	2"	17"		IF 3 55003	.860	1-3/4"—2-1/4"	1-7/16"	14"
	FF 618 55268	.625	1-3/4"—2-1/4"	2"	18"		IF 5 55005	.985	1-3/4"—2-1/4"	1-7/16"	14"
	FF 619 55269	.625	1-3/4"—2-1/4"	2"	19"		IF 7 55007	.945	1-3/4"—2-1/4"	1-7/16"	14"

In some cases, engine overheating can be traced to a lack of air movement through the radiator. As we have learned about roadsters, with their open engine compartments, air doesn't always make it through the radiator. Instead, it takes another path of less resistance, much to the dismay of our overheating engine. Often by replacing the original fan blade assembly with one that has more blades (and a better pitch) you can aggressively draw more air through the radiator at idle and low engine rpm, thus solving your over-heating problem.

Also important is the distance between the fan and the radiator. In order for a fan to be effective it must be close to the radiator to draw the air through. About one inch of clearance is a common standard and a goal to strive for. In addition, the fan should be located in the middle or upper third of the radiator, because that is where the warm coolant enters the radiator—from the top.

In some applications a fan shroud attached to the engine side of the radiator may help your cooling problem. A fan shroud can act as a guide to channel incoming air through to the engine. Fan shrouds became popular in the early 1960s for performance and heavy-duty applications. Today, they are an integral part of cooling system design.

For the majority of cooling system applications you can make your own shroud to direct the airflow. Or, fan shrouds are available from the aftermarket and high-performance catalog vendors as well as the local auto parts stores or parts counter of the car manufacturer. Some of the best advice is to go to a car show and look for the same model car as yours with the same engine and options. Talk to the owner and see what experiences he has had and if his combination is working. In most cases, you can learn plenty from someone who has already "been there and done that" and you just might gain a friend along the way.

Electric Cooling Fans

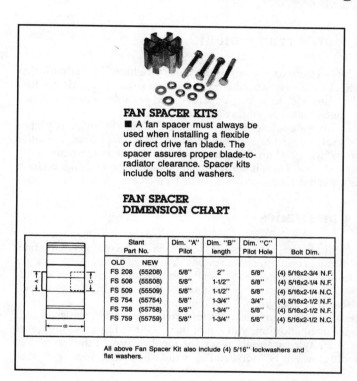

FAN SPACER KITS

■ A fan spacer must always be used when installing a flexible or direct drive fan blade. The spacer assures proper blade-to-radiator clearance. Spacer kits include bolts and washers.

FAN SPACER DIMENSION CHART

Stant Part No.		Dim. "A" Pilot	Dim. "B" length	Dim. "C" Pilot Hole	Bolt Dim.
OLD	NEW				
FS 208	(55208)	5/8"	2"	5/8"	(4) 5/16x2-3/4 N.F.
FS 508	(55508)	5/8"	1-1/2"	5/8"	(4) 5/16x2-1/4 N.F.
FS 509	(55509)	5/8"	1-1/2"	5/8"	(4) 5/16x2-1/4 N.C.
FS 754	(55754)	5/8"	1-3/4"	3/4"	(4) 5/16x2-1/2 N.F.
FS 758	(55758)	5/8"	1-3/4"	5/8"	(4) 5/16x2-1/2 N.F.
FS 759	(55759)	5/8"	1-3/4"	5/8"	(4) 5/16x2-1/2 N.C.

All above Fan Spacer Kit also include (4) 5/16" lockwashers and flat washers.

In some hot rod and racing applications, there just isn't enough room to install a fan clutch or a fan shroud, or fit any other type of big fan between the engine and the radiator. In many cases, the original plan includes stuffing ten pounds into a five-pound sack, so anything extra is out of the question.

It is in cases such as these that an electric radiator cooling fan can save the day. These fans mount directly to the radiator, either on the engine side or the grille (front) side, and help move (draw or push) air through the radiator. Electric radiator cooling fans can also be used along with an engine-driven fan to help in high-performance applications where everything is a tight fit and the frontal area of the radiator is limited.

Over the following pages you will learn that a "pusher" style of electric radiator cooling fan is designed to be mounted on the front side of the radiator and pushes air through the core. In contrast, a "puller" style electric radiator cooling fan is designed to mount on the engine side of the radiator and pulls air through the radiator.

Puller-style electric radiator cooling fans are often used to replace engine-driven fans. The purpose is to save engine horsepower while at the same time allow everything to fit and still get the hood closed.

When mounting your electric radiator cooling fan it should be installed in the upper third of the radiator, where the warm coolant enters the radiator. You see lots of electric fans mounted in the middle or lower part of the radiator. By the time the coolant gets to the bottom of the radiator, chances are the fan isn't going to be of much help—too little, too late!

Also, when you receive your fan, take a look to be sure you have the correct fan blades for your application—don't assume somebody else got it right. **The rule is the curve or pitch of the fan blade should always face the engine, no matter what!** Most fan blades will be marked as either pusher or puller blades. After installation (and assuming you have followed all of the directions to a "t"), double check your work. If you have installed a pusher fan, *carefully* hold a shop rag behind the fan and the rag should be drawn towards it. If it is blown away from the fan, your fan motor is wired backwards or you have the wrong fan blade on your fan.

In contrast, if you mounted a puller fan to the radiator, again *carefully* hold a shop rag behind the fan and it should be blown away (towards the firewall). If that happens, you got it right! You would be surprised at the number of electric radiator cooling fans that are running "backwards" on cars. Of course, then the heating problem is going to be worse. Not only is the fan running backwards trying to push air against the airflow coming through the front of the radiator, there is now more restriction of that airflow through the radiator because of the fan. So you hear, "Yeah, I installed one of them electric radiator cooling fans—darn thing didn't help a bit!"

Electric Fan Thermostats

Another word to the wise concerning electric radiator cooling fan thermostats. Think about where the most logical place would be to take a temperature reading: the engine block or the radiator; then look at where most electric fan thermostat probes are located. The engine block should be the obvious choice, as that is the reason for all of this coolant stuff in the first place, right? So why do most kits offered position the probe into the radiator? Because it's cheaper! If you cannot find a thermostat kit for an electric cooling fan that fits into the engine block, you just have to look harder.

This also applies to your engine temperature senders (sometimes you see them mounted in the upper radiator hose). Suppose your thermostat in the engine sticks closed and the coolant temperature in the engine block climbs to 240 degrees. What temperature will the radiator hose be showing if there is no warm engine coolant in the radiator? If all of your temperature senders are somewhere besides the engine, you could be in trouble and not know it—until it is too late!

Electric Fan Arrangement

Also, in some applications where the cooling system uses a large "cross-flow radiator" (a radiator that flows the coolant horizontally instead of vertically), it may work better to use two smaller electric cooling fans instead of one big electric fan. The smaller fans will draw less amperage, and are able to cover a greater part of the radiator core while at the same time create less of an airflow blockage.

Fan motor size is also important to electric radiator cooling fans. In this case, bigger is better. A bigger fan motor will have to work less hard, and therefore, will last longer and use fewer amps than a smaller motor, which will be overworked, run hotter and have a short lifespan, resulting in poor performance.

Think about this from a common sense point of view. Does it seem logical that a fan motor designed for a 10-inch diameter fan could be large enough and powerful enough to run a 14- or 16-inch electric fan? Not likely!

Fan Blades

Fan blades are another tricky subject. You will see straight blade, curved blade, and S-shaped blade fans with all sorts of different pitch on the blades. Again, common sense applies. You want the fan with straight blades and the most aggressive pitch you can find if you are going to be in the air moving business. Of course, a more aggressive pitch on the blades, along with more blades (10 is common for the bigger high-output fans) will require a bigger motor to power those blades (because you are moving more air).

If you want to get into the cheap fan business you could just put a flatter pitch on fewer fan blades, which would then allow a smaller fan motor to be used. In addition, you could then sell the fan as a "universal fan" that would work as either a pusher- or puller-style by simply reversing the direction of the fan motor. You could then sell the fan a lot cheaper, and because it is "universal" it would fit everything. Well, that is exactly what some companies do!

Universal electric radiator cooling fans are quite common and much cheaper to build. But like anything else, you get what you pay for and electric cooling fans are no exception. If you are serious about solving your overheating problem and decide an electric radiator cooling fan is what you need, buy one that is designed specifically for your application. One with a good-size fan motor and lots of blades having an aggressive pitch; one that will move some "serious" air.

Tech Tip

Be wary when you watch fans being demonstrated at car shows and trade events. Oftentimes, they are just turned on and running in a display rack, which doesn't take a lot of horsepower but does move a lot of air. **Look for demonstrations where the fan is actually blowing air through a radiator core (making sure the core has a reasonable amount of fins per inch). This way you can see how much air the fan is actually capable of moving through a radiator.** Electric radiator cooling fan blades that are curved or "s" shaped are quieter than conventional straight fan blades, but you also give up some performance. It is a choice *you* have to make. Personally, I buy the straight blades, and move some air.

There are many more different fan blade shapes out there besides the "s" and straight blades. When you read the advertisements, they all claim to be the best on the market, but remember this analogy when looking at cooling fan blades: Think of an airplane or a helicopter. Both are in the air moving business, and neither one would fly if their blades weren't efficient. If there was a better design for an airplane propeller or a helicopter blade, don't you think that is what they would be using?

Installation Kits

Finally, there is the cooling fan installation kit. It should contain all of the necessary mounting hardware along with the correct on/off switch and inline fuse with all necessary related hardware. Instructions are a good way to check out a fan. If the installation kit is complete with all of the necessary hardware you need, and the instructions are easy to read and make sense, then chances are you are looking at a quality cooling fan.

In the case of mounting the fan, actual metal brackets are better than the nylon wire ties that pass through the radiator core. These wire ties will eventually wear a hole in the radiator core, especially if your fan has a good-sized motor on it.

Electric cooling fan installation should not be limited to just the radiator, either. In the case where you have a big-block engine under the hood (its size alone can create quite an air dam), you may want to think about installing a pair of ten-inch electric fans in the inner fender panels, for instance, to help move air through the underhood area. Sometimes (as we have learned earlier), the air is getting through the radiator okay, but then needs to be given some further direction underhood.

Summary

In an upcoming chapter, when we design and build our own cooling system, we will learn about underhood pressure and how to direct air to our advantage. We will also learn about hood louvers and how they can help with the underhood air movement.

Finally, we will learn how to make our own tools, or better yet, borrow a set of unique HVAC (heating, ventilation, air conditioning) tools from your friendly neighborhood HVAC technician that identifies low-pressure areas. Once identified, low-pressure areas can be used to direct and channel the hot air away from the engine compartment.

We have done well so far, but if you notice, things are slowly getting more complicated as we work our way into the modern stuff. If you can hang in there and keep making sense out of things as they get more difficult, you will be rewarded. While you may not care what happens to the modern cars, all of this information will be necessary as we design and build our own cooling system. That, my friends, is when things will start to get really interesting!

There are many more different fan blade shapes out there besides the "s" and straight blades. When you read the advertisements, they all claim to be the best on the market, but remember this analogy when looking at cooling fan blades: Think of an airplane or a helicopter. Both are in the air moving business, and neither one would fly if their blades weren't efficient. If there was a better design for an airplane propeller or a helicopter blade, don't you think that is what they would be using?

Notes

Chapter 18:
Coolant Plumbing

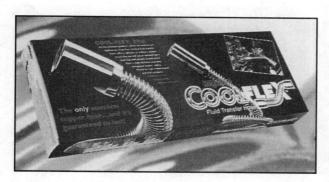

All of us have, at one time or another, tried to mix the old with the new, installing a modern engine in an older chassis for a street rod project, or tried to build a race car using parts sources from here, there and everywhere. And, as is usually the case, nothing fits and you must make everything.

Making engine mounts and transmission mounts is no big deal. Building and fabricating components is kind of fun until you get to the plumbing of the radiator to the engine. Who in the world makes a radiator hose that has a 1-1/2-inch inlet on one end, 1-3/4-inch on the other, is shaped like the letter "Z" (with two 180-degree bends) and is just 22 inches long?

Usually, you end up spending hours going through the "illustrated hose buyers guide" at the local auto parts store. After a two week exhaustive search you come home with a pair of rubber flex hoses (the closest thing you can find for your odd application) only to discover that you have to route the upper hose the long way around to straighten out the curves enough so the hose won't collapse and restrict your coolant flow. Boy, is that going to look like heck! A flex hose isn't exactly what you had in mind, but it will work until you can find something better.

If you have ever been in that "can't find a hose to fit" situation, then you can appreciate Cool-Flex. Cool-Flex is a seamless corrugated copper tubing that can easily be bent and shaped to connect to most any engine/radiator combination. Cool-Flex will not collapse; even 180-degree bends are no problem. Also, Cool-Flex is not affected by vibration, engine fluids, or high coolant pressure.

Where Did Cool-Flex Come From?

Cool-Flex, as we know it today, was developed by Total Performance (established in 1971) to meet the needs of the newly emerging hot rod aftermarket. Popular during this era were the "T-bucket" roadsters, hot rods based on a 1923 Model T Ford roadster.

Total Performance developed and began manufacturing its own line of products based on the 1923 Ford roadster. Total Performance offered its customers everything needed to assemble a complete car, right down to the step-by-step instructions. It also offered complete turnkey cars built to the customer's specifications.

Cool-Flex was one of the products developed by Total Performance during these early years. "Flex hose," as it was originally called, was developed for the T-bucket cars. Because the T-bucket radiators were short in height, and mounted close to the engine, it was difficult and sometimes impossible to find a radiator hose to fit. Cool-Flex became the perfect solution to tight-fit coolant plumbing. Because the original

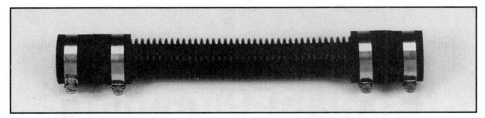

Original Cool-Flex.

application was mainly inhouse, Cool-Flex was originally only available in twelve-inch lengths.

The demand for Cool-Flex continued to grow, even though it was still only available by the foot. In 1988, Total Performance acquired Inglese Induction Systems, whose main product line was building Weber Carburetion systems for Ford and Chevrolet engines. With the success of the Inglese induction products, Cool-Flex was moved out of the Total Performance product line-up and into the Inglese product group.

In 1991, Harry Hibler, former publisher of *Hot Rod* magazine, agreed to publish a press release describing the Total Performance product, now known as Cool-Flex. That press release was the rebirth of Cool-Flex (which was also known as "flashy flex" at one time) and has resulted in the overwhelming popularity of the product.

It has been more than twenty years since Cool-Flex was introduced. Cool-Flex is now available in lengths of twelve, twenty-four and thirty-six inches. Cool-Flex heater hoses are also now available (sold in pairs) in forty-four-inch lengths to fit both three-fourths-inch and five-eighths-inch applications. And for the Chevrolet big-block engines there is even a Cool-Flex by-pass hose available for both the long and short water pumps.

Cool-Flex cover ends are now available in colors. Besides the original polished chrome, other colors available include: satin, a red or blue anodized finish and a black powder-coated finish. Also available is (24K) gold and chrome ends for use on show cars. The Cool-Flex hose is available in chrome and black powder coat only.

Cool-Flex is made in the USA and is guaranteed for life. As with most popular ideas that work, there are always a few imitation products that appear on the market; so it is with Cool-Flex. While imitation is said to be a sincere form of flattery, you should be aware that sometimes the imitation isn't that sincere!

For instance, you may see products similar to Cool-Flex on the market that are made of stainless (which tends to crack from vibration). Or, products made overseas (made from a cheaper grade of materials) that may look the same as Cool-Flex at first glance, but do your homework (read the warranty). Look at the fit and finish of the products. Then go buy the "original" Cool-Flex with twenty-plus years of experience and a lifetime warranty!

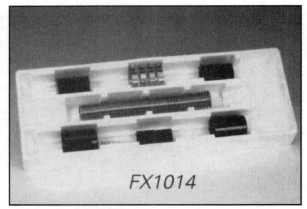

FX1014

Cool-Flex installation kit.

BBc Bypass Hose

FX4002

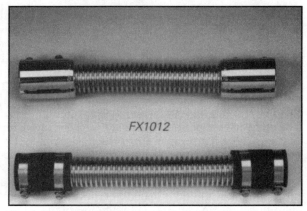

FX1012

Cool-Flex shown with (top) and without end covers.

Installing a Cool-Flex Hose

Installation is quite simple. First, you need to measure your existing hose or the length of the route the Cool-Flex needs to travel. In other words, you need to determine how long your coolant hose needs to be.

Next, you need to remove the original coolant hose. Now measure and mark the Cool-Flex hose at the correct length. Using a fine tooth hacksaw, cut the Cool-Flex to the correct length for your application. Remember your woodshop training in high school—measure twice and cut once. Then bend the Cool-Flex to the proper shape for your application. Now you are ready to install the hose clamps. The next step is to insert the rubber connector into the hose cover. Now connect the hose cover to the Cool-Flex hose. Next install the proper size reducer for your application, if needed (the reducer is glued to the radiator inlet, with glue supplied), onto the radiator inlet. Now press the hose over the reducer and tighten the hose clamps using a screwdriver. Do the same for the radiator outlet.

By the way, another possible advantage to the Cool-Flex hose is its larger physical diameter as compared to standard rubber coolant hoses. If your application is a big engine in a little chassis, the increased volume of coolant that the Cool-Flex hoses are able to provide could be of benefit to you. (You could enlarge your radiator inlet and outlet to take advantage of the full 1-3/4-inch size of the Cool-Flex hose.)

Refill the radiator, start the engine, and check for leaks. Remember, Cool-Flex is also available for heater hoses as well as some water pump bypass applications. The address for Cool-Flex is listed in Appendix B in the back of the book.

Cool-Flex Installation Tips

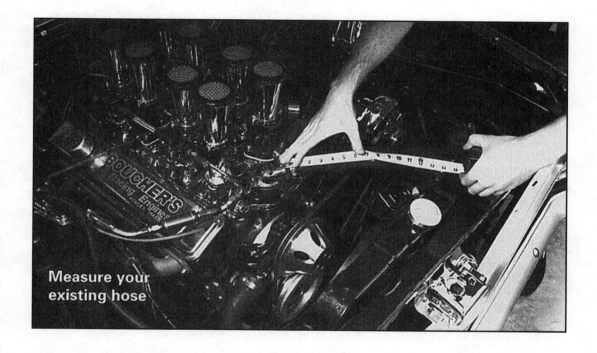

Measure your existing hose

Remove hose

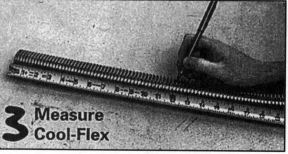

3 Measure Cool-Flex

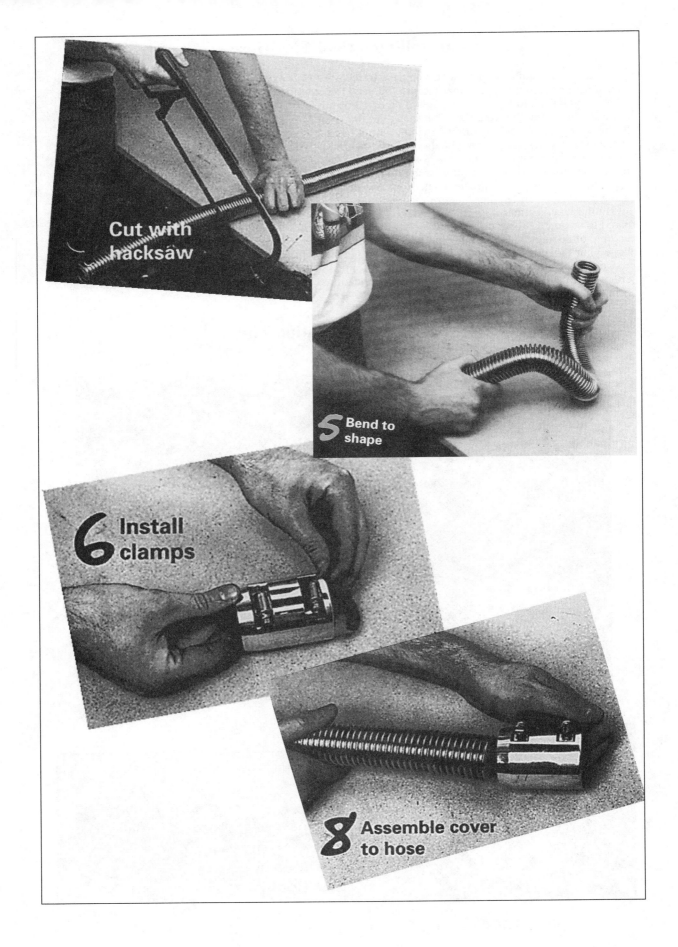

Cut with hacksaw

5 Bend to shape

6 Install clamps

8 Assemble cover to hose

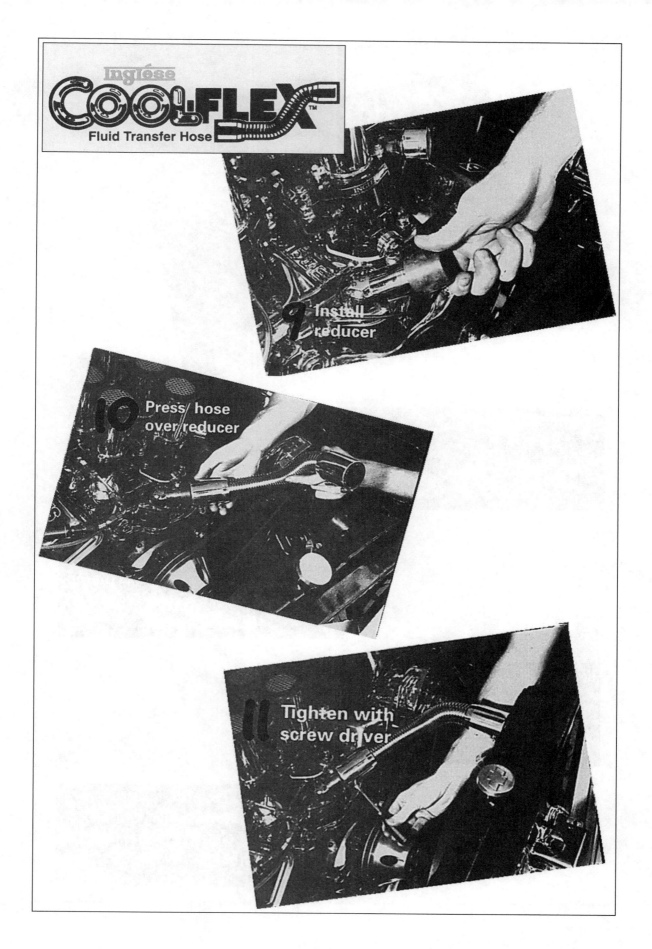

Inglese
COOL FLEX™
Fluid Transfer Hose

9 Install reducer

10 Press hose over reducer

11 Tighten with screw driver

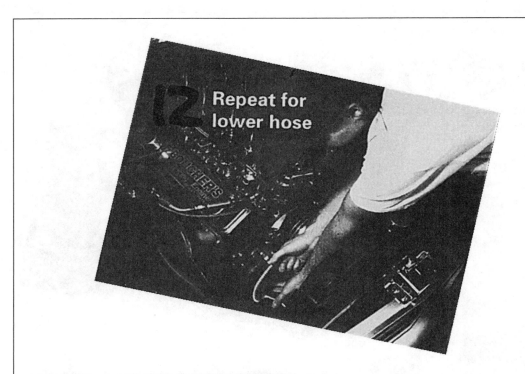

12 Repeat for lower hose

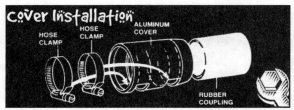

Cover Installation

HOSE CLAMP   HOSE CLAMP   ALUMINUM COVER

RUBBER COUPLING

Tech Tip
Before installing the reducer inserts, clean the rubber with soap and water to remove any residue from the release agent.

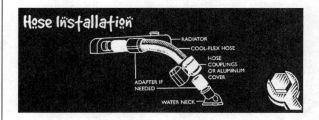

Hose Installation

RADIATOR
COOL-FLEX HOSE
HOSE COUPLINGS OR ALUMINUM COVER
ADAPTER IF NEEDED
WATER NECK

Tech Tip
Be careful when installing cool-flex hose, not to get close to your battery. You can arc the hose causing holes.

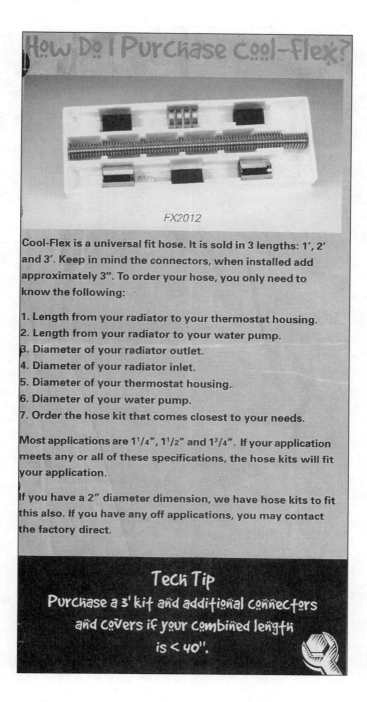

How Do I Purchase Cool-Flex?

FX2012

Cool-Flex is a universal fit hose. It is sold in 3 lengths: 1', 2' and 3'. Keep in mind the connectors, when installed add approximately 3". To order your hose, you only need to know the following:

1. Length from your radiator to your thermostat housing.
2. Length from your radiator to your water pump.
3. Diameter of your radiator outlet.
4. Diameter of your radiator inlet.
5. Diameter of your thermostat housing.
6. Diameter of your water pump.
7. Order the hose kit that comes closest to your needs.

Most applications are $1^{1}/_{4}$", $1^{1}/_{2}$" and $1^{3}/_{4}$". If your application meets any or all of these specifications, the hose kits will fit your application.

If you have a 2" diameter dimension, we have hose kits to fit this also. If you have any off applications, you may contact the factory direct.

Tech Tip
Purchase a 3' kit and additional connectors and covers if your combined length is < 40".

How to Purchase Cool-Flex

Again, the purpose here is to make you aware of some of the products that can help you solve your coolant system plumbing problems. Sometimes we need help just getting everything put together and hooked up. As street rodders and car builders, we tend to not follow the rules. So when we get into trouble we usually have nobody to blame but ourselves. The solution/challenge is, of course, to find a way to make it work anyway. That is what makes us so good at what we do.

For more information on Cool-Flex, see Appendix B at the back of this book.

Notes

Chapter 19: Airflow: Lessons From The HVAC Guys

If you recall in an earlier part of this book, I said that we would learn how to design a cooling system and that I would explain some of the things you need to take into consideration to do this. Well, this is one of those chapters and it is all about airflow.

We can learn some of the best lessons on airflow from the HVAC (heating, ventilation, and air conditioning) industry professionals, who have studied airflow for a lot longer than we have. It has just been within the last ten years or so that the automotive industry has begun to take a serious interest in airflow. In the old days, we didn't care about airflow; as long as our engine did not overheat, everything was fine with us. But today, it does matter. Engines produce a lot more heat than they used to and we depend on airflow more than ever, to remove that heat.

The HVAC people actually have a lot in common with us. For instance, they have what they call a heat exchanger—we have the same thing but we call it a radiator. They measure heat transfer and so do we; we just call it engine cooling. They build heat exchangers based on airflow just like we design radiators based on airflow, and so the list goes on. But the big difference between them and us is that they are way ahead of us when it comes to directing and controlling air, so let's see how they do it.

There are three basic tools the HVAC pros use that could be of benefit to us. Let's look at what each of these tools is designed to do, and then we can apply that knowledge to our project. The first tool is called an **Infrared Thermometer,** which can give you a digital reading of the surface temperature of an object almost immediately. The second tool is called a **Digital Micromanometer,** which measures differential pressures, calculates air velocity and volumetric flow rate. The third tool that can be of help to us is called a **Thermo-Anemometer,** which is used to measure cubic feet per minute (cfm) ratings and temperature. This tool can be used to measure and keep track of the minimum, maximum, and average cfm measurements.

For help with this chapter, I called on Rob Falke, who is the owner of Saunders Air Conditioning, located in Turlock, California. Rob also owns Balancing Ltd., an air balancing company. Rob is an NEBB certified air balancer (one of the few in the United States) and is also president of the National Balancing Institute, as well as a member of the Contracting Business advisory board. All of the people I spoke to within the HVAC industry recommended Rob as being the one that could best explain how airflow and air balancing works.

As Rob and I got into our discussion and I explained what I wanted to know, I began to realize that airflow and air pressure are a lot more complicated than I first realized. I also became aware of how much knowledge Rob has on airflow, a subject I considered pretty simple and basic up to now. Finally, I realized that we as an automotive industry have some catching up to do.

One of Rob's first basic explanations referred to the airflow in the ducts of your home or office. In many cases, part of the rooms seem to always be cold, while others seem to always be hot. Depending on which room you are working in, you or somebody else is constantly adjusting the thermostat up or down. That is an airflow problem.

Rob went on to explain that in most major office buildings of any size built today, the balance of airflow is worked out ahead of when the office building is actually built. An airflow cfm rating for each air duct is specified in the building blueprints. In contrast, many smaller houses and office buildings built prior to the 1960s were built using a simple formula based on the length and size of duct, and the size of the heating/cooling unit—not real accurate, but considered close enough at the time.

Meanwhile, let's look at the tools the HVAC people use that could be of benefit to us. From there we will learn how to use these HVAC tools for automotive applications, to help identify and fix our cooling problems. Finally, we will look at purchasing these tools, including what features that are important to look for. Then, no matter if you borrow or buy these tools, you will at least be using the best tools for the job.

Infrared Thermometer

Every object (including you) radiates invisible infrared based on its temperature. What an infrared thermometer is able to do is determine the temperature of an object through the use of a series of optics and a sensing element. An infrared thermometer detects the amount of radiant energy of an object (exactly what it sees), and is able to instantly display that temperature digitally.

This is a neat tool and you will find lots of uses for it besides solving cooling problems. One thing to remember is that the temperature reading you get is actually the surface temperature of what the infrared thermometer actually sees. So if you aim it at the top tank of your radiator, the reading you will get will be the temperature of the outside surface of the radiator tank, *not* the temperature of the coolant inside.

It is true that the coolant inside of the radiator does greatly affect the temperature of the radiator tank, but you need to remember what surface the temperature reading is actually of. If you need to know the temperature of the coolant inside of the radiator, you could check it by removing the radiator cap (*carefully* if it is hot) and aiming the "spot" at the coolant inside of radiator. You will then know the actual coolant temperature.

In summary, an infrared thermometer works best at measuring the difference in temperatures between two surfaces, such as the engine block area before the thermostat, and the radiator hose located after the thermostat. This simple test can tell you if the thermostat is opening properly, as well as help identify other similar problems.

Field of View

Just like a flashlight, an infrared thermometer records the temperature of just what it sees. And like a flashlight, the farther away you are from an object, the bigger the viewing area and the less accurate the reading. Known as the "field of view" (fov) the distance you are away from your target is expressed as a "ratio of distance to spot diameter." You need to divide the physical distance measurement between you and your target by the fov rating of your thermometer to determine the size of viewing spot of your thermometer.

Did I lose you? Thought so! Okay, suppose the infrared thermometer you borrowed from your HVAC technician neighbor has a rating of 10:1 spot diameter. That would mean that when you focus the thermometer on an object located approximately three feet in physical distance from you (such as your exhaust manifold), the spot diameter of your borrowed thermometer is 3.6 inches in diameter (10:1 field of vision, divided by 3.0 feet, the distance between the objects, equals 3.6, the spot diameter). So the temperature shown to you is the average temperature of the surface in that 3.6-inch diameter area.

In contrast, if your neighbor had one of the more accurate (and more expensive) infrared thermometers with a 33:1 ratio, then at that same three-foot distance away, the spot circle on your manifold would be 1.1 inch (33:1 field of vision, divided by 3.0 feet, the distance between the objects, equals 1.1 inch)—much more accurate than you need, but, hey, borrow what you can!

You can be more accurate with a 10:1 ratio infrared thermometer simply by getting closer to your target. To figure out where you are or exactly where you need to be, divide the physical distance to your target by the fov ratio of the thermometer you are using to learn the size of the spot diameter. In other words, if you need to know the exact temperature of a rear alternator bearing, you can figure out how far away from the bearing you need to be physically by dividing the size of the bearing surface into the field of view of the thermometer. The result will be the maximum distance you can be from the bearing surface and still get an accurate reading. For example, a 33:1 fov divided into a one-inch bearing surface (distance measured across the surface area) equals three feet, the maximum distance allowed between the bearing surface and the thermometer to still get an accurate reading. And you thought those HVAC people were so smart!

Emissivity

There is one more thing that figures into how well the infrared thermometer works (and not all infrared thermometer manufacturers talk about this) and that is emissivity or how reflective a surface is. Just like a mirror, a shiny metallic surface (such as your chrome valve covers for example) will reflect the temperature of things around or in front of itself, which can greatly affect the accuracy of the temperature readings.

Dark or painted surfaces (such as radiators) reflect very little and are usually not a problem. Officially, emissivity (the ability of an object to reflect light) is measured on a scale between 1.0 and 0.01. Most non-reflective objects are between the .70 and .95 range.

Some deluxe infrared thermometers will have an emissivity selector for either dark objects (.95) or light reflective objects (.70). Again, in most cases, for what you want to know, the emissivity selector is not something you need to worry about. You just need to know what it is, in case you borrow a high-dollar tool!

Also, an infrared thermometer will not read through glass or plastic. It will read the temperature of the first surface it comes in contact with. Distance is almost unlimited; you can take the temperature of a cloud in the sky, but in reality, the closer you are to the surface the more accurate the reading will be. On some shiny reflective surfaces, a piece of masking tape or black electrical tape will make the readings more accurate.

Temperature Range

Most (but not all) infrared thermometers will work in the temperature range that you need. The majority are designed to work in a range of between -40F to +950F, which is fine for most automotive applications. But some cheaper infrared thermometers do not have near enough range for automotive use and are also less accurate, so pay attention to the fine print. Better yet, ask someone who uses one everyday to make a recommendation or take this person shopping with you. A good infrared thermometer will last you a lifetime; a bad one and you are better off not having one at all.

Additional Features

One feature that is handy and something you should look for when buying your own infrared thermometer is a "laser marker." A laser marker will send out a laser beam of light to show you exactly where you are measuring. **The accuracy of a laser marker is important and should point to the center of the field of view. Some laser markers point to the spot circle, but are not accurate when it comes to where the actual reading is taking place.** By the way, there are two types of laser markers found on infrared thermometers: coaxial and offset. The coaxial laser points directly into the center of the fov while the offset points about one-half inch away from the center. While this really doesn't matter to us because our surface

Specifications			
Model	15005	15003	15002
Field of View	33 : 1	10 : 1	10 : 1
Response Time	1.5 seconds	0.8 second	0.8 second
Sighting Method	Coaxial Laser	Offset, pulse laser	None
Backlight	Auto Sentry	Automatic	None
Alkaline AA Battery life	100 hrs. (no light/laser)	30 hrs.	60 hrs.
Temperature Range	-4~752°F (-20~400°C)	-40~950°F (-40~510°C)	-40~950°F (-40~510°C)
Accuracy at 76°F (25°C)/E.95	±1%;±3°F (±2°C)	<0°C±3°C; 0°-200°C±2°C ; 200°-510°C ±2°C or 1% of reading	
		<32°F±4.5°F; 32°-392°F±3°F ; 392-950°F ±3°F or 1% of reading	
Hold Mode	Last Reading/Max (Peak)	Last Reading	Last Reading
Emissivity Ratio Adjust	Dark (.95)/ Bright (.70)		Fixed .95
Operating Environment	32° ~ 122°F (0 ~ 50°C) / 35 ~ 85% RH		
Scale/Resolution	C°/F° selectable / 1°		
Repeatability	1°C(2°F) or 1% of reading		
Optics/Sensing Element	Silicon lens/Thermopile/8 ~ 14 μm		
Protective Case	15101 or 15102	15104 only	15104 only
0.1° Resolution Models		15007 with laser	15004 no laser

Infrared thermometer model comparisons.

areas are usually large, if you are working on something with a small surface area, the coaxial laser would be the one to have. The offset laser can often point to the outer edge of the field of view, but both types will work okay for us. Just be aware of which type you are using. And be sure not to get your laser and infrared names mixed up. Laser is the beam of light that does the pointing; the infrared is what is reading the temperature.

Actual Use

So what if this is really an HVAC tool? That has never stopped us before. We, as car enthusiasts, can use any tool we want, so long as we understand how it is supposed to work. Okay, how do we use this infrared thermometer for automotive use?

Suppose you have a street rod, for example, a 1939 Chevrolet two-door sedan. It has a Chevy 350 cubic inch V-8 engine, automatic transmission, and the usual goodies such as air conditioning, power steering, tilt, cruise, etc. While this is not a unique combination (you have seen hundreds like it, at the Street Rod Nationals), your car has always had an overheating problem. You have tried all of the common solutions such as adding a fan shroud, adding an electric fan, and the dozens of other "fixes" acquired from magazines, fellow street rodders, and anybody who would listen to your problem long enough to offer a solution.

But the fact remains, after all of this expert help, you are still right back where you started, with no working solution. So how are you going to figure out what your problem really is? First, you have to determine if you have an airflow problem or an engine cooling problem. In other words, is your problem caused by airflow either not getting through the radiator, or stalling once it gets through the radiator and not drawing off any heat. Or, is there an internal engine cooling problem such as poor coolant circulation through the engine block or cylinder heads? Let's find out!

Taking Your First Readings

The first thing you need to do is warm your car to operating temperature. When the gauge in the dash reads 190 degrees (for example) and you have a 180-degree thermostat installed, odds are your thermostat is open and the coolant is flowing through your system. Now, take your infrared thermometer and measure the temperature across the top tank of the radiator in about three places (left side, middle, right side), then do the same thing across and down the front of your radiator core. Then measure the bottom tank. You should have about a dozen temperature readings by now.

If you find any reading that is much higher on one side than the other, you could have a coolant flow problem within the radiator, maybe a plugged tube or something that is restricting the coolant flow inside of the radiator.

Next, *carefully* remove the radiator cap and measure the temperature of the actual coolant. Now check the gauge inside the car to see if it is accurate. (I have seen them inaccurate by as much as twenty degrees.) If readings are matching (or close), put the radiator cap back on and take about a dozen temperature readings under the hood. Start at the engine side of the radiator and work your way around in a big circle, checking corners and firewall cavities, anyplace where the air might be bunching up or getting stuck in a corner.

The Box Fan Trick

With your car running in order to maintain operating temperature, plug in a box fan and place it on a stool in front of your car, so it is even with the front of your radiator. Turn the fan on high, as this will simulate you driving down the highway. With the fan on high, let it run for at least five minutes, again take temperature readings in the exact same places as you did before.

If there is a significant drop in temperature (20 degrees or more) from the previous readings, you have found at least part of your problem. You have an airflow problem—the air is getting through the radiator, but is stalling and not moving out from under the hood and, therefore, is not drawing off any engine heat. Eventually what happens is that enough air builds up under the hood to actually block completely the incoming airflow through the radiator.

Also, if the temperature of the radiator core reads twenty degrees difference from one "side" to the other, you have a radiator problem, an obstruction of some kind, or at the least a coolant flow problem. This is something that needs to be looked into.

Okay, but suppose everything still reads warm and the fan-in-front-of-the-radiator trick didn't help. What now? It is time to look elsewhere for hot spots in the engine block and cylinder heads. Start by taking a number of readings on the engine block, water pump housing, thermostat housing, front of cylinder head, middle of cylinder head, and rear of cylinder head. Note the temperature difference at all of these locations. Is the front side of both the left and right side about equal or is there a twenty-five degree difference between the right side and the left side? How do those temperatures compare to the radiator temperatures you took earlier? Is there a big difference?

If there is a big difference, of say forty degrees, odds are you are not getting the warm coolant to the radiator. This could be the water pump cavitating (pumping coolant vapors instead of coolant), or a "hot spot" could be creating a vapor barrier that is blocking the circulation of the coolant flow (common to the rear cylinders) through the cylinder heads.

Remember, water separates from the antifreeze as it begins to turn into a vapor, and that happens above 212 degrees Fahrenheit (depending on the pressure in the system). So if your temperature reading is 250 degrees at number eight cylinder, wouldn't that qualify as a hot spot?

What is a Manometer and What Can It Do For Us?

In order to understand what a manometer does, we first have to understand air velocity and how it is measured. There is actually two different measurements for airflow velocity: "standard" and "actual." The indicated reading shown on most all manometers is a standard or "mass" velocity and is the velocity that a mass of air would be moving if the temperature were at "standard" conditions.

Like most test instruments there has to be a "standard" or a known value to begin with, so some kind of norm can be established. In the case of manometers, the "standard" is 70 degrees Fahrenheit at 14.7 pounds per square inch at atmosphere (psia). While that doesn't really mean much to us, the reason most air velocity is measured that way is because it is the most accurate measurement of the heat-carrying capacity of the air.

In some applications, it is better if the air velocity measurement is given in "actual" velocity. This is the velocity at which a small particle of dirt would be traveling, if it were in the air stream being measured. It is the "actual" air velocity measurement and the one that makes the most sense to us. To convert air velocity "standard" readings to "actual" velocity readings, you need to compensate for temperature, barometric pressure, and humidity. I don't care if you learn that formula or not, I just wanted you to know how it is done. If you are into that sort of thing, you can follow through and learn it. As for the rest of us, we are going to proceed and learn more about airflow and velocity.

Measuring Airflow Velocity

What real benefit do we get from measuring air velocity? Remember, **we said that in order for air to flow easily through the radiator, we needed to have a low-pressure area behind the radiator. That is one of the things that a manometer can do, measure pressure. A low-pressure area on the engine side of the radiator will help draw air through the radiator**. (Air always flows in the direction from a high-pressure area to a low-pressure area, so sayeth the HVAC pros.)

Once we have established that we do, indeed, have a low-pressure area on the engine side of the radiator, we can then measure the velocity of the airflow through the radiator. By measuring the airflow on the front side of the radiator, then on the engine side of the radiator, we can determine exactly how much airflow is available. We can then figure out how much of that front-side airflow is actually making its way through the radiator. We will also be able to figure out how much heat the airflow is transferring from the radiator. This will help us to figure out if the radiator and the airflow together are doing their job. This also will help us determine how much of an obstruction that electric fan is, and the air conditioning condenser, and whatever else we have stacked in front of the radiator.

You can also measure and figure out if that air dam under the front of the car is doing any good. Or, maybe you need to add one. Make one out of heavy cardboard first, and see if it helps. By taking a number of readings in front of the radiator, you can actually find out where the path of air is.

Oftentimes, you will find that there is plenty of airflow available on the front side of the radiator, but because components such as electric fans and air conditioning condensers are blocking the front of the radiator, not much of the available air is getting through the radiator.

Where is the Air Going

Next, you need to find out what happens to the air after it gets through the radiator. You begin by measuring the airflow on the engine side of the radiator, and then compare those numbers with the amount of airflow available on the front side of the radiator. If the measurements are close, you are in good shape, so far, and it is time to move on. If you are not doing well (a large gap in the numbers), maybe you need to work on removing some of the obstructions from in front of the radiator. Or, figure out a way to re-route the airflow to increase that airflow through the front of the radiator.

If all is well, you need to continue to measure the air velocity under the hood just like you did with the infrared thermometer. You will find that some of those places where the air was the hottest under the hood were also the places where the air velocity is the slowest. Once you take the readings under the hood and around the engine, you should have a clear map of where the air is going once it is under the hood.

If you find a place under the hood where both the temperature is high and the airflow is low, then you have found a problem spot where air is stalling. What you may also find is that there is a higher pressure under the hood area than there is in front of the radiator. This happens because the air that has flowed through the radiator could not exit out from under the hood. It then continues to accumulate under the hood, creating a high-pressure area and eventually slowing or stopping the flow of incoming air through the radiator.

This is a common occurrence in street rods. Often, a skinny four- or six-cylinder engine is replaced with a small-block (or, in some cases, a big-block) V-8 engine. As a result, the new engine is creating a big air dam that not only blocks the flow of air through the radiator, but also through the engine compartment as well.

If you find a place under the hood where both the temperature is high and the airflow is low, then you have found a problem spot where air is stalling. What you may also find is that there is a higher pressure under the hood area than there is in front of the radiator. This happens because the air that has flowed through the radiator could not exit out from under the hood. It then continues to accumulate under the hood, creating a high-pressure area and eventually slowing or stopping the flow of incoming air through the radiator.

So what you are doing is finding where the air is going now, where it is being blocked and where it needs to be going. Locating where the air is bunching up under the hood is a step in the right direction. Early Ford V-8s of the 1930s and 1940s had this problem of air bunching up under the hood (which added to the overheating problem they already had). This is why you saw so many Fords running around with their hood sides removed. They were letting the trapped air out to improve the cooling of the engine.

Since thermal air velocity sensors are sensitive to changes in air density and air velocity, all thermal anemometers indicate velocities with reference to a set of standard conditions. For TSI instruments, standard conditions are defined as 21.1° C (70° F) and 101.4 kPa (14.7 psia). Other manufacturers may use different values.

The indicated velocity is called "Standard" or "Mass" velocity. This is the velocity that this mass of air would be moving if the temperature and pressure were at standard conditions. It is usually the most useful measure of airflow because it defines the heat-carrying capacity of the air.

In some applications it is desired to correct standard velocity readings to actual velocity. Actual velocity is the velocity at which a microscopic particle of dust would be traveling if it were in the air stream. To convert the velocity you need to compensate for temperature, pressure and humidity. Below is a table showing the differance between standard and actual velocity at some typical conditions.

Measurement Conditions	Measured Velocity	Actual Velocity	% Difference
16°C (60.8°F), 30% rh, 760 mmHg	5 m/s (984 ft/min)	4.88 m/s (961.04ft/min)	2.5
26°C (78.8°F), 70% rh, 740 mmHg	5 m/s (984 ft/min)	5.00m/s (984.50 ft/min)	0.0
34°C (93.2°F), 30% rh, 760 mmHg	5 m/s (984 ft/min)	5.14 m/s(1011.85 ft/min)	2.7
34°C (93.2°F), 80% rh, 760 mmHg	5 m/s (984 ft/min)	5.07 m/s (998.83 ft/min)	1.4
34°C (93.2°F), 80% rh, 780 mmHg	5 m/s (984 ft/min)	4.95 m/s (973.96 ft/min)	1.0

Correcting Mass Velocity Readings To Actual (Dry Air) Velocity

I) Correct for temperature and pressure

In Degrees Fahrenheit

$$V_{act} = V_{std}\left[\frac{460 + T_{amb}}{460 + 70}\right]\left[\frac{760}{P_{barometric}}\right] \text{ or}$$

In degrees Celsius

$$V_{act} = V_{std} \left[\frac{273 + T_{amb}}{273 + 21.1} \right] \left[\frac{760}{P_{barometric}} \right]$$

Where: T_{amb} = Ambient temperature (°F or °C)
$V_{act.}$ = Actual velocity (corrected for temperature and pressure)
V_{std} = Measured standard or mass velocity
$P_{barometric}$ = Total air pressure (barometric pressure in mmHg)

II) Correct for Humidity Effects

When humidity is high a significant fraction of the air is composed of water vapor. In most cases, the effect of humidity on air at room temperature and below is negligible. However, at higher temperature and relative humidity, the effect on the readings may be more of a concern.

1) Determine the dewpoint temperature of the air stream being measured.

If using a VELOCICALC Plus Model 8360 the dewpoint can be read directly. Alternately, a psychrometic chart can be used if the ambient temperature and relative humidity are known.

2) Look up the vapor pressure that coincides with the dewpoint temperature from Table 1 (page 4)

3) Calculate the dry air mass flow velocity

$$V_{act\,dry} = \frac{D_{dry}\,V_{act}}{D_{total}} = \frac{P_{barometric} - P_{vapor}}{P_{barometric} - 0.3783\,vapor} \; x \; V_{act}$$

Where: $V_{act\,dry}$ = Actual velocity corrected for humidity effects
V_{act} = Actual velocity corrected for temperature and pressure
D_{dry} = Density of dry air
D_{total} = Total air density
P_{vapor} = Vapor pressure in mmHg
$P_{barometric}$ = Total air pressure (barometric pressure in mmHg)
$0.3783 = (1 - R_{dry}/R_{vapor})$

R_{dry} = Gas constant of dry air = $2.153 \dfrac{mmHg\ m^3}{Kg\ °K}$

R_{vapor} = Gas constant of water = $3.461 \dfrac{mmHg\ m^3}{Kg\ °K}$

Example 1:

You want to convert standard air velocity measurement to actual air velocities. The air temperature is 26°C, with relative humidity of 70%, dew point of 22°C and a pressure of 740 mmHg. The measured velocity is 5 m/s.

$$V_{act} = 5.0 \left[\frac{273 + 26}{273 + 21.1} \right] \frac{760}{740} = 5.2 \; m/s$$

From Table 1: $P_{vapor} = 19.84$ mmHg

$$V_{act \, dry} = \frac{D_{dry} \, V_{act}}{D_{total}} = \frac{(740 - 19.84) \; 5.2 \; m/s}{740 - 0.3873 \, (19.84)} = 5.1 \; m/s$$

Example 2:

You want to correct your air velocity measurement for humidity effects. The air temperature is 72°F, with relative humidity of 60%, dew point of 62.5°F (16.9°C) and a pressure of 780 mmHg. The measured velocity is 500 ft/min.

$$V_{act} = 500 \left[\frac{460 + 72}{460 + 70} \right] \frac{760}{780} = 489 \; ft/min$$

From Table 1: $P_{vapor} = 14.53$ mmHg

$$V_{act \, dry} = \frac{D_{dry} \, V_{act}}{D_{total}} = \frac{(780 - 14.53) \; 489 \; ft/min}{780 - 0.3873(14.53)} = 483 \; ft/min$$

Table 1: Dew Point vs. Vapor Pressure

Dew Point °C	Vapor Press mmHg	Dew Point °C	Vapor Press mmHg	Dew Point °C	Vapor Press mmHg	Dew Point °C	Vapor Press mmHg
-50	0.029	-7	2.550	16	13.64	39	52.51
-45	0.054	-6	2.778	17	14.54	40	55.40
-40	0.096	-5	3.025	18	15.49	41	58.42
-35	0.169	-4	3.291	19	16.49	42	61.58
-30	0.288	-3	3.578	20	17.55	43	64.89
-25	0.480	-2	3.887	21	18.66	44	68.35
-24	0.530	-1	4.220	22	19.84	45	71.97
-23	0.585	0	4.580	23	21.09	46	75.75
-22	0.646	1	4.920	24	22.40	47	79.70
-21	0.712	2	5.290	25	23.78	48	83.83
-20	0.783	3	5.680	26	25.24	49	88.14
-19	0.862	4	6.100	27	26.77	50	92.6
-18	0.947	5	6.540	28	28.38	51	97.3
-17	1.041	6	7.010	29	30.08	52	102.2
-16	1.142	7	7.510	30	31.86	53	107.3
-15	1.252	8	8.040	31	33.74	54	112.7
-14	1.373	9	8.61	32	35.7	55	118.2
-13	1.503	10	9.21	33	37.78	56	124.0
-12	1.644	11	9.85	34	39.95	57	130.0
-11	1.798	12	10.52	35	42.23	58	136.3
-10	1.964	13	11.24	36	44.62	59	142.8
-9	2.144	14	11.99	37	47.13	60	149.6
-8	2.340	15	12.79	38	49.76		

The Thermo-Anemometer

A Thermo-Anemometer is a another tool used by HVAC personnel to measure airflow in cubic feet per minute (cfm). We, as car enthusiasts, can use that same thermo-anemometer to measure airflow through the radiator as well as under the hood of the car.

One of the things you will learn quickly as you begin to measure airflow and air pressure is that it does *not* always behave as you would think it should. And just because you install an electric fan on the front of the radiator with a rating of 2500 cfm does *not* mean you are going to get all 2500 of those cfm through your radiator to solve your cooling problem. It will depend on the thickness of your radiator, the number

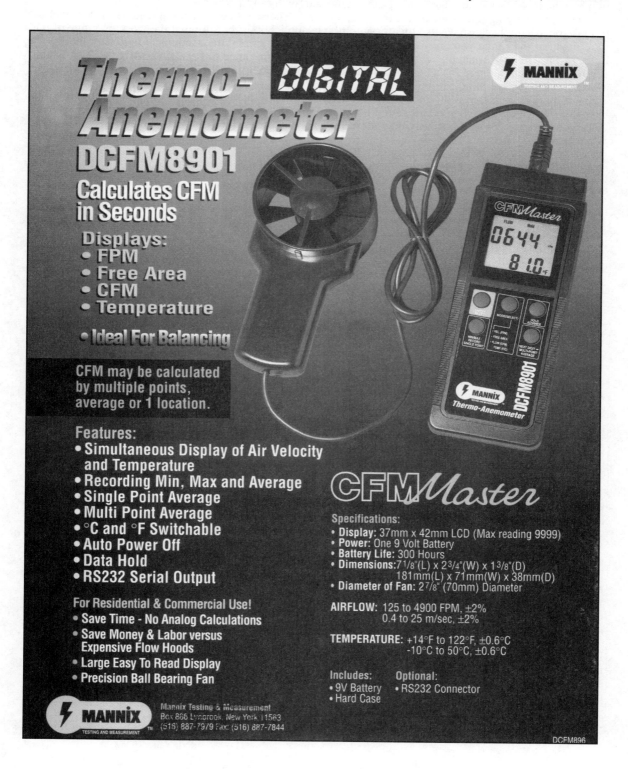

of fins per inch, and the amount of airflow into the front of the radiator that actually determines how much of that 2500 cfm gets through the radiator.

A Thermo-Anemometer is used to measure actual airflow in cubic feet per minute ratings so you actually see how much air is flowing through your radiator. It can also be used to see exactly where the air is going once it passes through the radiator.

Sometimes you will find that the air passes through the radiator at different speeds, stalls once it is through the radiator, or bunches up in a corner. The difference in cfm measurements (airflow speed) you get may surprise you. Measuring the airflow in front of the radiator and then behind on the engine side can be a big clue as to what is really happening to your airflow. This tool measures temperature as well, so you will be able to see if the air passing over the engine is drawing off any heat.

The accompanying photo shows a commercial HVAC Thermo-Anemometer and some of the features to look for. Again, because we use this for automotive applications, be sure that the working range of the tool is within the range you are likely to encounter. As an example, the accompanying chart shows the range of the Thermo-Anemometer pictured. It has a temperature range of between +14F to +122F, which is more than enough range for a heating and air conditioning duct, though it may not be enough for some air readings under the hood.

By using a manometer, a thermo-anemometer or an infrared thermometer to help you identify what is happening to your airflow, you can gain a much better understanding of where your problem is located. Once you have that figured out, solving your problem becomes much easier.

More Hot Air

One more thing (related to airflow) that affects what we do is known as the "Bernoulli's Principle." The

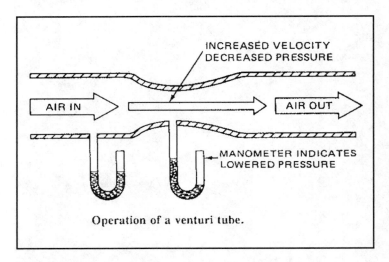

Operation of a venturi tube.

Bernoulli Principle states: "The total energy of a particle in motion remains constant at all points on its path, in a steady flow therefore at a higher velocity the pressure must decrease." That is the official explanation; here is what it means in real life:

Suppose you have a formation of soldiers marching down a street twenty abreast. They march until they reach a narrow alley where there is room enough to only march ten abreast. According to the Bernoulli rule, the men marching through the alley must march twice as fast as they did when they were marching in the street in order to maintain the same rate of travel as they had before.

This same thing happens quite often in automotive applications. Let's use a simple carburetor as an example. Air is drawn into the top of the carburetor and down into the bottom of the carburetor, into an area known as the venturi. This venturi area is smaller in diameter than the air intake area of the carburetor, so a low-pressure area is created just like when the soldiers arrived at the narrow alley.

We know from the example above that a low-pressure area will be created in the venturi of the carburetor. We also know that atmospheric pressure is present inside of the fuel bowl of the carburetor (just like it is inside of the cooling system). Now we have atmospheric pressure in the fuel bowl of the carburetor and a low-pressure area in the venturi of the carburetor. The outlet of the fuel bowl is located in the venturi, so what is going to happen to the fuel inside of the fuel bowl? Correct, the fuel is going to be pushed out of the fuel bowl by the atmospheric pressure, into the venturi of the carburetor, where it will mix with the intake air. This is how a carburetor "draws" fuel from out of the fuel bowl.

Now it becomes clear that a carburetor does *not* "suck" the fuel out of the fuel bowl as is often thought. Instead, the fuel is drawn into the air mixture as a result of the low pressure created in the venturi area of the carburetor. Once the fuel is mixed with the air, the mixture is drawn into the intake manifold, which is a big opening and a high-pressure area. This difference in pressure is what helps draw the fuel/air mixture through the carburetor.

Second Part of the Rule

The temperature of the air inside of the carburetor is also affected by the low-pressure area created. The second part of Bernoulli's rule says that things will remain a constant, so when the velocity goes up (the soldiers have to march faster) the pressure will go down, and the temperature will follow an equal amount.

And when the velocity slows down (when the air passes into a big opening) and returns to normal, the pressure will go back up and the temperature will also rise an equal amount. (This should all start making sense about now.) Just one more thing: Remember in our chapter on atmospheric pressure we said there were other things that could effect the atmospheric pressure, such as humidity and outside temperature? That is also true in this case. For example, when the fuel is pushed into the venturi by the atmospheric pressure, it (the fuel) evaporates rapidly. The quick evaporation of the fuel cools the air, the carburetor base, and the water vapor (humidity) trapped in the fuel. If the fuel has a high humidity (water vapor) content and the outside temperature is low enough, the cooling effect cools the carburetor base to below 32 degrees Fahrenheit. The carburetor base will frost over, ice will form (inside of the carburetor), and the fuel mixture will be stalled, resulting in poor engine performance.

Most of us have seen frost form on the base of a carburetor, but were never sure why it happened or how to explain it. Now you should understand why it happens and be able to explain it. The cure for the frosty carburetor was, of course, the manifold heat riser, which used engine heat to warm the base of the carburetor and intake manifold.

Okay, so what does all of this have to do with a cooling system anyway? Quite a bit, actually, because your cooling system is also affected by this Bernoulli Principle. Stop and think about how your cooling system is laid out. You have a big air intake area that directs air into the smaller core surface area of the radiator, then possibly through a shroud of some sort, then back into a large opening known as the engine compartment. Doesn't that layout seem remotely familiar?

It has been since the 1980s that automotive engineers have really begun to study and take advantage of airflow. As cars have become smaller and more aerodynamic, the size of the radiators and the grille openings have both been reduced at a time when engines are running hotter for cleaner emissions. So the balance between clean emissions and engine cooling is becoming narrow, with not much margin for error. In order to gain back some sort of control, the engineers began installing air dams and air ducts to guide air through the cooling system. Those air dams are not just for looks; a modern vehicle will quickly overheat without them in place.

By controlling and guiding the air (when building our own cooling system), we can also take advantage of the increased cooling benefits. Often, something as simple as an air dam below the grille can direct enough increased airflow through the radiator to lower your engine operating temperature twenty degrees or more. Imagine, the aviation and HVAC people knew this all the time.

Thanks to Don "Packy" Rankin (FAA certified airframe and powerplant instructor/inspector) for getting me straight on Bernoulli's Principle and how it applies to what we are trying to accomplish. Without his help, I couldn't have understood it well enough to explain it to you.

Notes

Chapter 20:
Brass/Copper Radiators and Performance Cooling

Just like a stock engine application, the stock cooling system is designed to cool a specific engine/horsepower combination. If you up the compression ratio of the engine to create more horsepower, more heat is going to be generated inside of the engine. Depending on the design of the original cooling system, and the application it fits into, you may or may not be able to modify the stock cooling system enough to match the increased engine output.

In most racing applications, along with many, if not most all, street rod and custom car applications, it is clear from the start that the original cooling system is not going to work, no matter how much you modify

things. Now it is time to design and build your own performance cooling system and we already know the radiator is the most important part of any cooling system. You have to get that right or nothing else will work as planned.

In street rods, racing, and most high-performance applications, the job the radiator has to do is a lot more difficult, and the margin of error a lot smaller than a stock OEM application. Therefore, you will need to do your homework, and study all of the variables that could affect the outcome of your new cooling system. One of your first decisions involves the material used in the radiator's construction. Should you use a radiator made from brass/copper or aluminum and what exactly is the difference between the two?

For background information on copper/brass radiators, I called upon Don Armstrong, owner of U.S. Radiator. Don and his company are not the only ones making copper/brass radiators (there are lots of reputable companies out there), but I called on Don, in part, because of his thirty-plus years of experience. U.S. Radiator manufactures a number of different radiators for a variety of applications, including street rod, muscle car, custom car and industrial applications. After designing and building radiators for over thirty years, Don knows plenty about radiators.

What Is The Difference Between Brass/Copper and Aluminum?

Let's compare the two materials. For those of you who like the technical stuff, brass (the common material used in conventional radiator construction) is actually a gold-colored alloy metal, made up of copper and zinc, usually 60 to 68 percent copper and 32 to 40 percent zinc. Brass has a low melting point and a good heat conductivity rating, which means that it is efficient at transferring heat. Brass also has properties that make it easy to shape and solder.

Copper is a reddish metal that has a high heat conductivity rating, which means it also transfers heat well. In fact, copper is second only to silver in its ability to transfer heat through itself. Most brass/copper radiators have a brass tank on the top and bottom of the radiator, with the tubes in the core being made of brass, and the cooling fins being made of copper.

How Come the Radiator isn't Made of One Material—Either Brass or Copper?

It is because of the physical properties of the materials. Brass is a soft metal that is easy to form and solder or braze (it accepts vibration well, for example), but is not as efficient at transferring heat as copper.

Copper transfers heat through itself well (second only to silver), but is a brittle material and can easily be damaged by vibration. Therefore, copper is the best material to use in the construction of the actual radiator fins, while brass, because of its flexibility, is the best material for the tanks and tubes.

The heat transfer properties of different common metals is measured as a form of resistance. In other words, the ability of the metal to transfer heat through itself is measured, and then given a rating. On a scale of 1 to 100 (the higher the number the better the heat transfer ability), copper's rating is in the 90s, brass is in the high 40s, as is aluminum, and lead (the bonding material of most non-aluminum radiators) is somewhere in the 20s.

How Is A Modern Copper/Brass Radiator Manufactured?

When a brass/copper radiator is manufactured, the top and bottom brass tanks are forged and shaped. Then the core itself is assembled using brass tubes and the correct amount of fins per inch for the application. The outside surface of the brass tubes (inside of the core) are coated with a fine layer of lead. Then the radiator is assembled and baked in an oven. During this process, the temperature should be hot enough to make the lead melt away (at the point of contact) so the copper and brass bond together with the lead acting as the bonding agent.

The oven temperature and the thickness of the lead coating on the tubes is critical. There are a number of things that can affect this process and if not carefully watched, can result in a below average radiator. If the oven is too hot, the lead melts and flows away—no bonding occurs. If the oven is too cold, the lead fails to melt properly and weak bonding takes place. The radiator will then have a short service life.

If the coating of lead on the tubes is too thick or is uneven, then besides the poor bonding of the materials, the thick lead deposits will cause poor heat transfer (remember, lead has a heat transfer rating in the 20s—not good). Ideally, the oven temperature and the thickness of the lead coating should be checked at least hourly during the manufacturing process.

One of the best ways to check the strength of a radiator is to physically tear the radiator apart to see how well the fins are bonded to the tubes. When the fins are pulled apart from the tubes, the brass tube walls should be exposed where the bonding occurred. This is something U.S. Radiator does on a regular basis to ensure the quality of its radiators. It also buys and tears apart other companies' radiators to see how well they are constructed.

The control of the lead, its thickness and its melting point is critical and can have a great effect on how efficient an individual radiator will be. For example, you can select three different radiators, all exactly alike in physical dimensions, core thickness, and design, and their ability to cool can vary up to fifteen percent as a result of how well the lead was controlled when the radiator was assembled.

Aluminum Radiators

Aluminum, in contrast, has the advantage of being about one-third lighter than copper and brass, and can be brazed together without the use of lead. Aluminum does not corrode with lime and hard water deposits, etc., as easily as brass or copper. Aluminum core radiators, while not as efficient as copper core radiators (based on same size and construction), are much cheaper to build.

In fact, if you were to weigh the amount of materials needed to build a copper/brass radiator, you would have about twenty-two pounds of materials. In contrast, the same size aluminum radiator would require about eight pounds of materials. Therefore, aluminum radiators are only about one-fourth as expensive to build as the same size brass/copper radiator. Aluminum as a raw material is also cheaper than brass or copper. Buying the initial equipment to vacuum braze aluminum radiators during assembly is more expensive.

The downside of an aluminum radiator is that its heat transfer rate is only forty-nine percent as efficient as copper. For most racing applications, aluminum radiators can be designed (using thicker cores) to be almost as efficient as a comparable brass/copper radiator while still providing a weight savings. Also, aluminum radiators are not quite as strong as brass/copper radiators, so for industrial and rough service applications, brass/copper is still used.

Aluminum does have the ability to transfer the heat from a liquid faster than copper does. So, like most things, there is a tradeoff. Depending on the application, one type of radiator may work better than another in certain situations. This is why you cannot make the blanket statement: "Copper/brass radiators work best in all automotive applications," because it is not true, and it is not that simple!

Modern Copper and Brass Radiators

We tend to think of radiators as something that has not changed much in the last 40 years, but nothing could be farther from the truth. For instance, prior to the 1950s, most radiators were of the vertical flow staggered tube design. The staggered tube design often allowed the air to flow through the radiator too fast, which resulted in not much heat being drawn from the radiator. Then in the late 1950s, the inline tube design was introduced, which helped cooling efficiency because it slowed the air as it passed through the radiator core so more heat could be drawn from the fins. In the mid-1960s, with the change in car design (aerodynamics) came the introduction of the cross-flow radiator.

High-Efficiency Radiators

It was in the early 1980s that the high-efficiency radiators came about. First introduced by the Japanese automakers, they determined that by reducing the size of the fins from one-half to three-eighths inch you could get the same cooling effect with a radiator that weighed twenty-five percent less. In addition, more tubes could be added to the core in the space formerly taken up by the fins. The result was a radiator that was more efficient, weighed less, and was cheaper to build.

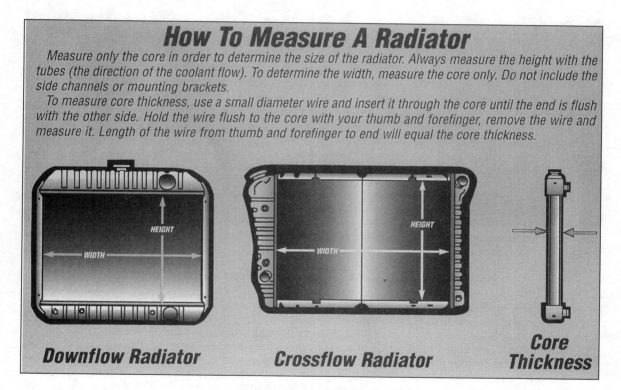

How To Measure A Radiator

Measure only the core in order to determine the size of the radiator. Always measure the height with the tubes (the direction of the coolant flow). To determine the width, measure the core only. Do not include the side channels or mounting brackets.

To measure core thickness, use a small diameter wire and insert it through the core until the end is flush with the other side. Hold the wire flush to the core with your thumb and forefinger, remove the wire and measure it. Length of the wire from thumb and forefinger to end will equal the core thickness.

Downflow Radiator

Crossflow Radiator

Core Thickness

Radiator Testing

"One of the things I wanted to know is how you test a radiator," Don explained. "Everybody says their radiator is better than the next guy's, but how do you prove it? We listened to that argument for years, then we designed and built our own state-of-the-art cooling system simulator. It is to cooling what an engine dyno is to building engines. Testing thermal dynamics and heat transfer requires a machine than can simulate most any kind of driving condition. Our cooling system simulator does that and much more. We can test virtually all types of radiators including aluminum and specialty radiators.

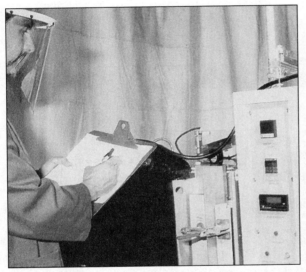

U.S. Radiator's cooling system simulator in operation.

How Does The Cooling System Simulator Work

"Our cooling system simulator heats an antifreeze mixture from ambient (room temperature) up to 200 degrees Fahrenheit, where it then flows through an actual working cooling system. The coolant flow can be varied to simulate engine temperature BTU (British thermal unit) output and engine rpm.

"The radiator being tested is mounted in a wind tunnel fixture where exact control of airflow and air temperature can be maintained. Radiator efficiency is then measured in degrees of temperature drop from inlet to outlet. The coolant flow rate through the radiator and cooling system can be varied from eight to sixteen gallons a minute (equal to coolant flow of OEM design water pumps). The airflow through the radiator can also be varied from 150 feet per minute all the way up to 500 feet per minute. This simulates driving conditions from idle all the way up to 3000 rpm or about 60 miles per hour. The simulator is able to test various radiators of the same size and construction to determine the actual working efficiency of the radiators. In addition, new radiator designs can be tested.

"Through intense coolant simulator testing we have learned that the core design has more effect on heat transfer than the material (copper vs. aluminum) the core is made of. There are many other factors to consider that can directly affect the cooling system, such as the airflow both in front of and behind the radiator, as well as the fin density of the radiator and the core's thickness."

OPTION-1:
O.E.M. Type, Tube & Center
Standard automotive core serpentine fin, with in-line tube construction 1/2" tubes on 9/16" centers. Available in normal duty, heavy duty and Desert Cooler®.

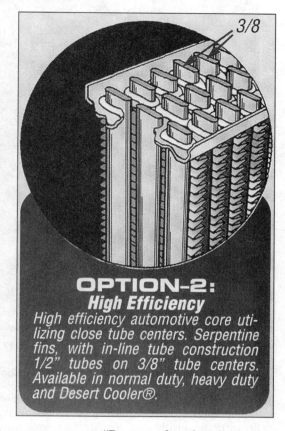

OPTION-2:
High Efficiency
High efficiency automotive core utilizing close tube centers. Serpentine fins, with in-line tube construction 1/2" tubes on 3/8" tube centers. Available in normal duty, heavy duty and Desert Cooler®.

OPTION-3:
Tubular / High Strength
Heavy duty core designed for maximum strength, louvered or dimpled flat plate fin. Tubular construction in a staggered pattern with 1/2" tubes on 5/8" centers. Available in normal duty, heavy duty, and Desert Cooler®.

Don went on to say, "Because of our location next to the Mojave Desert and Death Valley, we have the perfect environment for field testing radiators. In fact, it was because of this hot desert environment that we invented what we call our Desert Cooler radiator back in the early 1960s (which has become one of our best sellers). Besides building the Desert Cooler radiators and the street rod radiators we are well-known for, we also build OEM radiators for the U.S. Army, U.S. Air Force, airport tugs, forklifts, drilling rigs and a host of other industrial applications. We offer four different optional radiators depending on the application:

"Unique to our catalog is our illustrated radiator guide which not only lists the radiator application, but also the physical core dimensions of the radiator—a great help when building a street rod. We also have included tech tips and listed the core options available for each application...."

Another thing I wanted to know was the difference between an automotive radiator and an industrial radiator and would an industrial radiator work for an automotive application and vice versa?

Don answered, "Industrial radiators are typically about forty percent less efficient than a comparable (height, weight, and thickness) automotive radiator. That is because they are designed for a totally different environment. If you think about where industrial radiators are used it makes a lot of sense."

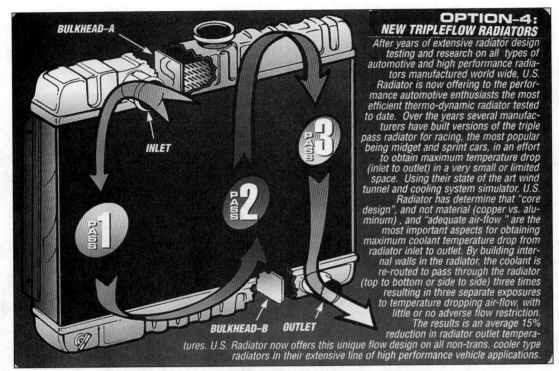

Flow Options

For example, we build a radiator for a diesel engine-powered New York City street sweeper where the radiator is tucked inside of the sweeper and surrounded by dirt bins and street sweeping equipment. Airflow for this radiator is almost non-existent and what little there is, actually comes from the engine compartment and is blown away from the engine (just the opposite of a conventional radiator cooling system) so the dirty air surrounding the street sweeper is not drawn into the engine compartment.

Without question, strength and reliability are the most important concerns when building industrial radiator applications. You do not want to be removing the 100-pound radiator from a street sweeper very often. So to design in the strength we need and the internal cooling ability that does not restrict the airflow, we use a staggered tube flat fin design. While not the best design for heat transfer, this design does give the radiator good strength and reliability. Then because we have the room (something usually not available in automotive applications) we can build the core thicker (to offset the inefficiency) to provide the cooling capacity we need based on the application.

The New York City street sweeper radiator we described is an extreme example, but clearly shows the difference in design between automotive and industrial applications. The street sweeper's radiator is a whopping 5.5 inches thick, 9 rows of tubes wide by 31 inches tall by 29 inches wide and actually weighs nearly 100 pounds. But knowing the environment the radiator is being used in and the way it will be taken care of (it is cleaned daily using a high-pressure power washer), you can imagine what that environment would do to a conventional automotive radiator. The vibration alone from the diesel engine would shake a conventional automotive radiator apart in a matter of a few months. High-pressure power washing an automotive radiator would also flatten all of the cooling fins, making the radiator worthless.

Industrial Radiator Design

The staggered tube flat fin design is common to most all industrial radiators. But while it is a stronger design, it is less efficient. **In most industrial environments, the strength of the radiator is the most important concern. In contrast, automotive applications need the heat transfer ability of the radiator and not the strength**, so most automotive radiators are built using the more efficient inline tube design.

So it becomes clear that the two types of radiators are designed for two completely different environments. And, while they might physically interchange, you should now understand the difference in their design.

More Advice

Use a little common sense. If something seems too good to be true, it usually is. Think about how your cooling system works, then read the product instructions carefully. If the instructions read okay and agree

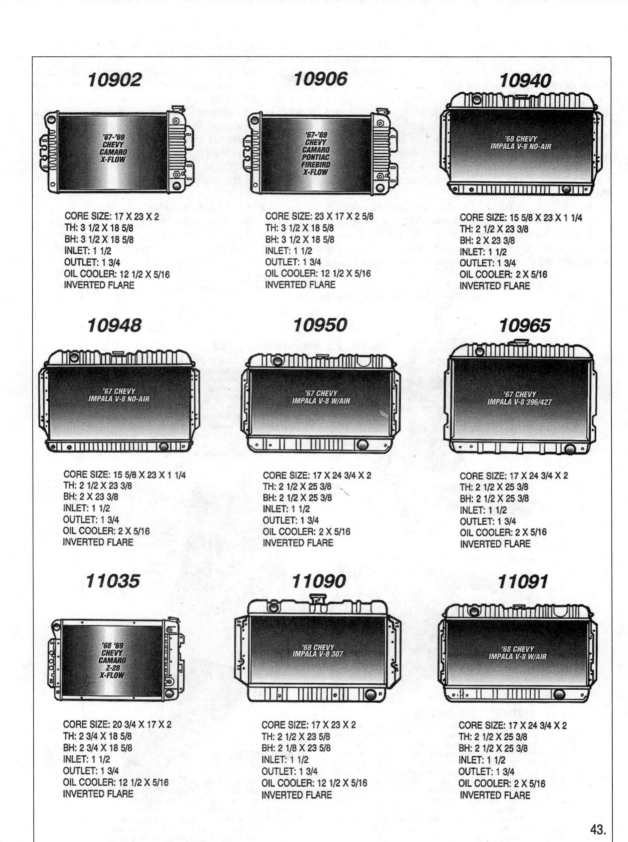

10902

'67-'69
CHEVY
CAMARO
X-FLOW

CORE SIZE: 17 X 23 X 2
TH: 3 1/2 X 18 5/8
BH: 3 1/2 X 18 5/8
INLET: 1 1/2
OUTLET: 1 3/4
OIL COOLER: 12 1/2 X 5/16
INVERTED FLARE

10906

'67-'69
CHEVY
CAMARO
PONTIAC
FIREBIRD
X-FLOW

CORE SIZE: 23 X 17 X 2 5/8
TH: 3 1/2 X 18 5/8
BH: 3 1/2 X 18 5/8
INLET: 1 1/2
OUTLET: 1 3/4
OIL COOLER: 12 1/2 X 5/16
INVERTED FLARE

10940

'68 CHEVY
IMPALA V-8 NO-AIR

CORE SIZE: 15 5/8 X 23 X 1 1/4
TH: 2 1/2 X 23 3/8
BH: 2 X 23 3/8
INLET: 1 1/2
OUTLET: 1 3/4
OIL COOLER: 2 X 5/16
INVERTED FLARE

10948

'67 CHEVY
IMPALA V-8 NO-AIR

CORE SIZE: 15 5/8 X 23 X 1 1/4
TH: 2 1/2 X 23 3/8
BH: 2 X 23 3/8
INLET: 1 1/2
OUTLET: 1 3/4
OIL COOLER: 2 X 5/16
INVERTED FLARE

10950

'67 CHEVY
IMPALA V-8 W/AIR

CORE SIZE: 17 X 24 3/4 X 2
TH: 2 1/2 X 25 3/8
BH: 2 1/2 X 25 3/8
INLET: 1 1/2
OUTLET: 1 3/4
OIL COOLER: 2 X 5/16
INVERTED FLARE

10965

'67 CHEVY
IMPALA V-8 396/427

CORE SIZE: 17 X 24 3/4 X 2
TH: 2 1/2 X 25 3/8
BH: 2 1/2 X 25 3/8
INLET: 1 1/2
OUTLET: 1 3/4
OIL COOLER: 2 X 5/16
INVERTED FLARE

11035

'68 '69
CHEVY
CAMARO
Z-28
X-FLOW

CORE SIZE: 20 3/4 X 17 X 2
TH: 2 3/4 X 18 5/8
BH: 2 3/4 X 18 5/8
INLET: 1 1/2
OUTLET: 1 3/4
OIL COOLER: 12 1/2 X 5/16
INVERTED FLARE

11090

'68 CHEVY
IMPALA V-8 307

CORE SIZE: 17 X 23 X 2
TH: 2 1/2 X 23 5/8
BH: 2 1/8 X 23 5/8
INLET: 1 1/2
OUTLET: 1 3/4
OIL COOLER: 12 1/2 X 5/16
INVERTED FLARE

11091

'68 CHEVY
IMPALA V-8 W/AIR

CORE SIZE: 17 X 24 3/4 X 2
TH: 2 1/2 X 25 3/8
BH: 2 1/2 X 25 3/8
INLET: 1 1/2
OUTLET: 1 3/4
OIL COOLER: 2 X 5/16
INVERTED FLARE

43.

Sample page from U.S. Radiator catalog showing core dimensions.

with how you know a cooling system works, the product might be worth a look. But if the instructions are general and promise a miracle cure in twenty minutes, you had better look further.

As a final bit of advice Don went on to say, "There are four important things you need to consider when designing a cooling system. First, is the water pump and its flow rate (you do not want the water pump to be the cause of a restriction in the cooling system). Most high-flow water pumps work well. Second, is the engine fan. I use a six- or seven-blade aftermarket engine-mounted fan on most of my personal vehicles, and have had great success, in part, because I am not blocking the flow of air through my radiator. Third, is the radiator core. It should be designed properly for the correct airflow, fins per inch, and tube size to match your application and driving conditions. And, finally, is the thermostat. Robertshaw thermostats work well (including the new balanced-flow series). The main thing is that the thermostat does not cause a restriction in the cooling system after it is open. The flow of the thermostat should be able to match the flow of your water pump."

The important thing is to do your homework and make sure everything is working together. For example, a high-flow water pump connected to a restrictive 1950s-design radiator is not a good combination.

In addition to the specialty radiators, U.S. Radiator also offers electric radiator cooling fan kits, air conditioner condensers and a host of other cooling system accessories. It also offers a complete line of diagnostic equipment to help you solve your cooling system problems.

DIAGNOSTIC EQUIPMENT

DIGITAL THERMO-ANONOMETER

If your car runs cool at 30 MPH plus, but, heats up at idle or low speed, chances are, you have an airflow problem. Changing fan blades, adding shrouds, airdams or electric fans can help but, measuring the actual improvement requires the proper equipment. Our New Digital Thermo-Anemometer allowing the pros and hobbist alike to see and measure airflow increase step-by-step during the modification process.

We now offer a High Quality Digital Instrument which measures air flow in...MPH, Km/Hr., Meters/Sec. or Knots while measuring the temperature in either Cº of Fº at the same time. A must for professional car builders and a true time and money saver for the hobbist. Unit comes complete with monitor, cord and hand held measuring fan, batteries not included.

The Desert Cooler®

DIGITAL FLOW-METER

We now offer in our complete line of cooling diagnostic tools, instruments designed to help professionals better understand cooling system failures. Our new Digital Flow-Meter quickly and accurately measures coolant flow in gallons per minute at various RPM's while testing the vehicle in a garage or on a road test (this unit is portable and can be used while driving your vehicle). Obvious mechanical failures such as worn bushings and seals are easy to see and diagnose, but inadequate flow and cavitation caused by worn impellers can only be revealed by accurately measuring the coolant flow while vehicle is running at idle or test driven. The battery operated Digital Flow-Meter is light weight and portable with an easy reading lighted dial. Unit comes complete with a 1-1/2" I.D. connection, wiring harness and easy calibration procedures. Installation is simple, unit plumbs directly into top radiator hose with wiring harness plug-in. The length of wires on harness will easily reach from vehicles engine compartment to inside most vehicle cabs. Batteries not included.

DIGITAL TEMPERATURE GUN

Last but not least we have now added a battery operated Hand Held Digital Temperature Gun to our line of cooling diagnostic tools. The Temperature Gun is designed to give accurate, instant temperature readings. Professional car builders and hobbiests alike will find many uses for this new infra-red gun including, temperature gauge verification and radiator temperature drop. Unit is ideal for checking thermostat opening and closing temperatures for sticking thermostats and for checking radiator cores for hot spots which would indicate blockage. Unit is hand held, light-weight and portable with a lighted dial for easy reading. Batteries not included. 35.

Notes

Chapter 21:
High-Performance Thermostats

In order to keep you from being confused about what you read about which kind of radiator, I am going to slip in this short chapter covering high-performance thermostats. While this chapter is not long, you will learn a lot in a short time.

We know that the thermostat is supposed to make sure the coolant inside of the engine block is recycled until the engine reaches operating temperature. Ideally, the faster that happens the more efficient the engine will be and the less sludge that will be allowed to build up inside of the engine.

Once the engine is warmed to operating temperature, the ideal thing then would be to get rid of the restriction created by the thermostat, so the cooling system could work more efficiently. We, of course, know that is not possible, so the next most likely thing would be to increase the efficiency of the thermostat by increasing its flow rate when it is open.

If you decide to install one of the high-flow water pumps to increase your coolant flow you should consider replacing your stock thermostat as well. **Research has shown that under hard acceleration at high rpm, the pressure buildup in the engine block (in part, from the high volume water pump) is enough to force an original equipment manufacturer (OEM)-type thermostat closed, causing a major restriction in the coolant flow and not doing much to help your overheating problem.**

You may be surprised to learn that OEM thermostats flow between eight and ten gallons per minute (usually closer to eight than ten) at idle, while a high-performance thermostat flows between twelve and fourteen gallons per minute. Also, it is important that the pressure between the engine block and the radiator be somewhat equal. The Robertshaw thermostats balance the pressure in the cooling system as well as increase the flow rate, so they offer a big advantage other than the increased flow rate.

A tip for you late Flathead Ford owners: a Robertshaw thermostat, part #330 series, is the high-flow balanced thermostat for a Chevrolet 350 cubic inch V-8 and, as it turns out, will also fit the 1949-1953 Ford Flathead as well. (The phone number for the Robertshaw company can be found in Appendix B in the back of this book.)

Many early Flathead Ford owners also use this same series of thermostat in the earlier engine blocks. This is accomplished by clamping the thermostat in the upper radiator hoses (there was no provision for thermostats in the earlier flathead engine blocks).

Extra Performance BALANCED THERMOSTATS — Built To Take The Pressure

HOW THE BALANCED THERMOSTAT WORKS.

CLOSED POSITION   **OPEN POSITION**

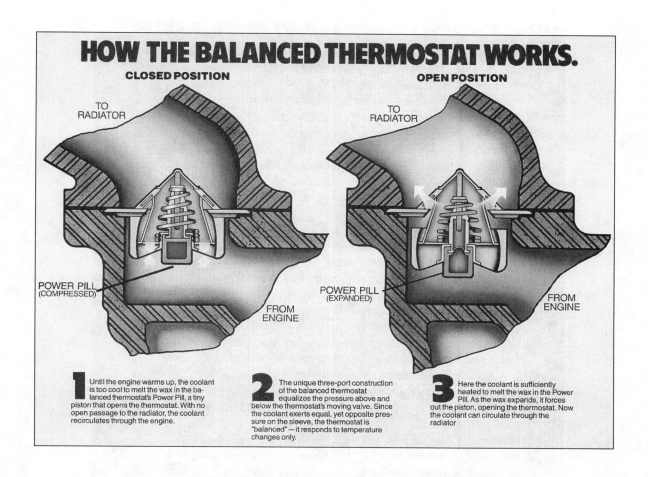

1 Until the engine warms up, the coolant is too cool to melt the wax in the balanced thermostat's Power Pill, a tiny piston that opens the thermostat. With no open passage to the radiator, the coolant recirculates through the engine.

2 The unique three-port construction of the balanced thermostat equalizes the pressure above and below the thermostat's moving valve. Since the coolant exerts equal, yet opposite pressure on the sleeve, the thermostat is "balanced" — it responds to temperature changes only.

3 Here the coolant is sufficiently heated to melt the wax in the Power Pill. As the wax expands, it forces out the piston, opening the thermostat. Now the coolant can circulate through the radiator

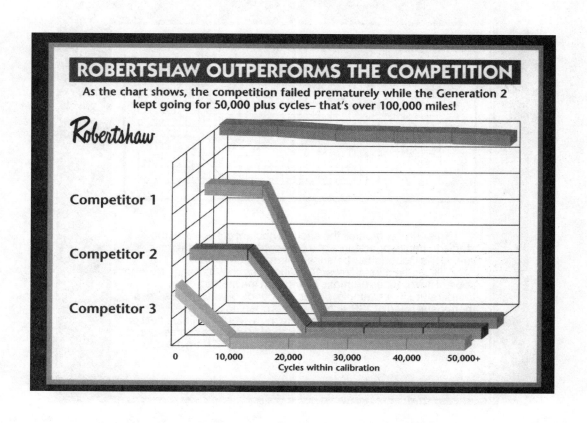

ROBERTSHAW OUTPERFORMS THE COMPETITION

As the chart shows, the competition failed prematurely while the Generation 2 kept going for 50,000 plus cycles– that's over 100,000 miles!

The smaller engines in today's cars operate at higher RPM's. And higher RPM's mean higher water pump pressure against the bottom of the thermostat, keeping it closed much longer than it should. This "unbalanced" pressure can cause the engine temperature to fluctuate greatly, stressing the cars' power plant to the point of failure.

To eliminate the effect of coolant pressure on the thermostat's start-to-open temperature, Robertshaw engineers designed the "balanced sleeve" thermostat. We think it's the best automotive thermostat on the market today. Here's why:

Unlike conventional thermostats, the balanced thermostat doesn't overreact to sudden, substantial changes in water pump pressure. The balanced thermostat's unique design makes it almost immune to the wide swings in pressure that occur at high RPM's so it's virtually free from overshoot cycling, where coolant temperature and coolant pressure fight for control of the thermostat. Even with engine speeds at "red line" RPM, this ruggedly-built thermostat opens at the correct temperature to properly control the engine.

The secret is a balancing seal inside a tough 1½" protective sleeve. The balancing seal eliminates the effect of water pump pressure on the thermostat's opening temperature. The result: The Robertshaw balanced thermostat distributes coolant uniformly, regardless of RPM.

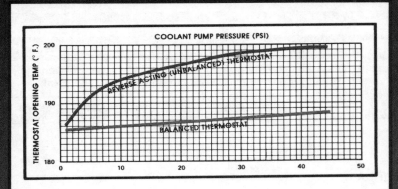

This chart compares the effect of coolant pressure on the start-to-open temperatures of a conventional thermostat (blue line) and a Robertshaw balanced thermostat (red line).

With conventional "reverse acting" thermostats, high pressure coolant flow causes dramatic changes in the start-to-open temperature. For example, under 30 pounds of water pressure, a thermostat rated at 185° actually starts opening at 198.5°.

Wide swings in coolant pressure, however, have little effect on the Robertshaw balanced thermostat. At 30 pounds of pressure, its start-to-open temperature has changed only 2° from the rated temperature.

Advantages of the Robertshaw Balanced Thermostat

- Fast response to temperature changes.
- Unaffected by pressure changes.
- Self-cleaning design prevents entrapment of foreign matter.
- No "cycling" in stop-and-go traffic.
- Durable two-piece construction of Power Pill.
- Fully-seated valve.

The Power Pill®

This is the heart of a Robertshaw thermostat. Its job: to detect minute changes in the temperature of the coolant, and to quickly activate a precision-engineered piston that opens and closes the thermostat valve. Compared to the thermal elements in some thermostats, Robertshaw's Power Pill has major advantages:

RAPID RESPONSE

The Power Pill's piston is activated by a temperature-sensitive mixture of metallic powder and wax. Some thermostats use an all-wax charge, which responds slowly to temperature changes. Other brands mix copper powder with the wax for faster response, but the copper quickly separates from the wax. Robertshaw developed a process to maintain suspension of the copper powder in the wax, so the fast response doesn't deteriorate and the thermostat will not "stick-open" to cause the engine to run cool.

RELIABLE PERFORMANCE

Most manufacturers use a one-piece rubber diaphragm to seal the charge and activate the piston. If the rubber part wears out, the thermostat fails. Robertshaw uses two separate parts: a diaphragm to seal the wax, and a stem seat that activates the piston. Even if the stem seat wears out, the thermostat is still operable.

PRECISE PERFORMANCE

Every Robertshaw Power Pill is calibrated to bring the thermostat's start-to-open temperature within strict tolerances.

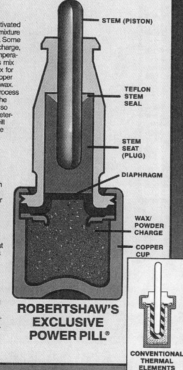

STEM (PISTON)

TEFLON STEM SEAL

STEM SEAT (PLUG)

DIAPHRAGM

WAX/ POWDER CHARGE

COPPER CUP

ROBERTSHAW'S EXCLUSIVE POWER PILL®

CONVENTIONAL THERMAL ELEMENTS

How Two Thermostats Respond To Pressure

1 BALANCED SLEEVE THERMOSTAT

Three openings in the bottom of the sleeve allow the water pump pressure to act on a balancing seal inside of the sleeve. Counteracting forces eliminate the effect of water pressure on the thermostat's opening temperature. So the balanced thermostat responds only to temperature changes.

2 REVERSE POPPET THERMOSTAT

For a conventional, unbalanced thermostat to open, it must overcome water pump pressure on the poppet. But this thermostat can overreact to pressure drops when it opens. Result: the valve opens and closes repeatedly as temperature and pressure fight for control of the thermostat.

Advantages of the Robertshaw Generation 2™ Thermostat

• Brass Components • Total Accuracy • OEM Tested and Approved
• Stronger Sealing Area • Long Life • Domed Diaphragm • Security
• Double Wall Separation

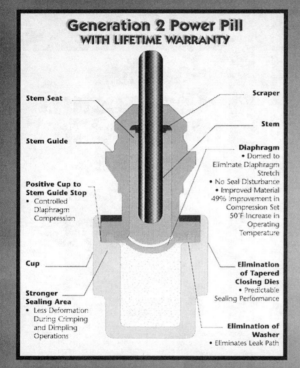

Generation 2 Power Pill
WITH LIFETIME WARRANTY

- Stem Seat
- Stem Guide
- Positive Cup to Stem Guide Stop
  - Controlled Diaphragm Compression
- Cup
- Stronger Sealing Area
  - Less Deformation During Crimping and Dimpling Operations
- Scraper
- Stem
- Diaphragm
  - Domed to Eliminate Diaphragm Stretch
  - No Seal Disturbance
  - Improved Material 49% Improvement in Compression Set 50°F Increase in Operating Temperature
- Elimination of Tapered Closing Dies
  - Predictable Sealing Performance
- Elimination of Washer
  - Eliminates Leak Path

What does a 5% to 7% loss in thermostat performance do?

- Fuel to air ratio will be computer adjusted, decreasing performance.

- Fuel mileage will be reduced.

- Overall driveability will be affected.

- Acceleration will be lost.

- Passenger compartment will feel the loss of heater performance.

• Robertshaw's Generation 2 provides a double wall separation between the special power pill charge and the thermostat stem. This double wall separation eliminates any of the damaging effects of coolant contamination in the power pill. This contamination will reduce the life of a thermostat almost immediately, but with the new Generation 2 this is eliminated!

• This same double wall separation in the power pill also protects against corrosive damage caused by the wax in the power pill against the stem insert. The power pill's special wax charge is very corrosive to the stem insert. Any contact between the two will reduce the thermostat's life significantly, but with the new Generation 2 this is eliminated!

• Robertshaw's special top secret power pill charging method helps make the Generation 2 the most accurate thermostat that will never lose its calibration over its lifetime. We are so confident in our design that Robertshaw will stand behind each and every Generation 2 thermostat with a Lifetime Warranty. Never again will you need to replace your thermostat... GUARANTEED!

Notes

Chapter 22:
Aluminum Radiators

Meanwhile, now that we understand the basics of a copper/brass radiator, let's take a trip over to Fluidyne Racing Products. Fluidyne builds custom aluminum radiators, and has an excellent reputation within the industry. Fluidyne is involved in virtually every aspect of racing and high-performance cooling system design. Fluidyne designs and manufactures its own radiators and cooling system products. It also has an excellent research and development department with two Ph.D. engineers on staff.

Because high-performance radiators and cooling systems are designed and built so differently than conventional stock cooling systems, we need to first look at what is different and why. Most performance racing radiators today are made of aluminum because of the weight savings, with an aluminum radiator (of equal size and construction) nearly one-third lighter than a brass radiator.

Basic Radiator Construction

We already know that a radiator uses engine coolant, along with airflow, to draw the heat from the engine. The heat from the engine coolant is released through the radiator fins when the engine coolant passes through thin tubes surrounded by cooling fins attached to the core of the radiator. To increase the efficiency of the radiator tubes, thin fins are attached to the tubes providing an additional source of cooling. Attached to each fin is a series of tiny louvers (you will need a magnifying glass to see them, but they are there), which can also affect the airflow and the efficiency of the radiator.

The number of louvers, their height, and their angle of attack can all be changed to redirect the airflow through the radiator and to make it more efficient. The more aggressive (the sharper the angle) the louver is in relation to the tubes, the slower the air will pass through the radiator and the more cooling effect the air can provide.

What Is Different About a Fluidyne Aluminum Radiator?

Also important is the size of the radiator tubes themselves. Fluidyne uses two different sizes of radiator tubes, depending on the application. The smaller size tube is 0.9875 or just under one inch while the larger size is 1.6 inch or 40mm. Fluidyne builds single-row radiators using its big diameter tubes, but uses the smaller tubes for most all of the other (two-, three- and four-row) radiators.

According to Gary Johnson, owner of Fluidyne, when you put water through a large radiator tube you get what is called "laminar flow." This is where the coolant nearest the walls of the tube slows way down, but the coolant in the center of the tube keeps moving. This makes the transfer of heat inefficient, because the slow-moving coolant creates a barrier that blocks the transfer of heat.

In contrast, a smaller diameter tube will create more turbulence or "tumbling" of the coolant. This creates better cooling, because more of the coolant is being exposed to the outside of the radiator tube. Therefore, in most cases, one big radiator tube is not nearly as efficient as four smaller tubes when it comes to removing heat from the engine coolant.

If a large-tube radiator is being used because of size restrictions, you can improve the cooling effect of the radiator by making the tubes oval in shape. This causes the coolant inside of the tubes to tumble, which breaks up the heat molecules and transfers them into the fin area of the radiator.

Besides the vertical and horizontal tube design radiators common to the industry, Fluidyne has also developed a "slant tube" radiator design. This design is unique in that the tubes are slanted in the core. The air coming in from the bottom of the car does not have to change direction to come in contact with the tubes. This design greatly improves the efficiency of the radiator.

Fin Density

As the radiator core becomes thicker, the number of fins per inch should be reduced. That is because it is more difficult for air to pass through a thick radiator. With fewer fins, the air will have an easier time getting through the radiator. Sixteen to eighteen fins per inch is about normal for the average two-row radiator. The fin count should be reduced to about twelve fins per inch in the thicker four-core radiators.

When designing any type of radiator, it is important to have a good volume of coolant flow through the tubes, and good airflow through the radiator. If either one of these is off balance with the other, it will greatly reduce the cooling ability of the radiator.

Finally, our last concern should be the sizing of the radiator, in other words, the "core face" or the actual number of square inches of frontal surface area. The core face is determined by the size of the opening at the front of the car, the depth of the core, and the number of fins per inch.

> **When designing any type of radiator, it is important to have a good volume of coolant flow through the tubes, and good airflow through the radiator. If either one of these is off balance with the other, it will greatly reduce the cooling ability of the radiator.**

This Really Works

Let's look at some racing radiator applications, to see what difference radiator construction really makes. According to Fluidyne, most Saturday night racers with modified stock engines usually run a two-row radiator. The NASCAR Busch Series racers with their 700 horsepower engines along with the NASCAR truck series racing teams run a three-row radiator, although somewhat larger in physical size.

The NASCAR Winston Cup Series racers, driving on the superspeedways, want the maximum amount of cooling from the radiator, with the minimum amount of exposed core area—it's an aerodynamics thing. So the Winston Cup teams use a four-row radiator. But it is not as simple as all that. As radiators become thicker, air begins to stack up in front of the radiator, creating a high-pressure area. This causes the air that cannot go through the grille opening or radiator to go up over the top of the race car, creating downforce (which is good), but also adding air drag (which is bad). The secret is to balance the downforce against the amount of airflow needed to keep the engine cool.

There is another benefit to running a thicker core for the Winston Cup cars. Less underhood airflow results in a smaller low-pressure area under the hood. A low-pressure area under the hood tends to create lift—not a good thing at 200 mph.

If a four-row Winston Cup radiator is designed and built correctly, with the right balance of fins vs. tubes, the radiator should be able to keep the engine in the 190-degree operating range. While 190 degrees is considered to be too cool for the engine to make good horsepower, it allows for a cooling system reserve and another trick. Just a two-inch wide strip of duct tape applied to the "grille" mesh fronting the radiator can provide between 50 and 75 pounds of downforce on the front of the car. That allows the stock car to go faster into the corners and can help to improve the car's handling (how each tire grips the racing surface). As a result, the race teams are able to control the operating temperature of the engine (while also changing the handling characteristics of the stock car) simply by adding or removing the duct tape across the mesh fronting the radiator. It is true that the engine operating temperature can be raised or lowered (as much as 30 degrees) this way. But in order to be able to do that, the radiator has to be able to cool the car with the reduced airflow. Pretty sneaky!

Fluidyne has also done extensive wind tunnel testing. One interesting thing learned from this testing was that **no matter how fast a car is traveling, the airflow through the radiator is equivalent to about thirty-three to forty percent of vehicle speed, depending on the thickness of the radiator**. Many racers wrongfully assume that the faster you go, the more air flows through the radiator. In reality, the area in front of the radiator is just so big and there is only so much air you can fit into that space. The rest will go to one side or the other or up over the top of the car.

Also, the amount (volume) of air sitting in front of the radiator is not the same volume of air that is going through the radiator. If that were actually the case, the fins in the radiator (which, by the way, range between .004 inch and .008 inch thick) would be bent flat and crushed.

At the 2-1/2-mile Daytona International Speedway in Florida, for example, when a Winston Cup stock car is racing 190 mph around the racetrack, the airflow through the front of the radiator is *not* 190 mph. Because of the thickness of the radiator core, and the pressure drop caused by the restricted airflow through the radiator core itself, the effect on the front of the radiator is equal to about 55 mph.

The Backside of the Radiator

Likewise, the control of airflow on the back (engine) side of the radiator is a result of the pressure drop between the front and back of the radiator (as well as tube design and arrangement). The amount of airflow allowed to flow through the radiator is also determined by the density of the radiator. The denser (closeness of fins) the radiator, the slower the speed of the airflow will be. It can be slowed enough where the air will actually stall (stop flowing altogether). This can be both a good thing and a bad thing.

If the airflow is stopped completely, it takes away the low-pressure area under the hood, which eliminates the lifting effect. But the airflow through the radiator is also used to help with the cooling of the engine. Even if the air flowing through the radiator is no longer cool (after it has absorbed engine heat from the radiator) that airflow helps to keep air movement going under the hood. If there is no air movement underhood, the engine and exhaust heat will remain trapped under the hood causing a major buildup of heat.

So to design the ideal racing radiator, you need to find the balance between the radiator, water temperature and a certain amount of downforce. By changing the airflow through the radiator, you can also affect the aerodynamics on the back side of the radiator. The balance of the airflow can be controlled by the density of the fins in relation to airflow.

For most applications, a thinner radiator works better. The only way you can benefit from a thicker radiator is if you have enough air velocity available to push the air through the thicker core. **A thinner radiator can actually transfer more heat and do a better job than a thick core radiator, in most applications**. Oftentimes, the pressure buildup in front of a thick radiator gets to a point where no matter how fast you drive, you will not be able to get any more flow through the radiator. There is just too much radiator density for the amount of airflow present.

Exit Air

The next most important element of airflow and radiator design is what happens to the air after it has passed through the radiator and across the engine. The airflow must have some kind of exit path in order to keep from building pressure under the hood. If there is no exit path, then no matter how big your radiator is you will still battle overheating problems.

Fenderwell openings and wheelwell openings can make a big difference in how well the air exits from under the hood. Think also about the cowl induction area (carburetor air intake area) below the windshield. If air is flowing from the outside, into the windshield cowl and then down into the engine compartment, you could unknowingly be building pressure under the hood behind the radiator. If this air begins to dam up, the airflow through the radiator can be greatly reduced or in the case of a thick core radiator, may even stall.

For example, most hot air from under the hood of a Winston Cup stock car exits into the wheelwell opening, where there is a venturi (vacuum) effect present that can actually help draw off the heated air from under the hood. The airflow in the wheel openings also helps to cool the brake rotor assemblies on its way by—another benefit. In NASCAR, nothing is left to chance.

Airflow acts differently in different vehicles. For instance, the new NASCAR truck series vehicles, because of their more square shape and taller height, actually have more trouble with the airflow under the hood causing lift. To overcome the lifting effect, the teams are using larger and thicker radiators (which hold more coolant). This increases the weight on the front of the truck so the teams can attempt to balance the lifting effect and have better control of the truck, while also gaining some coolant reserve.

NASCAR teams spend a great deal of time and money trying to figure out how to control airflow. Downforce is created as air moves over the surface of the car. Downforce helps to hold the car on the track at high speeds and also allows the driver to go faster into a corner. The goal is to manage the airflow, over, around, under, and through the car so the minimum amount of drag is produced while the maximum amount of downforce is captured.

Air Flow and Horsepower

Back in 1998, when the new-design Ford Taurus was introduced to replace the Ford Thunderbird, there was a lot of discussion among the NASCAR officials and other non-Ford teams about the aerodynamic shape of the new car (which, by the way, was the first four-door model approved for NASCAR competition since the organization's inception in 1948). Because of the much improved aerodynamics of the new Taurus over the older Thunderbird design, the new shape was said to be worth a twenty-five to thirty horsepower advantage because of the reduced wind drag. The result was a four to five mph speed advantage. In NASCAR, where new developments result in tiny fractions of horsepower gains or speed advantages, the Taurus was a huge step forward.

Air Flow and Safety

Airflow technology is becoming important as a safety concern as well as a speed advantage. If you will notice most of the Winston Cup and Busch Series stock cars have a 1.5-inch strip of metal attached to the outside of the back glass on the driver's side of the race car. This strip is designed to interrupt the airflow, to prevent the lifting effect that normally occurs when the car begins to spin.

Cars are also being built with air flaps in the cowl area and rear portion of the roof for the same reason. In the event of a spin, the cowl flaps and/or roof flaps are designed to open automatically to help release the air buildup under the hood and/or in the cockpit. This along with the metal attached to the back glass, are designed to work together to keep the car from lifting and turning over in the event of a high-speed spin.

Meanwhile

The secret to making a cooling system work is to make sure you have at least some pressure drop between the front and rear of the radiator. The more of a pressure drop you can create, the better your radiator will be able to cool. Part of ensuring that you have a proper pressure drop is to be sure that you have established airflow exits under the hood.

A two-row radiator with a poor airflow exit can back up as much air as a four-row radiator can with a good exit. The pressure difference would still be the same. That is why there are no hard and fast rules for choosing a radiator. You have to consider all of the possibilities that could affect the end result.

Air Drag

When we talk about air drag, there are actually two different kinds: one is the drag caused by airflow through the radiator, which helps to cool the engine. While this drag can create a downward force, it is not the ideal way, mainly because it is hard to control. The other way to create air drag is by closing off the grille opening at the front of the car. This will cause the airflow to go up over the body of the car. By building downforce in this manner, the air is easier to control and the air drag on the car itself is reduced, resulting in a faster car.

Cooling Fans

Every racer, car builder, and radiator company seems to have a different idea about the value and type of fans that should be on a race car. Some want electric fans because they do not want the horsepower drag associated with mechanical engine-driven fans. Some racers want metal blade mechanical fans because they move more air.

Actual wind tunnel tests have proven that the horsepower drag from a mechanical fan is 2.7 horsepower on a Winston Cup racing engine, while the coolant temperature was reduced by 25 degrees. On the other hand, an electric fan (depending on the size and brand) was proven to be only about two-thirds as efficient. But electric fans can be an advantage in the event the race car is involved in a crash. Because most electric fans are attached to the radiator, a "slight misalignment" from a wreck might not be a problem, whereas a metal blade fan could easily damage the radiator in the same situation.

Three Types of Aluminum Racing Radiators

Vertical flow radiators were once the standard radiator design, until about the 1960s. Vertical flow radiators have the tubes inside of the radiator mounted vertically inside of the core, so the coolant enters the top of the radiator and flows from there to the bottom.

Next came the cross-flow radiator design. As cars became more aerodynamic in design (shorter hoods) and the engines more powerful, a better, more efficient radiator design was needed. With the introduction of the cross-flow design came increased frontal area, more tubes, and better cooling efficiency.

Dual pass is the latest innovation in racing radiators. A dual pass radiator uses a "splitter plate" inside of the radiator to separate one of the tanks. The hot coolant enters the radiator, then drops down to the splitter plate and travels across the top part of the core. The coolant next flows down over the top of the oil cooler, makes another pass through the second half of the radiator, and finally exits the radiator. The benefit of this radiator design is that the coolant is being exposed to the air twice. It is the equivalent of running the engine coolant through two separate radiators.

Dual pass racing radiators are not a "cure all" for every application. In some applications where a high-flow water pump is being used, a single pass radiator works best. The dual pass radiator can reduce the flow rate of the coolant by up to thirty percent. But if a dual pass radiator is used along with an OEM-design water pump, the dual pass radiator can increase the efficiency of a high-performance cooling system by as much as twenty percent.

Another unique aluminum radiator design that Fluidyne has developed is called the circular flow design. Instead of building a conventional dual-flow radiator where a splitter plate is installed horizontally (which causes the coolant to flow through the radiator twice), the circular flow radiator design has the splitter plates installed vertically, which causes the coolant to flow from back to front, then to the back of the other half of the radiator, on to the front again and finally out of the radiator. This design, while not common, does work well in certain specialized racing applications.

Fluidyne is a registered ISO-9001 and QS-9000 company, which means its products meet international standards for quality assurance and design standards. Many countries outside of the United States recognize and endorse the ISO standard ratings and have adopted them as local standards.

Now that we understand how an aluminum radiator is designed to work, I asked Gary Johnson of Fluidyne to list the most common mistakes people make when selecting an aluminum racing radiator. Here is his answer:

"The most common mistake, by far, is the customer tries to buy too big of a radiator for his application. Many racers that call us for a radiator are convinced that they need nothing less than a four core radiator the size of a king size mattress. All of the wrong information they have collected over the years has told them that bigger is better. They see the big NASCAR racing teams use big radiators so naturally they assume that technology applies to them, also, and nothing could be further from the truth.

"Here are some examples, and, by the way, our two core aluminum radiator will cool most any street rod or Saturday night racer application without any problem. **The secret to any radiator is airflow; you have to get the heat transferred out of the fins and the fins have to be in contact with the air in order for the heat to be drawn off. So naturally, the thicker the radiator, the less air flows through the radiator and the less efficient the radiator is.**

"You also have to take into consideration what the vehicle is, and how it is going to be driven. A street rod cruising a fairgrounds at 30 mph is much different than an Indy (open wheel) race car making laps at 150 mph. Besides the airflow difference, the construction and shape of the cars, and everything else surrounding the radiator is much different between the two.

"On a scale of one to ten, here is how the difference in aluminum radiators stack up: a vertical flow design would be a nine, while a cross-flow design would be a ten, a vertical splitter design would be an eleven, and the circular flow design a twelve. But there are other factors, such as the airflow to the radiator and the environment it is going to be used in, that really decide which radiator design to use.

"A properly designed cooling system can be equal to or, in some cases, more efficient using a simple cross-flow radiator than a poorly-designed system that uses a more expensive circular flow radiator."

Things That Make an Engine Run Hot

Aside from a poorly designed cooling system, there are a number of things that can make an engine run hot, according to Gary Johnson. The radiator often catches the blame instead of the actual problem. They include:

1) "Timing is important. Every engine makes horsepower differently. For example, the General Motors V-6 engines that are used in the late model stock cars—the trick with them is to retard timing as far as you can go and still keep the engine running. These engines then develop a nasty attitude and run like an engine with 12:1 compression. But at the end of the race, the cylinder heads are glowing cherry red! You can't expect a cooling system to keep up with that abuse.

2) "Airflow into the cooling system; if you don't have good airflow to the front of the radiator and then through the radiator, your cooling system is not going to work well, no matter how big of a radiator you buy.

3) "Cylinder head gaskets and how well they seal is important. Through our research we have found that a leaking cylinder head gasket can leak the combustion chamber gases into the coolant, which causes the coolant to be heated excessively. At the same time, the coolant does not leak into the cylinder, therefore, the problem does not show up as a cylinder head gasket failure.

4) "High oil temperatures. A car running oil temperatures of 300 degrees will cause the coolant in the engine to overheat as well, because the oil is already saturated with heat and is not able to draw off some of the engine heat as it should. In contrast, if the engine oil temperature is around 190 degrees it can help draw off some of the engine heat. The simple rule that applies here is that oil can help the radiator, but the radiator cannot help the oil.

5) "The age of the aluminum radiator itself (and the care it has had) can make a big difference in its cooling ability. As radiators age, a corrosive film develops both on the inside and the outside surfaces of the radiator. As a result, this film acts as an insulator, trapping the heat inside of the radiator. It is important that when an aluminum radiator is drained that the cap is replaced to seal out the air and reduce the corrosion effect.

6) "Radiator additives can shorten a radiator's useful life. Read the labels carefully. I have seen some really strange things put into radiators such as concrete patch (silicone silicate), which is normally used to seal cracks in concrete walls to keep out moisture. An additive like that might work to stop leaks, but the radiator itself won't last the season with that kind of additive inside. Most NASCAR teams have three different aluminum radiators (set up for the different types of tracks, and the amount of airflow available). All three are replaced at least every season, sometimes more often.

7) "Salt water is damaging to aluminum radiators, and many races are held on and around beaches, which increase the exposure to salt water. It is interesting to note that salt water, while highly corrosive, is actually better than pure water at dispersing heat! It is true that the alkali in the salt water helps to carry away the heat.

8) "Water pump speed. Often, you will hear people say you need to slow the coolant flow so it spends more time in the radiator and has a chance to cool more. While the idea is correct, the reason they believe it works is not. The correct reason you want to slow the flow of coolant is so the coolant doesn't foam, and air doesn't get trapped in the cooling system. Neither air nor foamy coolant can provide any cooling benefit. Also, despite what you may have been told, you do need to run a thermostat in your street engine. Running a street car without a thermostat will make your overheating worse, in most cases. This is because the thermostat acts as a restriction in the cooling system to build pressure behind the coolant pump, so air isn't drawn into the pump. Race cars that do not run thermostats use what are called "restrictor plates" instead, which—not to be confused with the carburetor restrictor plates mandated by NASCAR for the two largest superspeedways to "slow" cars to under 200 mph—are big flat washers with a five-eighths-inch hole in the center to accomplish the same thing as having a thermostat in place. This also helps build pressure against the coolant pump.

9) "Also, high-pressure cooling systems can cause overheating. Some NASCAR teams have tried thirty-pound pressure radiator caps. While it does raise the boiling point of water to over 300 degrees, it also swells and distorts the radiator. In addition, the flat/oval-shaped tubes inside of the radiator become round and twisted and eventually become pinched off at the top and bottom of the radiator, restricting the flow of coolant. This is sometimes difficult to detect at first glance, but there is little doubt the radiator is ruined. If the cooling system is designed properly, a fourteen to eighteen-pound cap should be more than sufficient for most applications. We test each of our radiators using twenty-four pounds of pressure to ensure there is a margin of safety."

Aluminum Radiator Construction

It was in the early 1970s that the first aluminum radiators were tried in racing applications. It was "King" Richard Petty who got one of the first aluminum radiators that was a whopping five rows thick! It looked like a massive radiator and it was. It also came with an outrageous (for the time) price tag of $2,800 per copy!

So why the five rows thick? Because the technology had not been developed to braze aluminum together successfully. One of the problems was that if the fins and the tubes were assembled too closely together, an arc would occur as the radiator was being brazed inside of the furnace, which immediately burned a hole in the tube of the radiator.

Because there was no immediate solution to the problem, extra rows of tubes were added to the radiator. When a leaking tube was discovered, it was simply pinched off, because there was (in theory) plenty of extras. This is also why the early aluminum radiators used epoxy to set the tanks—it provided an access to the tubes in case of a leak, and there were plenty of leaks in those early days!

Today, most all quality aluminum radiators are manufactured using the Nocolok Process, which eliminates all of the arcing and problems associated with building aluminum radiators. As a result, the cooling fins can be placed next to the edge of the radiator for increased cooling, and the radiator itself is stronger because there is no epoxy used. Best of all, there is no worry about leaks.

Because of the high initial cost of buying the equipment associated with the Nocolok Process, some aftermarket companies elect instead to vacuum braze the fins and tube (core assembly) together. A high grade epoxy is then installed around all of the tubes as they pass from the sheet tube area (around the tubes) into the tank. This type of radiator is not quite as strong, nor as efficient, as a Nocolok Process radiator, because the epoxy material used has a tendency to block the heat transfer. In addition, the cooling fins cannot run all the way to the edge of the tube sheet area because there has to be room remaining for the epoxy sealer.

Fluidyne is the only (as this book is being written) aftermarket company that is building aluminum radiators using the more expensive Nocolok Process. In addition, there is only one other major aftermarket aluminum radiator company that owns a furnace and is set up to build its own cores. Most aftermarket aluminum radiators are "assembled" using the epoxy sealing process. The epoxy process has been around for a number of years and is still being used in many applications.

The original equipment manufacturers (OEM) first used epoxy welded radiators beginning about 1987, and continued to use them through the 1994 model year. Since then, they have made the investment in equipment to build radiators using the Nocolok Process. Ford's radiator plant, as of 1998, was building 70 Nocolok Process radiators per hour.

Economy Racing Radiators

Did you ever wonder where the really cheap racing radiators come from and if they are really any different from the more expensive ones? Here is how some companies do it cheaply. They buy (in large truckload quantities) all of the radiator core assemblies left over from the "Big Three" automakers (Chrysler, Ford and General Motors), epoxy tanks to them and then sell them as racing radiators.

While there is actually nothing wrong with these radiators in most cases (they are new radiators...), they are not designed or engineered for actual racing applications. As a result, these radiators will not perform as well, or survive as long, when they are used in an actual (hard use) racing application. Just another example of "You can't get something for nothing."

Although you may not recall the Fluidyne name, you have seen the company's handiwork in a host of racing applications. Its customer list is packed with names from NASCAR, the World of Outlaws sprint car series, Dodge Viper racing team as well as being the "Official Radiator of IROC" (International Race of Champions).

Notes

Chapter 23:
More "Cool" Stuff

Besides all of the trick radiators and thermostats, cooling hoses, and related components we have already learned about, there are a few more things that we need to discuss, in case you are working on a "You'll never fit that in there and drive it" project..

Street and Performanc

I spoke with Mark Campbell, of Street and Performance, a company well-known for its ability to build cars with blown (supercharged) engines that will live on the street. I asked Mark if it was reasonable to expect a blown (supercharger-powered) car to be able to cruise a fairgrounds, or be driven in stop-and-go traffic without overheating. Here is his answer:

"Of course that is reasonable, but you have to set up the car correctly first. Don't run timing way advanced, and don't put a big thick radiator in front of the engine (which I see happening to all types of street rods). A thick core radiator makes it difficult for the air to circulate through the radiator, especially at idle and slow speeds. A thick core radiator can also limit the airflow at highway speeds. If the radiator is too thick, the air will flow to either side or up over the top of the radiator instead of through it.

"Another important thing is to be sure all of the sheet metal panels are replaced under the car. If you remove the panel that goes between the radiator and the grille, for instance, when you are stuck in traffic, the engine fan will draw the hot air out from under the car and right back through the front of the radiator. So you are just recycling the hot air. You need to have that sheet metal in place, so the air being drawn into the radiator has to come from the front of the car through the grille opening, and not from under the car.

"The cause of many street rods overheating is poor airflow through the engine compartment and where it is directed after it leaves the car. Big-block cars, especially, generate a lot of engine heat and you can't expect the radiator and cooling system to do it all. You need to have good airflow both in the front of the radiator and beyond, so once the air has absorbed the engine heat, it can be drawn away from the car and replaced with fresh air.

"At the same time, you do not want the airflow too fast, or it will not have enough time to absorb any of the engine heat. You have to find the balance between good airflow and good air/heat absorption. We offer a number of cooling system accessories to help keep your engine cool (see Appendix B for contact information)."

Many thanks to Mark for taking time out of his busy schedule to share some of his tech tips with us.

Weiand High-Flow Water Pumps

Weiand is another company well-known in hot rod circles, having been around since 1930. The company has literally grown up with hot rodding, and true to form, has been doing its share of work in the engine cooling department. What follows are some of the products the company offers to improve cooling system performance.

Weiand's series of cast-iron water pumps—an improvement of the stock design cast-iron pumps, which require less horsepower. They work well in the "claimer class" racing divisions.

Weiand aluminum "Action-Plus" series water pumps—these pumps are thirty to fifty percent lighter than stock OEM pumps, and feature a heavy-duty shaft with a five-eighths-inch pilot. They are designed to limit cavitation and work well on high-performance street applications.

Weiand Team G water pumps—these are designed for oval track competition and will provide ample coolant flow under the most demanding racing conditions. These pumps feature a whole list of improvements over stock water pumps. One of the things unique to Weiand is that the company has built its own water pump dynamometer test stand. This water pump dyno can be used not only to test existing pumps, but also to aid in the research and development of new pump designs.

Every Weiand water pump is pressure tested before it leaves the factory to ensure there will be no water leaks once the pump is installed. For drag racing applications, Weiand also offers electric water pumps for cooling, without robbing valuable horsepower. These electric pumps can be either manually or thermostatically controlled.

Weiand Cooling System Accessories

In addition to the water pumps, both electric and mechanical, Weiand also offers a host of cooling-related accessories for performance applications.

Weiand is a company well-known to many hot rodders. Weiand was started in 1930 by Phil Weiand and first offered speed parts for the early automobiles. It was in 1937 that Weiand introduced its first product, an aluminum performance intake manifold for the Flathead Ford. The Weiand Flathead Ford intake manifold was the first aftermarket aluminum intake manifold on the market. Aluminum high-compression cylinder heads for the Flathead Ford soon followed after the war ended. Hemi engine manifolds were

Six Decades of Progress

WEIAND

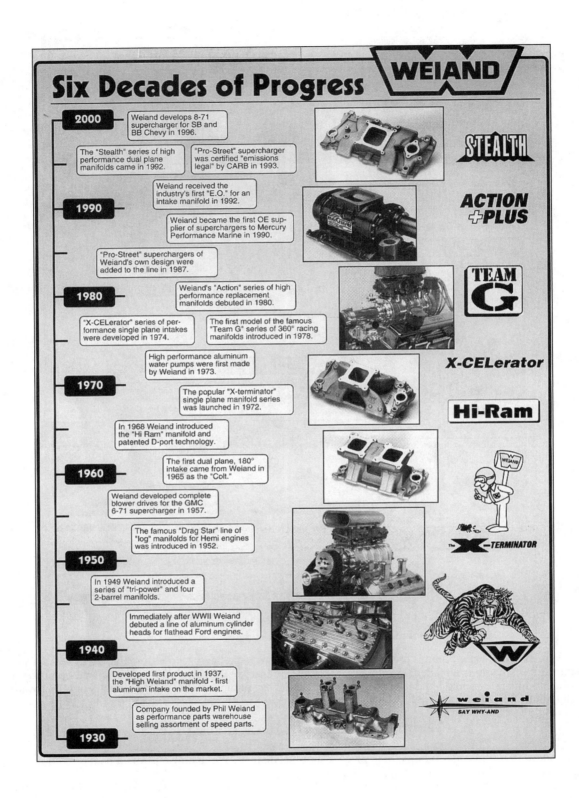

2000

Weiand develops 8-71 supercharger for SB and BB Chevy in 1996.

The "Stealth" series of high performance dual plane manifolds came in 1992.

"Pro-Street" supercharger was certified "emissions legal" by CARB in 1993.

Weiand received the industry's first "E.O." for an intake manifold in 1992.

1990

Weiand became the first OE supplier of superchargers to Mercury Performance Marine in 1990.

"Pro-Street" superchargers of Weiand's own design were added to the line in 1987.

1980

Weiand's "Action" series of high performance replacement manifolds debuted in 1980.

"X-CELerator" series of performance single plane intakes were developed in 1974.

The first model of the famous "Team G" series of 360° racing manifolds introduced in 1978.

High performance aluminum water pumps were first made by Weiand in 1973.

1970

The popular "X-terminator" single plane manifold series was launched in 1972.

In 1968 Weiand introduced the "Hi Ram" manifold and patented D-port technology.

The first dual plane, 180° intake came from Weiand in 1965 as the "Colt."

1960

Weiand developed complete blower drives for the GMC 6-71 supercharger in 1957.

The famous "Drag Star" line of "log" manifolds for Hemi engines was introduced in 1952.

1950

In 1949 Weiand introduced a series of "tri-power" and four 2-barrel manifolds.

Immediately after WWII Weiand debuted a line of aluminum cylinder heads for flathead Ford engines.

1940

Developed first product in 1937, the "High Weiand" manifold - first aluminum intake on the market.

Company founded by Phil Weiand as performance parts warehouse selling assortment of speed parts.

1930

STEALTH

ACTION +PLUS

TEAM G

X-CELerator

Hi-Ram

The X-TERMINATOR

weiand
SAY WHY-AND

Water Pumps ACTION-PLUS Aluminum/Mechanical

WEIAND

WEIAND's lightweight, performance aluminum mechanical Water Pumps give a weight savings of 30-50% over stock cast-iron pumps. All water pumps feature a heavy-duty shaft with a 5/8" pilot. WEIAND's high-performance Action-Plus Water Pumps use high-quality, heavy-duty, precision bearings that have twice the load capacity of most stock pumps.

The stamped steel impellers will not crack, fatigue or corrode and are designed to limit cavitation at high rpm. All pumps are designed with the necessary bracket bosses and water connections to fit popular street applications. WEIAND's high-performance Action-Plus Water Pumps are a **MUST** for today's hotter running engines!

Note: Action-Plus water pumps are **not** for competition, use Team G pumps on **page 50-51.**

Aluminum Short Water Pumps

Chevrolet Small Block V-8 and 90° V-6
Part No. 8208   ACTION-PLUS Aluminum water pump, Satin
Part No. 8208P   ACTION-PLUS Aluminum water pump, Polished*
Fits 1972 and earlier trucks, 1968 and earlier cars short water pump applications. 1969 and later application may require #8207 water pump spacer kit for correct alignment.   Shpg. wt. - 6 lbs.

Part No. 8207   Water pump spacer kit, Satin
Part No. 8207P   Water pump spacer kit, Polished
Use on 1969 and later Chevrolet small block V-8 and 90° V-6 for correct pulley alignment.
     Shpg. wt. - 2 lbs.

Chevrolet Big Block
Part No. 8212   ACTION-PLUS Aluminum water pump, Satin
Part No. 8212P   ACTION-PLUS Aluminum water pump, Polished
Fits short water pump applications.   Shpg. wt. - 9 lbs.

See photo at bottom of page for polished version.

#8208

#8207

#8212

Aluminum Long Water Pumps

Chevrolet Small Block V-8 and 90° V-6
Part No. 8240   ACTION-PLUS Aluminum Water Pump, Satin
Part No. 8240P   ACTION-PLUS Aluminum Water Pump, Polished
Fits 1969 to 1986 passenger cars and 1973 to 1986 light trucks. Will not fit Corvette. Use #8208 or #8222.   Shpg. wt. 8 lbs.
NOTE: *Not for use on serpentine drive belt equipped vehicles.*

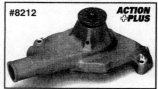

#8240

Chevrolet Big Block
Part No. 8242   ACTION-PLUS Aluminum Water Pump, Satin
Part No. 8242P   ACTION-PLUS Aluminum Water Pump, Polished
Fits 1969 to 1987 big block passenger cars and light trucks originally equipped with a long style pump.
Will not fit Corvette. Use #8212 or #8224.   Shpg. wt. 11 lbs.
NOTE: *Not for use on serpentine drive belt equipped vehicles.*

#8242

Water Pump Dimensions

Description	Dimension A
Small Block Chevy Short Water Pump	5.625"
Small Block Chevy Long Water Pump	6.90"
Small Block Chevy "Corvette" Water Pump	5.80"
Big Block Chevy Short Water Pump	5.75"
Big Block Chevy Long Water Pump	7.25"

Dimensions apply to all Chevy Mechanical Water Pumps in this catalog.

◄— **A** —►

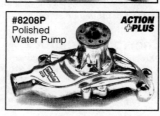

#8208P Polished Water Pump

Water Pumps

 WEIAND has an extensive line of belt-driven aluminum water pumps that include **TEAM G models for competition applications**. They are offered for both "standard" and "Corvette" small block and big block Chevy.

The WEIAND TEAM G competition pump is ideally suited to oval track competition. It is designed to provide an ample flow of coolant under the most demanding race conditions. And to achieve these goals, each unit contains the following features:

1. Rugged 356-T6 aluminum alloy casting with extra reinforcements
2. Hefty 3/4" shaft with 5/8" or 3/4" fan snout
3. Extra heavy-duty bearings
4. Housing counterbored for bearing retention
5. Adjustable cam thrust stop (S/B only)
6. Highly efficient design cast alloy impeller
7. Optional slotted mounts with locking adjuster to allow setting belt tension
8. 1/2" NPT auxiliary outlets
9. Precision machined 1/2" steel billet hub (dual bolt pattern)
10. Smooth, efficient flow passages
11. Severe-duty seal assembly

There is nothing finer in terms of performance and reliability than a WEIAND TEAM G competition aluminum water pump. There are special design features that are exclusive to WEIAND. And extensive test data confirms that nothing out-flows or out-lasts a WEIAND pump!

TEAM G Short Water Pumps

Chevrolet Corvette Small Block

Part No. 8220 Standard aluminum **TEAM G** water pump, Satin
Part No. 8221 *Adjustable* aluminum **TEAM G** water pump, Satin
Fits 1971-82 Corvette water pump applications. Has 3/4" fan snout. Adjustable model (#8221) has slots and locking adjusters.
Shpg. wt. - 7 lbs.

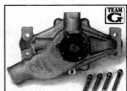

#8220

Chevrolet Small Block V8 and 90° V6

Part No. 8222 Standard aluminum **TEAM G** water pump, Satin
Part No. 8223 *Adjustable* aluminum **TEAM G** water pump, Satin
Fits 1968 and earlier short water pump applications. Converts to long design with part no. 8207 spacers. Has 5/8" fan snout. Adjustable model (#8223) has slots and locking adjusters.
Shpg. wt. - 7 lbs.

#8223

Chevrolet Big Block

Part No. 8224 Standard aluminum **TEAM G** water pump, Satin
Fits short water pump applications.   Shpg. wt. - 9 lbs.

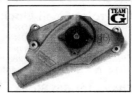

#8224

TEAM G Long Water Pumps

Chevrolet Small Block V8 and 90° V6

Part No. 8241 Standard aluminum **TEAM G** water pump, Satin
Fits 1969 to 1986 passenger cars and 1973 to 1986 light trucks. Will not fit Corvette. Use #8208 or #8222.   Shpg. wt. 9 lbs.
NOTE: *Not for use on serpentine drive belt equipped vehicles.*

#8241

Chevrolet Big Block

Part No. 8243 Standard aluminum **TEAM G** water pump, Satin
Fits 1969 to 1987 big block passenger cars and light trucks originally equpped with a long style pump.
Will not fit Corvette. Use #8212 or #8224.   Shpg. wt. 11 lbs.
NOTE: *Not for use on serpentine drive belt equipped vehicles.*

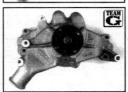

#8243

Accessories Cooling System

Water Flow Restrictor Plates

Mounts under water neck on intake manifold. Supplied with 3 different sized plates (5/8", 3/4" and 1" opening) to restrict water flow for improved heat dissipation and cooling. Allows you to control water flow for optimum efficiency. Fits all GM V-8s, GM V-6s and small block Fords.

Part No. 8229 - Water Flow Restrictor Plates (set of 3)

#8229

Water Pump Pulley Spacer Kit

Universal kit works with just about any GM or Ford water pump with a 5/8" or 3/4" shaft. Fits between the water pump pulley and drive flange. Contains two 1/16" and one 1/8" shims. Allows placement of water pump pulley in perfect alignment with other components.
Part No. 8230 - Pulley Spacer Kit (set of 3)

#8230

Thermostat Housing

Facilitates use of AN -16 stainless steel braided line upper radiator hose. Precision machined aerospace alloy aluminum component has recess to accommodate thermostat or flow restrictor plate (P/N 8229). Mounting hardware also includes O-ring.
Part No. 8231 - Thermostat Housing

#8231

Thermostatic Switch Assembly

Designed for use with WEIAND TEAM G electric water pump and similar 12v units. Toggle switch has three stationary settings; manual "on,""automatic" and "off." In automatic mode, pump is activated when water temperature reaches 165°F (± 5°F) and turns off when temperature drops to 147°F (±5°F). The standard on/off modes override any automatic functions. Requires a 10-amp circuit fuse (not included).
Part No. 8228 Thermostatic Switch Assembly

#8228

Water Pump/Radiator Hose Adapters

Precision machined from aerospace aluminum alloy and hard anodized for extra durability. Facilitates use of all popular type radiator hose setups with WEIAND electrical water pumps.
Part No. 8225 - Adapts 1" NPT to AN-16 hose
Part No. 8226 - Adapts 1" NPT to 1-1/4" hose
Part No. 8227 - Adapts 1" NPT to 1-3/4" hose

#8225   #8226   #8227

introduced in 1952, followed by supercharger blower drives in 1957. The innovations continued throughout the years. Weiand introduced its high-flow aluminum water pumps in 1973, long before high-flow pumps became popular for street use. Twenty-plus years of experience has served the company well.

Brodix Racing Products

In an earlier chapter, we talked about how the 1998 Corvette and Camaro/Firebird engines were plumbed from the factory with coolant lines out of the rear of the cylinder heads. Wait, I can see your mind is racing forward; you are no doubt wondering if that same setup would work on your big-block Chevrolet

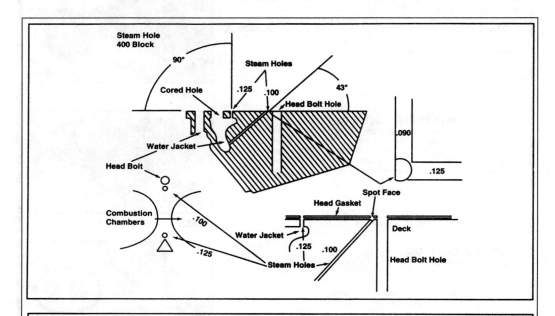

ITEMS NEEDED:

1   **.125 Drill 2 in. long**
1   **.100 Drill 4 in. long**
1   **.125 End Mill 2 flute for spot face**
1   **Sharp Center Punch**
1   **Scribe**

Scribe holes to match gasket. Center punch 90° holes, spot face 45° holes, then center punch. Drill approximately 2 1/2 in. deep into water jacket.

**STEAM HOLES ABSOLUTELY MUST NOT LAP OVER
INTO THE HEAD GASKET SEALING RING AREA.**

For increased water circulation between heads & block the following
3/8" holes may be drilled in the block to match cast holes in head:

THIS IS AN OPTIONAL OPERATION

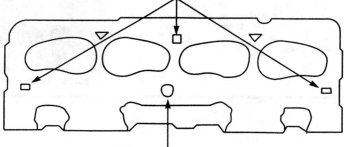

Enlarge small hole in head gasket to 3/8"

3/8" holes must be punched in head gasket. A hardened leather punch is acceptable for this.

Recommended Water Circulation System

Brodix recommends this type of plumbing to any Canted Valve, 18º or 15º cylinder head. Any holes tapped into the cylinder should be at least 3/8 and in some instances 1/2 pipe thread. The hose size generally accepted is at least -8 and in some instances as large as -10 or -12.

engine in your 1934 coupe as well. You're in luck! Brodix describes how to modify (drill and tap) your cylinder heads and how to plumb them into the cooling system.

This setup really does work well because, as we learned earlier, the buildup of vapor in the rear of the cylinder heads is often the cause of coolant flow being restricted (because of the vapor barrier created), which causes the already established hot spot to grow larger, making the problem worse. As much as a thirty degree difference in operating temperature has been achieved by tapping into the back of the cylinder heads.

If you are running a high horsepower engine in a street rod or racing application, it might be worth your time to install this kit. Even standard street rod applications can benefit because of the lack of airflow associated with most engine-chassis combinations.

The accompanying photos (courtesy of Brodix) show the template for modifying the cylinder heads and the gasket. Also shown is the correct size of plumbing line to use and the correct routing. The modified thermostat housing is available from Brodix. If you are interested in doing this, check with your local performance machine shop, which should already be aware of this procedure, or consult Brodix for more information (see Appendix B).

Notes

Chapter 24: Best of the Old and the New

There are times in life when a project calls for the best of the old and the new. This may include the use of modern technology, while still maintaining the integrity of the old design and styling. For example, suppose you were building a really first-class street rod, say a 1936 Ford. You want the radiator to be made from German Silver to reflect the character of the car. You also want the radiator to be of the original design and appearance, but you are replacing the original Ford engine with a modern Chevrolet LT-1 performance small-block engine for increased reliability and performance.

You also want to incorporate air conditioning into the car, which means you will need an air conditioner condenser, electric fan, and, perhaps, a fan shroud and overflow recovery tank. Your car will have an automatic transmission, so the new radiator will also need accommodations for automatic transmission cooling lines. How would you design and build a radiator with all of these features that is still able to retain the original design appearance of the 1936 Ford radiator?

Shown here is a 1933 Ford polished German silver street rod radiator set up for an LT-1 with an electric fan, fan shroud, hidden overflow tank, and AC condenser.

You could go visit the BrassWorks, which has built just such a radiator. BrassWorks has a well-known reputation for building some of the best hand-crafted radiators available. The quality is outstanding. The company builds many one-of-a-kind radiators, and is able to incorporate many modern features into vintage-looking radiators—often considered impossible. A quick tour through the BrassWorks' catalog shows examples of some of its quality work. It has built hand-crafted radiators for vehicles such as the 1957 Chevrolet, 1924 Ford-based hot rods, 1948 Chrysler firetruck, 1936 Ford and even a 1920s Speedster featuring a Livington Super "V" radiator (considered the ultimate racing radiator of its time).

BrassWorks is also able to recreate the exact original radiators for famous marques such as Mercedes-Benz, Bugatti and Rolls-Royce. Besides hand-crafting a completely new radiator, BrassWorks is also able to recore and restore vintage radiators to original specifications.

BrassWorks Water Pumps

In addition to its radiators, BrassWorks also offers a line of high-output water pumps. Because many overheating problems can be traced to poor coolant circulation, increasing the coolant flow through the engine and radiator can often solve an overheating problem, especially when the overheating occurs at idle and low rpm (such as with the air conditioning on high, while idling in traffic).

BrassWorks' FlowKooler high-output water pump doubles the flow of engine coolant at idle and low rpm. Once the engine reaches about 3500 rpm, the flow rate returns to normal to prevent too much coolant flow at high rpm.

The FlowKooler features a specially designed impeller for increased efficiency, along with an anti-cavitation design that helps prevent water pump cavitation. Independent tests have shown that a FlowKooler

In The Details

Every radiator is custom-built to order by a craftsman for a customer who cares how it looks. Hidden overflow tanks, polished fan shrouds, secret pressure caps built inside original-style filler necks, and oddly-shaped, sized, or positioned inlets and outlets are no problem.

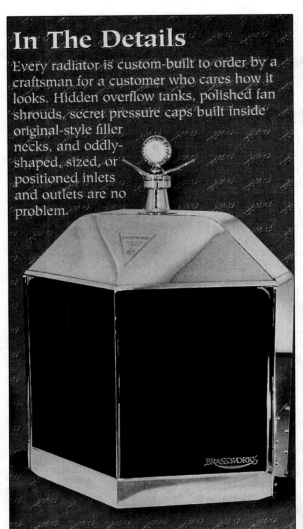

water pump will flow twenty percent more coolant at 2000 rpm (engine rpm) and 100 percent more coolant flow at 900 rpm engine speed. Research has also shown that a FlowKooler water pump creates twenty-two percent more coolant pressure inside of the cooling system (which helps to suppress engine hot spots, steam pockets and premature detonation).

In addition to the higher output at low speeds, BrassWorks' FlowKooler water pump has been proven to be up to thirty-two percent more efficient than some OEM-style water pumps. As a result, the engine operating temperatures can be reduced as much as thirty degrees in traffic.

BrassWorks has sold over 60,000 FlowKooler water pumps and the unique design of the water pump is patent pending. The accompanying charts illustrate the coolant flow at various engine rpm as well as the gallons per minute rate as compared to other water pumps. For more information on BrassWorks radiators or its line of FlowKooler water pumps you can contact the company direct (see Appendix B in the back of this book). By the way, BrassWorks recommends Robertshaw "high-performance balanced thermostats" (discussed in Chapter 21) for use in its cooling systems (again, see Appendix B).

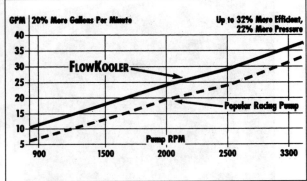

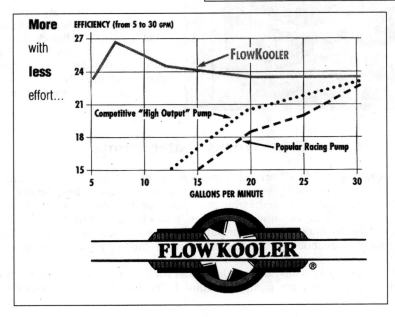

HOW TO ORDER A FLOWKOOLER WATER PUMP

1) What thermostat do you want? What thermostat do you need? We recommend and sell Robertshaw high-flow Extra Performance thermostats for use with our FLOWKOOLER water pumps (this is not a standard Robertshaw reverse poppet OEM-style thermostat as sold over the counter in parts stores). The Extra Performance thermostat allows the increased output of our pumps to flow easily throughout the cooling system. They are what are called "balanced sleeve" thermostats. They are cleverly designed to respond only to temperature changes, not pressure changes. This means that they are not affected by pump pressure surges on the back side of the opening (OEM-style reverse poppet thermostats are adversely affected by pressure surges). If you don't get an Extra Performance thermostat from us when you buy a FLOWKOOLER water pump, get one from somewhere else, because without a balanced sleeve thermostat, the full potential of the FLOWKOOLER water pump is not going to be realized.

The EPA would like to see a higher opening temperature (205°) for a cleaner-running engine. Most street rodders want to maximize their cooling, so they tend to select 180° or even 160° opening settings. We stock all four settings for most applications (160°, 180°, 195°, and 205°), so the choice is yours. For most applications, we'd go with the 180° setting unless you've really got a hot-running engine on your hands. The 160° setting, if you live in a cold climate, is going to make heater use a bit marginal in the winter, and (summer or winter), the 160° setting will, in theory, wear out your engine faster due to the cooler operating temperature of the oil and friction surfaces.

2) Do you want stock cast iron, aluminum, polished aluminum, or chrome? If you want chrome, you're out of luck. We do not sell polished chrome water pumps because all our pumps are brand new (and come with a lifetime replacement warranty). They are not the rebuilt old-style pump (with the heater hose outlet located off on the side of the pump, as opposed to the new, less aesthetically pleasing location on top of the pump) preferred by most chrome pump customers.

We do carry small block Chevy "short" aluminum water pumps and can also provide them in polished aluminum if desired. No aluminum "long" pumps are available. Many of the other stock water pumps we offer are also made out of aluminum (most Ford, Chrysler, and Pontiac, for example), and can therefore be custom polished at extra cost (cost varies depending on pump).

Our cast iron pumps are the least expensive and constitute the bulk of our sales. Most of our customers are not show car owners; they're generally street rodders or stock car, truck, or RV owners who want to solve an overheating problem as inexpensively as possible.

STANDARD, REVERSE ROTATION, AND OPEN WATER PUMPS
(CLOCKWISE, COUNTERCLOCKWISE, AND BI-DIRECTIONAL)

Refer to the belt path diagram under the hood, typically located on the fan shroud or front fender brace, or locate the water pump pulleys on the vehicle.

Compare the diagrams below. Water pump pulleys running on the **inside** surface of the belt indicate a **Standard Rotation** water pump (grooved side of belt).

Water pump pulleys running on the **outside** surface of the belt indicate a **Reverse Rotation** water pump (flat or smooth side of belt).

CAUTION: STANDARD AND REVERSE ROTATION WATER PUMPS ARE NOT INTERCHANGEABLE.

Serious engine damage can result from the use of the wrong pump.

When the question arises, "Is this a standard or reverse rotation water pump?", the customer's own vehicle holds the clearest answer. Under the hood on most late-model light trucks and automobiles, is a belt path diagram. Locate the water pump pulley on the diagram (on the front of the engine if you cannot find the diagram). Simply determine if the water pump is driven by the inside or outside of the belt.

EXAMPLES OF OPEN IMPELLER AND DIRECTIONAL IMPELLER CHAMBER DESIGNS

Open or Bi-Directional Impeller Chamber Design
(FlowKooler Water Pump #1659)

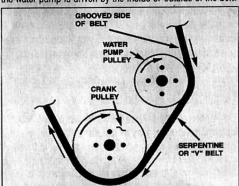

Standard or Clockwise Rotation Water Pump
(inside of belt)

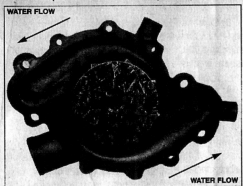

Standard or Clockwise Directional Impeller Chamber Design (FlowKooler Water Pump #1731)

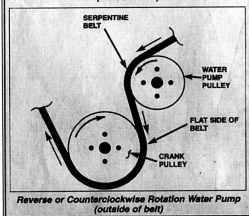

Reverse or Counterclockwise Rotation Water Pump
(outside of belt)

Reverse or Counterclockwise Impeller Chamber Design (FlowKooler Water Pump #1660)

FLOWKOOLER WATER PUMP INSTALLATION INSTRUCTIONS

BEFORE INSTALLING YOUR NEW FLOWKOOLER WATER PUMP

1) Disconnect battery.

2) Drain coolant. Thoroughly flush and drain the cooling system.

3) Check hoses, clamps, radiator. Examine the hoses, clamps, and the radiator and cap. Repair or replace if necessary.

4) Gain working room. If necessary for working room, remove the radiator, fan shroud, and other components. A few minutes spent analyzing adjacent components and removing those in the way may save you hours of lost labor.

5) Remove belts. Remove all belts that ride on the fan pulley.

6) Remove the fan. Remove the fan and inspect it carefully. **Important:** A flying fan blade can be deadly! If you detect any evidence of cracks or bends in a fan, replace it. Never try to straighten or repair a fan.

7) Inspect fan clutch. If a fan clutch is present, check it for evidence of fluid leakage. If the fan spins more than five revolutions when turned by hand, the fan clutch mechanism should be replaced. *Faulty fan clutches are a major cause of overheating.* (See Fan Clutch Overview, page 32.)

HOW TO INSTALL YOUR NEW FLOWKOOLER WATER PUMP

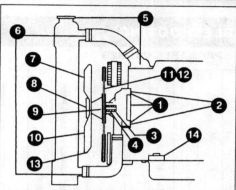

1) Flush cooling system if it shows signs of corrosion. Clean pump impeller cavity and gasket surface. Tighten back plate mounting bolts where applicable.

2) Position new gaskets after coating them on both sides with sealer. Check rivet head clearance with open back impeller chamber type pumps before coating gaskets (see instructions in box).

3) Carefully install new pump. *Do not strike shaft!* Tighten pump bolts hand-tight, then torque them in a criss-cross pattern to manufacturer's specifications. **Note:** On some applications, it is necessary to apply a sealant to the mounting bolt threads. If there are traces of old sealant on bolts, or evidence of corrosion of the bolts (from contact with coolant), clean threads and apply sealant.

4) Turn pump shaft by hand. It should move freely.

5) Check thermostat and radiator cap. Replace if they show signs of sticking or leaking.

6) Connect hoses and fill cooling system. Check for leaks. Fill system according to manufacturer's procedures.

7) Check fan blade for cracks, bent blades, loose rivets, etc. *Never straighten a bent blade!* If any defects are found, replace the entire fan.

8) Check fan clutch (if used) for loss of oil, looseness, or wobble. A bad or misaligned clutch will damage pump. (See Fan Clutch Overview, page E.)

9) Check that the fan pulley (or clutch, if used) sits square on the pump hub. Using lockwashers, torque bolts evenly to assure wobble-free operation.

10) Rotate fan by hand and check for fan wobble: ³⁄₃₂″ maximum at outer edge (with no fan clutch); ¼″ maximum with fan clutch.

11) Check belts for cracks, frayed edges, missing sections. If in doubt, replace belt(s).

12) Adjust fan belt(s) to proper tension, using commercial tension gauge, if available. Or lay straight edge between alternator and pump pulley and adjust belt deflection to ½″ to ¾″. (See vehicle manufacturer's specifications for recommended tension.)

13) Check fan clearances at blade tip, between fan and shroud, and fan and radiator.

14) Check motor mounts for wear or splitting. Check bolt tightness, cracked or damaged rubber in mounts. A broken motor mount will let the engine "rise up" under load, causing the fan blades to contact the shroud, hoses, etc.; this results in damage to all, including the water pump.

15) Start engine and run until normal operating temperature is reached. Check for leaks and for smooth operation. *Never stand in line with or near fan when revving engine!* For your own protection, the hood should be closed when revving engine.

Note: Many things can cause water pump failure, including defective, crooked, or unbalanced fans; defective or unbalanced fan clutches; excessive (too tight) fan belt tension; dirty cooling systems; insufficient clearance between fan and shroud or radiator; loose or broken motor mounts. *Check everything when you have the chance; help avoid future water pump failures.* This product intended only for use as originally specified by the OEM manufacturer and/or the catalog.

Caution: The addition of more water than recommended will raise the freezing protection temperature and weaken the corrosion inhibitors. Refer to specifications for the cooling system capacity for all vehicles.

Note: The system must be maintained with the correct concentration and type of antifreeze to prevent corrosion damage. The coolant normally contains a 50/50 mix of water and permanent coolant.

COMMON WATER PUMP FAILURES AND THEIR CAUSES

BROKEN WATER PUMP HOUSINGS AND SHAFTS COMMONLY CAUSED BY:

1) Excessive vibration & unbalance due to:
- Bent, cracked, or broken fan.
- Fan not squarely mounted on the shaft.
- Cracked or bent pulleys due to improper handling or installation.

2) Belts too tight:
- Over-tightened belts cause overloads on the bearing, greatly reducing its operating life.
- They also impose a powerful bending force on the shaft, causing it to deflect substantially from true center rotation. The result is large unbalance and early shaft fracture.

SEEPAGE FROM THE WEEP HOLE

Seepage from the weep hole is a sure sign of seal failure. The life of the seal can be greatly extended by performing regular maintenance on your cooling system.

Periodic inspection of hoses and coolant recovery tank will assure coolant levels are correct and that no atmospheric contaminants that can cause oxidation and sludge build-up are present. Sludge build-up in the cooling system is a primary cause of seal failure as well as reduced cooling system efficiency.

WATER PUMP TROUBLESHOOTING

PROBABLE CAUSES

SYMPTOMS	Low coolant level	Air pocket in coolant system ❶	Faulty fan clutch	Inoperative electric coolant fan	Restricted exhaust system	Retarded spark timing	Bolts go through into cooling system ❷	Mounting surface unclean	Gasket misaligned	Pump bolts not properly tightened	Rust deposits from mounting surface entering pump	Pump installed without gasket	Excessive side play in pump ❸
Overheating	●	●	●	●	●	●							
Leaks at water pump bolts							●						
Leaks at gasket								●	●	●			
Scraping noise when pump shaft is turned											●	●	●

❶ Allow engine to cool; restart and run with radiator cap removed and fill as necessary.
❷ Apply sealant to threads.
❸ Bearings damaged from over-tight belt.

Note: A common cause of overheating in cars equipped with electrically-operated radiator fans is a malfunction in fan control circuits. This may be a blown fuse, a faulty thermoswitch, etc. After the FlowKooler pump is installed and the cooling system refilled, run the engine until the coolant reaches the temperature at which the fan should switch on. If it does not do so, refer to the manufacturer's recommendations for troubleshooting the fan circuit.

Chapter 25: The Dragnet Pages

Many of you may recall the old "Dragnet" television series where Sgt. Joe Friday (portrayed by actor Jack Webb) always asked for "Just the facts." Well, the fact is, by the time you have reached this stage in the book, you have read and tried to retain so many facts and figures that your brain is overheated and ready to boil. These next few pages contain a few of the important facts that you need to remember:

1) Thermo-syphon cooling systems do not use a mechanical engine-driven water pump, but instead depend on the expansion of the coolant inside of the engine to force the circulation of coolant through the cooling system.

2) Plain water is the best disperser of heat. Antifreeze is added to a cooling system to correct the pH level of the water, but provides no actual cooling benefit. Water, while good at transferring heat, also is corrosive to the cooling system.

3) The boiling point of water at sea level is 212 degrees Fahrenheit. The higher you are above sea level, the lower the boiling point of water is, and the sooner it will boil.

4) Engine cooling systems are pressurized to raise the boiling point of water. For every pound of pressure in the cooling system, the boiling point of water will rise by three degrees.

5) Water boils when the atmospheric pressure and vapor pressure become equal.

6) When measuring the pH of engine coolant (using litmus paper), 7.0 is considered neutral. Most new ethylene glycol (EG) antifreeze solutions will test above 12.0, so as the additives separate from the coolant over time, the pH level will remain above 7.0 for the rated life of the antifreeze, usually two to four years.

7) Atmospheric pressure affects both the boiling point of water and the engine compression pressure.

8) A fanbelt gets its strength from the tensile cord. High-cord fanbelts are manufactured using more tensile cords (than a center-cord belt), which makes the high-cord belts stronger than a comparable center-cord belt.

9) Electrochemical degradation (ECD) can occur whenever a conductive fluid (such as water) comes in contact with the different metals of a cooling system.

10) Never mix EG and PG (propylene glycol) coolants together in the same cooling system. EG and PG coolants each require their own special type of antifreeze hydrometer.

11) EG antifreeze is toxic. One ounce can kill a 50-pound child.

12) Pusher electric radiator cooling fans mount on the front side of the radiator and are designed to "push" air through the radiator.

13) Puller electric radiator cooling fans mount on the back (engine) side of the radiator and are designed to "pull" air through the radiator.

14) In a vertical flow radiator, the coolant flows vertically, from top to bottom.

15) In a cross-flow radiator, the coolant flows horizontally, from side to side.

16) In radiator design, thinner works best in most applications because of the increased airflow through the radiator.

17) The faster you drive, the more "air" that will flow through the radiator is *not* true. No matter how fast you drive the pressure against the front of the radiator is equal to about forty percent of the vehicle's speed.

18) One of the key things to remember about any cooling system is that there must be a difference in air pressure between the front side and the back (engine) side of the radiator. This difference in pressure helps to draw the air through the radiator.

19) What happens to the air after it gets through the radiator is just as important as the amount of air that flows through the radiator in the first place.

20) High pressure under the hood can slow or even stop the flow of air through the radiator. This explains why an engine can run hot, even with plenty of air under the hood.

21) An easy way to determine if your overheating problem is airflow-related or coolant-related, is to park your car in the driveway and warm it to operating temperature. Place a box fan in front of the radiator. If the temperature drops, you have an airflow problem. If the temperature holds, you have a coolant-related problem.

22) When trying to solve an overheating problem, check the temperature of the coolant inside the radiator by using a kitchen thermometer (*carefully* stick it into the coolant at the radiator fill neck). You might be surprised to learn that your temperature gauge in the dash is wrong; some have been found to be "wrong" by as much as twenty degrees! **Note:** Do not reuse this thermometer for food preparation purposes.

23) Pusher-style electric cooling fans are normally considered to be about twenty percent less efficient than electric fans mounted on the back (engine) side of the radiator. This is due, in part, to the airflow restriction the pusher fan creates from being mounted to the front side of the radiator. Pusher fans are a good choice for auxiliary cooling.

24) When shopping for an electric fan, look at ones that are actually blowing through a radiator core. Any fan is able to move a lot of air if it does not have any restriction in front of it. Also, keep in mind, electric fans are good for idle and low speeds, and are of little or no use past about forty miles per hour vehicle speed.

24a) Remember when you are measuring your radiator for an electric fan, ask yourself, "How much of the radiator can I afford to cover with this fan?" You should have already identified the cause of your heating problem before you go shopping for an electric fan. This means that if your car is overheating while you are driving down the highway, installing an electric fan is *not* going to fix it!

25) There are three basic designs of water pump impellers: open blade, closed blade and scroll design. The scroll design is the most efficient, followed by the closed-blade design and, finally, the open-blade design. An open-blade impeller design can be modified into a closed-blade design to increase the efficiency of the water pump.

26) Staggered tube design radiators are not as efficient as inline tube design radiators. However, staggered tube design radiators are stronger and can be found in most industrial applications.

27) In brass/copper radiators, the top and bottom tanks are almost always made of brass, as are the tubes inside of the core (because of the flexibility of brass), while copper is used to build the fins because of its high heat transfer efficiency.

28) The heat transfer ability of metals (the ability of the metal to transfer heat through itself) is important and helps determine the efficiency of the radiator. On a scale of 1 to 100, silver is the highest in the upper 90s. Copper has a rating in the 90s as well. Brass has a rating in the upper 40s, as does aluminum. Lead, which is often used to bond the brass and copper together in a radiator, has a rating in the 20s.

29) Because lead solder is still being used to build conventional radiators, the non-toxic antifreeze solutions (such as Sierra brand) do not remain non-toxic once they are exposed to the lead and other chemicals inside of the radiator. They are, however, a big improvement over the conventional EG-type antifreeze solutions that are toxic by composition.

30) Conventional original equipment manufacturer (OEM) water pumps flow, on the average, between 10-12 gallons per hour at idle and 60-65 gallons per hour at high rpm. In contrast, high-flow water pumps (such as those built by Evans Cooling Systems) can deliver as much as 80-100 gallons per hour at high rpm.

31) Should there be any doubt that electrolysis really does take place in a cooling system, check it out for yourself! Connect the negative lead of your voltmeter to a good ground (clean metal-to-metal contact). Place the positive lead into the engine coolant. If you get more than a .5 volt reading, the pH of your cooling system is acidic and needs to be changed immediately.

31a) Unexplained random electrical and mechanical failures can (finally, after much grief) be traced back to the cooling system, where the coolant (as a result of electrolysis) has a voltage reading as high as 5.0 volts! Automatic transmissions that have been subject to repeated failure with no obvious mechanical defects, can be traced to electrolysis in the cooling system.

32) Aluminum radiators must be cared for properly. When not in use and with the coolant drained, the radiator should be sealed from the outside air. This prevents a thin layer of corrosive film from forming on the inside of the radiator, which can then reduce the radiator's cooling ability.

33) Be careful when adding any kind of coolant additive to an aluminum radiator. Read the label of the additive carefully to be sure it is designed for use with aluminum radiators, or else you may find yourself shopping for a new one.

34) The average horsepower draw of a mechanical engine fan is 2.5 horsepower, and it usually can provide for a 25 degree drop in coolant temperature. In contrast, an electric radiator cooling fan will require between 10-15 amps of electrical power and will be good for about a 17 degree drop in coolant temperature.

35) Engine lubricating oil can help the radiator with engine cooling by absorbing some of the engine heat. In contrast, the radiator cannot help the engine oil if it becomes saturated with engine heat.

36) Aluminum radiators have a limited lifespan as compared to brass/copper radiators. Over time, a thin corrosive film begins to cover both the inside and outside of an aluminum radiator. This film acts as an insulation barrier and slows the transfer of heat.

37) When comparing copper radiators to aluminum radiators, remember that copper transfers heat through itself better than aluminum, so copper is better at moving the hot air away from the tubes inside of the radiator. Aluminum radiators are better at transferring the heat out of the liquid coolant, so with increased airflow, an aluminum radiator can be made to be as efficient as a copper radiator.

37a) Again, it is an airflow thing. In racing applications such as NASCAR, there is plenty of airflow, so aluminum radiators are used because of their weight savings. In contrast, copper is used in industrial applications because of the lack of airflow and the increased efficiency of the copper fins at transferring heat away from the tubes with less airflow.

38) If you work for a NASCAR team and you are the radiator guy, your official title is the "Coil Man." You are in charge of making sure the correct radiator is in the car for the track you are racing at. You are also responsible for most everything else related to the cooling system and you had better not screw up!

Notes

207

Chapter 26:
Real Life Adventures

Okay, by now you should know how everything is supposed to work. But in real life, we know that not everything works as it should and not everything goes according to plan. This is true no matter if it is your first project car or your twenty-first project car. So, to make you feel better and help you realize that not everything bad happens only to you, I have come up with a few real life car-building stories. You have nothing to complain about!

Our first story comes from Brent Vandervort, owner of Fatman Fabrications (manufacturer of suspension products). Brent knew exactly what he wanted from his next car project; his goal was to build the ultimate highway car that would look good, ride well, run smooth, and...turn lots of heads. What follows is Brent's story:

"Like every rodder, my next project was going to be really special. I had located and purchased a really cherry 1949 Chevy fastback and a 500 cubic inch Cadillac engine to put in it. This car was to be my Americruiser—a great highway car that would get lots of 'oohs' and 'aahs'! When I mounted the Cadillac engine into the Chevrolet engine compartment, I found that it would barely fit and that I only had half an inch clearance between the back of the engine and the firewall, even after I moved the radiator forward and down. It was obvious there wasn't going to be room for a clutch-type fan, so I made an adapter to mount the stock Cadillac eighteen-inch-diameter steel fan to the engine.

"When I was finished, the fan was sitting really close to the radiator, but I thought things would be okay. However, the first time I started the engine in the car, it torqued over and proceeded to completely destroy my newly purchased hot rod radiator.

"I added a torque strap to the engine and took what was left of my hot rod radiator to the local radiator shop where they installed a new four-row core to my new/old tanks. I then installed a 750 cfm carburetor, and changed the rear end gears to 3:10 ratio. I had two-and-a-half-inch diameter exhaust and tailpipes installed, routing everything up over the rear axle. I was ready to cruise, or so I had thought.

"What a disaster! The engine ran 230 degrees at highway speeds, and I am eating up fanbelts every 40 to 150 miles, depending on the brand (and there *is* a difference, believe me). Every time I shut off the car or stopped for gas, the radiator overflow puked antifreeze all over my car and the ground! I had originally installed air conditioning, but it was pretty clear I wasn't going to get to use it with this combination."

Plan B

"Plan B was executed after much deep thought and lots of advice from everywhere and everyone. I tried the straight water fix, the Water Wetter additive fix, the 160-degree thermostat fix, and a host of other cures, none of which worked or even made a difference! Meanwhile, the original steel fan ate another radiator core. I was getting nowhere fast!

"So I switched to a big aluminum flex fan, added a shroud, a new three-row radiator, and an overflow tank. I also stuffed an enormous heater core (from a late model Lincoln) into the left-hand fender opening, (behind the wheelwell) with a gravel guard protecting it—desperate times call for desperate measures.

"I also changed the rear end ratio again, this time to a 3:00 gear set, thinking that if I could drop the engine rpm maybe things would run cooler. The thinner three-row radiator worked better than the four-row radiator it replaced, but my troubles were far from over."

Plan C

"I added a front 'chin' spoiler underneath the car below the grille, along with little air spoilers under the front fenders. On one of my trips, I noticed and could feel heat coming out of the glass well in the doors, so I figured heat was being trapped underneath the car.

Electric cooling fan used to extract heat from under the hood of Brent Vandervort's hot rod.

I installed a pair of twelve-inch electric fans to the inner fender panels to help remove some of the trapped heat under the hood.

"I also installed a new Edelbrock intake manifold and the original 925 cfm Quadra-jet carburetor (unique to the 500 cubic inch Cadillac engine). That seemed to help and I survived a cruising season by exercising great care. It was about this time that I began flying lessons and reading up on homebuilt aircraft. I soon realized that airplane designers spend the bulk of their time controlling heated air exit.

"In fact, the P-51 Mustang has a radiator located in the belly of the airplane that creates up to 150 pounds of thrust from the exiting air. I remembered from my college days about thermodynamics and how it works. I also recalled reading in one of Smokey Yunick's books about the hotter an engine runs, the more efficient it is, and the more horsepower it will make.

"In his book, Yunick explains how the boiling point of the coolant helps determine what the operating temperature of an engine should be. So I began doing a little homework and discovered that the Cadillac engine's temperature light was triggered to come on at 238 degrees. I also learned that a 500 cubic inch Cadillac engine has the same size valves as a 283 cubic inch small-block Chevrolet! No wonder it likes a richer mixture and low rpm."

Plan D

"Armed with this information, I began to realize that my problem was largely exit airflow. So I added a pair of cool looking teardrop vents to the hood, using 1936 Plymouth hood trim. I also wrapped the exhaust with heat wrap from the engine, back to the mufflers. I also redid the tailpipes so they exited under the axle, and much straighter than before. You could actually feel that the exhaust was hotter as it exited. The common bubble-type floor insulation didn't do much, so I spent the big bucks and bought some high-quality insulation, like they use in the race cars, and that made a big difference.

"I also changed rear end gears again, this time to a 2:47 ratio. I replaced the 16-pound radiator cap I had been using with a 22-pound cap. That raised the boiling point to 278 degrees, which I thought was good. My only concern was blowing radiator hoses, and swelling the radiator.

"The local racers have been using 22-pound radiator caps, and have had no problems, so I thought it was worth a try. So far, everything is working great. The engine temperature stays just over 190 degrees, the air conditioning now works great, and the engine doesn't overheat.

"Also along the way, I replaced my original air conditioning evaporator with a much larger one, which doesn't hide, but works much better. With all of these improvements, the highest temperature I have seen so far is 235-240 degrees, when I got stuck in a construction zone for forty-five minutes; but, I did not lose any coolant!

"I now believe, after all of this, that if your engine is not putting coolant on the ground, then it is not overheating, no matter what the temperature gauge reads!

"The following is also a list of common mistakes I have seen people make when building a street rod:

1) Too much engine, or the engine is too large to fit in the engine compartment and still allow for proper fan clearance.

2) Too wide of an engine, blocking the air from flowing out between the frame rails; also, too big of an engine, which results in too many square inches of engine surfaces to cool for the amount of airflow available.

Brent Vandervort's Cadillac-powered Chevy hot rod with 1936 Plymouth vents in its hood to aid cooling.

3) Many people needlessly worry about getting the cool air through the radiator when actually, they need to be more concerned about getting the hot air out from under the hood.

4) Using an inefficient but attractive mechanical fan. You should buy a fan for its air-moving capability, not its looks.

5) Too 'tall' of a gear in the rearend makes the engine run at higher rpm, which creates more heat! This is why the overdrive transmissions work well; you have the lower gears for good acceleration, and also the overdrive gears for highway cruising."

Brent agreed to share some of his experiences in the hope that other rodders might learn from his experiences. We owe Brent a huge debt of gratitude for taking the time out of his busy work schedule to share this information with us.

Rex Gardner and the 1998 Great American Race

Rex Gardner, as you may recall, contributed to the Flathead Ford chapter earlier in this book. In 1998, Rex decided (in part because of the Great American Race handicap system) to again team up with Gary Kuck to run a 1917 Hudson speedster in the Great American Race. The route for the 1998 race began in Tacoma, Washington, with overnight stops set up in Tricities, Washington; Boise, Idaho; Ogden, Utah; Steamboat Springs, Colorado; Littleton, Colorado; Hays, Kansas; Lee Summitt, Missouri; St. Charles, Missouri; Blue Ash, Ohio; Canton, Ohio; Olean, New York; Syracuse, New York; and Haverhill, Massachusetts (Boston area).

One of Rex's concerns was that the trip, nearly 4,600 miles in length, involved altitudes above 7,000 feet on at least three occasions, with one mountain road above 10,000 feet. We all know by now what happens to the boiling point of engine coolant at higher altitudes, and how much harder an engine has to work at the higher altitudes.

Like the Model T Ford, the 1917 Hudson speedster had a non-pressurized cooling system, so the problem was how to keep coolant in the radiator while in the mountains. When Rex and I visited, I suggested he try some of the Evans coolant in his car. It was designed to work in a non-pressurized cooling system and had a boiling point of 370 degrees, so it seemed like the ideal solution.

I called Evans Cooling Systems and talked to Steve Pressley and explained the situation and asked if he had ever used Evans coolant in a vintage race car under similar conditions. "No," replied Steve, but he agreed it might be a good test. So we worked out a sponsorship arrangement between Evans Cooling Systems and Rex, and installed the Evans coolant in the Hudson Speedster for the 1998 Great American Race."

Rex Gardner and car owner Gary Kuck's 1917 Hudson speedster used in the 1998 Great American Race.

Rex Gardner's Comments

"First, a little more background on the car. This 1917 Hudson Indy Speedster was one of five cars built by the Hudson Motor Car Co. to advertise its new counter-balanced crankshaft engine. Hudson was the first to introduce this feature in 1915 and built the cars to show off the smoothness of the engine. To put things into perspective, the average horsepower rating of Indy race cars in those days ranged between 30 and 45 horsepower. The Hudson speedster boasted 76 horsepower.

"That amount of horsepower was unheard of at the time the engine was introduced, and when you look at how the engine is constructed, you come to realize how amazing it really is. The engine is powered by a single carburetor (using a variable venturi) bolted directly to the engine block.

"There is no outside intake manifold. Once the gasoline is inside of the engine block, it travels down in between the cylinders in runners (something like a water jacket passage) making various 90 degree turns before finally ending up at the intake valve. Two problems with this design are that first, the fuel is being preheated before it gets to the end cylinders (because of the fuel runners passing next to the middle cylinders), and second, the 90-degree corners and the vertical rise into the intake valve area makes it difficult to control the fuel flow.

"Another problem is that the center cylinders tend to run rich, while the end cylinders run lean (because of the increased distance the fuel has to travel). This makes it difficult to control the engine block temperature as well as the fuel mixture. It is without question a crude and inefficient way to meter fuel into an engine.

Race Preparation

"Originally, a long shaft driven off of the timing gear ran the distributor, water pump, oil pump, and the generator/starter combination. The water pump seal consisted of a bronze seal and rope packing. A few modifications were made to the car in the interest of safety and reliability. Those changes included modern seals for the water pump, a separate starter, alternator, and oil pump drive. The rest of the car remained stock.

"Cooling the engine was also a challenge because of the engine design. The coolant enters the lower right-hand side of the engine block, then travels up and along the full length of the engine. It makes passes around all of the engine cylinders and then up through the cylinder head before being returned to the radiator via a long tube located at the rear of the cylinder head."

"Because of the long distance the coolant has to travel before it is returned to the radiator, and because the back of the cylinder head is the last place the coolant reaches before it is returned to the radiator, the coolant temperature at the rear of the cylinder head always seemed to be at least 30 degrees hotter than the temperature of the coolant in the top tank of the radiator. This is due, in part, because the coolant has been picking up engine heat all through the engine block before it ever comes in contact with the cylinder head so the coolant has already absorbed plenty of heat by the time it reaches the back of the cylinder head."

Long tube used to return warm coolant to radiator.

The Route

"The 1998 Great American Race was, by far, the toughest of the twelve races I have participated in, and was more like an endurance race than a rally event. It was also the hardest race on the cars, by far. With the tough weather conditions and the difficult route, the cars really took a beating. Nearly thirty percent of the cars entered in the championship class of the Great American Race received at least one DNF (did not finish score) for a day as a result of breakdowns suffered that were serious enough that they were not to be able to finish the day.

"The championship class is the well-prepared, experienced teams and their cars, who take the race seriously. Problems included engine failures (often related to cooling), rearend failures and clutches and various driveline-related failures. One championship team went through three complete Flathead Ford engines, and still was unable to finish the race. On more than one leg of the tour, we drove the Hudson in second overdrive, pedal to the floor, and could barely pull the hill. Many others weren't so lucky.

Evans Coolant

"So...what happened to the engine temperature during all of this? The Evans coolant is some strange stuff. It seemed that regardless of the outside temperature, the coolant warmed to about 190 degrees and stayed there. One afternoon the high was 45 degrees (Fahrenheit) and the Evans coolant warmed up and stayed at 190 degrees all day long. Even on the hot days with 95 degree-plus afternoon temperatures, the coolant stayed right around 190 degrees.

"The only time the temperature went up was when we were really pulling the engine on a hill. Once on one of the really long, steep hills, the coolant temperature in the radiator got up to 235 degrees. I flipped the switch over to the cylinder head temperature and it just continued to climb, so when it got about three-fourths of the way over I flipped it back to the radiator coolant temperature. I was scared to look at the cylinder head temperature!

"Later, when we got home, I called Steve Pressley about the high temperature and he reminded me that the readings I was experiencing were a measure of the coolant temperature and not the actual engine surface temperature. The Evans coolant is more efficient at removing the heat from the metal surfaces than conventional antifreeze.

"I do know that, typically, the cylinder head temperature readings were about thirty degrees hotter than the coolant temperature (the sender was located in the top tank of the radiator). We never did lose any coolant and not one drop of coolant ever showed up in the overflow tank. Engine (premature) detonation was not a problem.

"Because of the color of the Evans coolant, leaks are easy to spot. We opened the hood one day to find a bright purple drip behind one of the water pump bolts. We tightened the bolt and the drip was gone. The color sure made it easy to spot coolant leaks.

"In comparison, in the 1997 event we did lose some water as did most everyone else. Although the route in 1998 was much tougher and there were lots more overheated cars, we never saw any coolant in the overflow tank—it all stayed in the engine. We were plenty nervous when the coolant temperature in the radiator climbed above 210 on a number of occasions, but, again, we never lost any coolant.

"The last day of the race was, by far, the most difficult. We were climbing some really steep, long hills (climbing continuously for up to five minutes at a time). Meanwhile, the instructions called for an increase in speed from thirty mph to forty-five mph, and it was pouring rain the whole time! We, like everyone else, were just lucky to climb the hill, let alone try and gain any speed! That is when the Evans coolant temperature got up over 220 degrees.

"I also noticed that the electric fan (which is on a thermostat) ran longer after we shut off the car with the Evans coolant installed. It must take longer for the Evans to release the heat it has absorbed.

Summary

"In summary, if you were to ask me if the Evans coolant works as advertised I would say, absolutely! It actually does have the high boiling point, doesn't boil out, and is non-corrosive to the cooling system. It does seem to run hotter than plain water."

•Rex Gardner

Appendix A

Just to put things in perspective and to confirm that you indeed are not the only one with a cooling system problem, I have also included a few overheating/cooling problems from Tom Brownell's "Q & A" column found in *Old Cars Weekly News & Marketplace*. As Tom is quick to point out, overheating problems are one of the most popular topics of discussion for his questions and answers-formatted column. Take a look at some of these, it might be just like looking in the mirror.

Q. I have a comment regarding Richard Phalen's coolant loss in his '49 Mercury. I have worked on many flathead Ford engines and have never seen one that runs coolant through the intake manifold. There are two passages that look as if they might carry coolant, but they are heat passages which allow exhaust gasses to warm up the base of the carburetor. I bet Mr. Phalen's problem is either a leaky head gasket of a crack in the block around the exhaust valve seat in one or more of the cylinders. I suppose he could have a leaky water pump, but I would think he would notice the moisture under the car. just one more thing, if there is a bad pump, one of the bolts that holds the water pump to the block is located inside the pump where the lower radiator hose connects. Once the lower radiator hose is removed the bolt can easily be taken out with a socket and an extension. William S. Braislin, Sherman, Conn.

A. Several readers joined Mr. Braislin in suggesting solutions to the problem of coolant loss from a 1949 Ford V-8. All ruled out the intake manifold, noting the lack of water passages to the intake manifold in flathead V-8 engines. Albert Remme of Dennison, Minn., and Larry Lavin of Iron River, Wis., suggest checking the radiator cap. Mr. Lavin writes, "I had the same problem with a 1951 Lincoln. I found out it was a weak radiator cap. When the radiator would warm up the pressure would push open the cap and water would seep out past the cap and go out the overflow. Your reader should try a new cap. It is chapter than tearing down the engine." Brian Gunther of Wilton, Conn., suspects a water pump and offers the following scenario. "When the temperature gets high enough one of the pumps could seep so that the coolant ends up on the outlet for the lower hose which could be hot enough to boil off the liquid before it hits the ground." Drawing on experience with water loss from a 1960 Ford 390 V-8, Coy Belcher of Shoals, Ind., writes, "I purchased this vehicle new and had water loss from the day I drove it away from the dealership. The dealer did everything he could think of to solve the problem, but it was to no avail. They changed radiator caps, the thermostat, all hoses, checked the radiator and heater cores, even removed and checked the heads and block. I discovered the cause one day while changing the oil when I noticed a large rusty spot on the underside of the block. On closer inspection I could see that water was seeping out through the casting. I might add that the block was not cracked. A knowledgeable mechanic advised me that it was more than likely a mold defect in the block. Since the leak was minimal and the vehicle was driven daily, heat from the engine kept the seepage dried off. Therefore no signs of rust appeared until after the car had been parked for a long period of time." Let me add to Mr. Belcher's statement that mold defects do occur. Recently Chrysler Corp. has had a run of mold defects with its V-8 and V-10 engines, with blocks even being replaced at dealerships.

Finally, Peter Drumsta of Tonawanda, N.Y., offers a test sequence to pinpoint coolant loss problems. He suggests: 1) running the engine to near operating temperature; 2) stopping the engine and disconnecting fanbelts; 3) draining engine coolant to a lever to remove the upper radiator hoses (Ford flathead V-8s had dual water pumps and upper and lower radiator hoses) at the thermostat housings; 4) filling thermostat housings with coolant to the level where you can see it; 5) starting the engine and letting it idle; 6) observing the water in the thermostat housings while accelerating the engine in short spurts. If the head gaskets are leaking of if there are other faults in the combustion chambers, bubbles will appear in the thermostat housings. If coolant is leaking into the cylinder combustion chambers, the coolant will smell burned. This style engine is prone to head gasket problem which will be detected by the above procedure. Resurfacing the heads and installing new gaskets should cure the problem.

"Regarding Dave Stegman's article about flathead Fords overheating, don't reduce the water flow rate to help a cooling problem," writes Robert Koken of Lancaster, Calif. We received several letters from flathead Ford owners warning against reducing the flow rate to cure overheating problems. "That's an old wives tale," Mr. Koken continues, "probably from observing that some cars overheated with the thermostats removed, but the overheating isn't because the water is flowing too fast. If it's dwelling too briefly in the radiator, it's also dwelling too briefly in the block. The only explanation for overheating when the thermostats are removed that I've thought made any sense is the possibility that the water pump(s) are sucking air at the seal when they are pumping against the resistance of the thermostats causing some of the water to go overboard and resulting in water loss. Millions of flatheads didn't have heating problems but when overheating exists, the solutions are to make sure the radiator has sufficient tubes and that the radiator is clean (rodding works well here). Aftermarket radiators typically have fewer tubes or fewer fins or restrict fan airflow in the tube spacing. Start with a good radiator core from a reliable rebuilder. Remember, any paint on a radiator reduces heat flow. Make sure the rebuilder uses very little paint. I have also seen cases where a pressurized radiator system cured a flathead overheating problem. Finally, don't use bug screens; some of them reduce radiator airflow a substantial amount."

William McLellan of Pasadena, Calif., also responded to Dave Stegman's advice for slowing down the flow rate by reducing the size of every other impeller blade on the water pumps. "My analysis shows that something is wrong here," Mr. McLellan writes. "In a typical radiator, the hot coolant (water) enters the upper radiator tank and descends through the radiator tubes. Heat is transferred from the tubes to the thin metal fins which provide a large surface area for the air coming through the radiator to pick up heat. This rate of heat transfer is proportional to the temperature difference between the water and the air. To see this, let's look at what happens as water from the block enters the radiator tubes at the upper tank. Assume that air flow through the tubes is held constant. As it descends, the water gets cooled by this air, let us say by 'A' BTUs/minute in the first inch of tubing. This same water will be cooled by 'B' BTUs/minute in the next inch, etc. B will be less than A because the water-to-air temperature difference is decreasing.

Now, if the water flow is reduced, the temperature difference between water and air at the various levels in the tubes will decrease as well because a lesser volume of water is being cooled per unit of time. For a brief while, the water that arrives at the bottom of the tubes and lower radiator tank will be at a cooler temperature than before (at the higher flow rate). But now for the rub! The total amount of heat extracted per minute from the water is less than before because the decreased temperature difference made the lower sections of the radiator (with the cooler water) less efficient. Because of the lower flow rate, the water entering the upper radiator will be hotter and eventually a higher difference between the upper and lower tanks will result as well, but this difference will not reduce the maximum temperature; in fact the temperature will increase. Therefore, I maintain that the shorter time the water spends in the core, the more total heat will be extracted per unit of time—and extracting heat per unit of time (not the exit temperature) is the measure of cooling. Don't trim those impellers!"

Ruben Strube adds these comments. "You can get a four-pound pressure cap; Ford made them for the '48 pickups and they fit from 1932 to 1948 passenger car radiators. Use the open-faced generator/water pump belt and it has to be so tight that you can barely turn the right-hand (or passenger side) water pump pulley by hand when the engine is not running. If it is too tight the rear generator bushing will fail. The reason for this tightness; the crank pulley feeds play to the right pump while the generator and left pump hold play back to it. A pressure cap and tension on the belt at the right-hand water pump pulley are the major items in overcoming overheating. Also use the coolest thermostats."

DeWitt Morgan, Jr., of Portland, Ore., also responded to the overheating Ford flathead issue stating that he found the problem on his 1936 Ford to be incorrect fan blade pitch. He replaced the fan with an original, which solved the overheating problem. "A retarded distributor replaced prior to the fan was part of the problem, too," Morgan writes.

The debate over the connection between flow rate and overheating of Ford flathead engines has been seen in the pages of this publication before. Overheating being the irksome problem it is, Ford flathead owners have found a variety of cures. However, before modifying the cooling system, the first place to check—as our reader Robert Koken advised—is the radiator. There is a difference between having a radiator cleaned by dunking in a hot tank and rodded. In the rodding process, the upper and lower tanks are removed and small diameter rods are actually run down through the tubes to remove all sediment and gunk. Then the radiator is thoroughly cleaned, the tanks soldered back onto the core and pressure tested for leaks. Mr. Koken's warning about aftermarket radiators with reduced cooling capacity should also be noted. Ford made oversize radiators available and installing one is a better way to cure an overheating problem than to doctor the cooling system.

Years ago flathead Ford V-8 station wagons were used to haul tourists up the Mount Washington (New Hampshire) auto road to the top of the second tallest peak east of the Rockies. The cars were equipped with oversize radiators and made the trip up and down the mountain many times a day. If overheating problems were a normal feature of the flathead V-8, Fords would have never been used for this grueling work.

Theodore Selling's solution proved to be mechanical. "I had an overheating problem with a 1962 Lincoln," he writes. "I tried the usual, boiling out the radiator and block, to no avail. Finally I decided to replace the water pump. Comparing the old and new water pumps, I realized that the impeller on the old pump had deteriorated to the point that it no longer circulated the water properly. The new pump cured the overheating problem."

Tom Osborne's solution sparkles with creativity. "I am a Model A Ford nut," he writes, "and have several low mileage 'A' Fords with the original round tube, three-row radiators. They always heat up doing a mountain climb in second gear. Having recently acquired a 1928 radiator to go with my '28 Fordor, I took the radiator to a local shop for cleaning. The owner, who has been in business for many years, checked the flow, said it was adequate and advised against rodding due to the general age, condition, etc. He said it should be fine, but said I should pour a quarter-cup of dish washing detergent in the radiator, drive the car all week, then dump out the coolant and repeat the process until the heat gauge indicated the radiator is clean. Have you ever seen a scuzzy dishwasher? Then you know this man is on to something.

"I installed the 'new' radiator on my Tudor and decided to add an extra step to the radiator man's advice. For the first week, I added a quarter-cup of water softener salt to the coolant and drove the car 50 miles. Then I flushed the system. For the next week I added both water-softener salt and a quarter-cup of dishwasher detergent. In two weeks, the temperature (registered on both the original working moto-meter plus a new mechanical gauge backup) dropped from a constant 180 degrees down to 120 degrees. In heavy traffic, 120-135 seems to be tops.

"My radiator man also advised that once I had the cooling system cleaned out to fill it with one-third Prestone (or other name-brand antifreeze) and the balance with distilled water. So far, no heating problems. Take a look inside your dishwasher...."

Appendix B

Companies and individuals mentioned throughout this book can be contacted via the following addresses and phone numbers. Many of these companies have Internet sites where you can find additional information about their products and services. By typing a company name and a few key words into most any Internet search engine, you can easily locate each company's current web site. If you do not have access to a computer (or the desire to run one) you can still contact the companies directly, and receive more information.

Sources

Evans NPG Cooling Systems
Richard Venza
446 Lancaster Ave.
Frazer, PA 19355
ph. 610-889-9933
fax. 610-854

Texaco Lubricants Company
Terri Parker-Consumer Relations
ph. 800-782-7852 ext. 4
2000 Westchester Avenue
White Plains, NY 10650
Available through local retail outlets
 (has website)

The Gates Rubber Company
Jim McClean-marketing
ph. 303-731-8170
990 South Broadway
PO Box 5887
Denver, CO 80217
Available through your local full line auto parts retailer.
 (has website)

AE Clevite Engine Parts
McCord Gaskets-Bob
ph. 734-975-4777
1350 Eisenhower Place
Ann Arbor, MI 48108
Available through your local full line auto parts retailer.
 (has website)

Pro-Blend MotorSport Products
PO Box 5854
Winston-Salem, NC 27101
ph. 800-331-9520
fax. 910-761-0388

Red Line
Synthetic Oil Corp.
6100 Egert Court
Benicia, CA 94510
ph. 707-745-6100

Fluidyne Radiators
ph. 800-266-5645-Gary Johnson (owner)
4850 East Airport Dr.
Ontario, CA 91761
fax. 909-390-3950
 (has website)

Stant Cooling Products
Stant Manufacturing
Connersville, IN 47331
Available through your local full line auto parts retailer
 (has website)

Inglese Cool-Flex
Fluid Transfer Hose
Div. of Total Performance Inc.
400 South Orchard Street
Wallingford, CT. 06492
ph. 203-265-3617
fax. 203-265-7414
 (has website)

U.S. Radiator
6710 South Avalon Boulevard
Los Angeles, CA 90003
ph. 909-279-8403
fax. 909-340-3423
 (has website)

Sanders Air Conditioning
Balancing Ltd.
Robert Flake
ph. 209-667-5500
fax. 209-634-0127
PO Box 1641
Turlock, CA
(airflow measuring equipment)

Street and Performance
ph. 501-394-5711
Hwy. 375
Mena, AK 71953
blown (supercharged) engines and TPI wiring harnesses

Brodix Manufacturing
ph. 501-394-1075
301 Maple Avenue
Mena, AK 71953

Weiand Automotive
2316 N San Fernando Road
Los Angeles, CA 90065
ph. 213-225-4138
High-flow cast-iron, aluminum, and electric water pumps

Paul Kosma
ph. 601-393-2290
4681 Lake Cove Road
Walls, MS 38680
Specializes in late-style Flathead Ford engines

Dave Lukkari
ph. 760-247-4282
20233 Encino Road
Apple Valley, CA 92308
Has used 409 Chevy water pumps
on Flathead Fords for years

Cornhusker Manufacturing
ph. 402-749-1932
RR 1 Box 47
Alexandria, NE 68303
409 Chevy water pump kits for Flathead Fords.

Robertshaw High Flow Thermostats
Tennessee Division
2318 Kinston Pike
Knoxville, TN 37919
ph. 423-546-0550
fax. 423-544-5193
Available through Auto Zone Auto Parts stores
and Summit Racing's mail order catalog
 (has website)

American Honeycomb Radiator Mfg. Co.
Neil Thomas-president
171 Highway 34
Holmdel, NJ 07733
Shop 718-948-7722
or 908-946-8743
Manufactures round, honeycomb and
square tube cartridge-type radiator cores

BrassWorks
289 Prado Road
San Luis Obispo, CA 93401
ph. 800-342-6759
Custom-built Brass and German Silver radiators
FlowKooler high-output water pumps

Cooling Systems Warehouse
Dept. BK
PO Box 434
Parkerford, PA 19457
ph. 888-990-2665
fax. 610-970-0286
Exclusive factory distributor of Evans NPG Coolant and related
cooling system products, including Robertshaw thermostats.
Also aluminum radiators, high-performance waterpumps, etc.

Rex Gardner
16001 Russell Road
Stilwell, KS 66085
Specializes in the early 21 stud Flathead engines,
engine rebuilding service available.

Fifth Avenue Antique Auto Parts
415 Court Street
Clay Center, KS 67432
ph. 785-632-3450
fax. 785-632-6154
Fifth Avenue manufactures 6 and 12 volt electric cooling fans,
gear driven auxillary electric fuel pumps, and 6 and 12 volt alternators.
Its products are designed for, and used by, the participants of the
Great American Race, and on vehicles used in Hollywood movie studio
productions. Its products can also be found on antique and collector
cars around the world. It is a specialty company known for solving
the drivability problems associated with vintage and collector cars.

Brent Vandervort
Fatman Fabrications
8621-C Fairview Road
Hwy 218
Charlotte, NC 28227
Complete chassis and front suspension kits for street rod projects including
the 1935-40 Ford as well as Mustang IFS kits, 1984-87 Vette, etc.

Prestone Products Corporation
39 Old Ridgebury Road
Danbury, CT 06810
Prestone has been making engine coolants and related products since 1927.
Prestone is available at most any auto parts store as well as most any full line
retail outlet.

About the Author

Randy Rundle

    Randy Rundle is the owner of Fifth Avenue Antique Auto Parts located in Clay Center, Kansas. Rundle has spent the last ten years preparing vehicles entered in the Great American Race, setting up these pre-1950s cars' electrical, fuel and cooling systems. In addition, he has also completed four movie projects for Hollywood studios, his most recent project being the movie "L.A. Confidential."

    Rundle's automotive electrical book, titled *Wired For Success: Auto Electrical Made Easy*, available through Krause Publications the publisher of this book, continues to be popular as a source for simple explanations and problem-solving information.

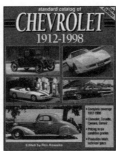
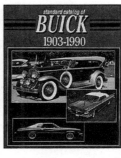

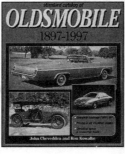
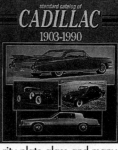
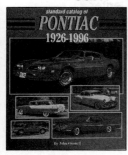
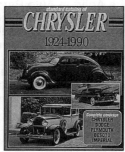
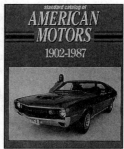

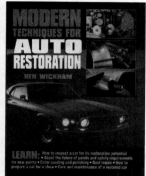
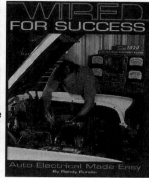

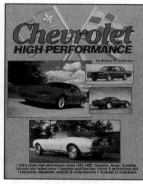

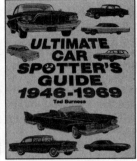

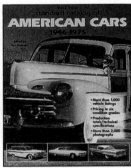